Secrets
of the
ENGLISH
WAR BOW

Also by the Author

The Crooked Stick: A History of the Longbow

The Romance of Archery: A Social History of the Longbow

Straight and True: A Select History of the Arrow

How to Shoot the Longbow

Of Bowmen and Battles

Secrets of the
ENGLISH
WAR BOW

HUGH D. H. SOAR

*with Joseph Gibbs, Christopher Jury,
and Mark Stretton*

WESTHOLME
Yardley

Published by Westholme Publishing, LLC

904 Edgewood Road, Yardley, Pennsylvania 19067

Visit our Web site: www.westholmepublishing.com

ISBN: 978-1-59416-126-1

Printed in the United States of America.

*In grateful acknowledgement of the skills and
dedication of past and present members of the*
MARY ROSE TRUST

Contents

The remains of a *Mary Rose* archer on the seabed. The spacer that holds remnants of his arrows is just below the archaeologist's scale at the top. The warship capsized and sank with great loss of life on July 19, 1545, just outside Portsmouth harbor. (*Copyright, Mary Rose Trust. May not be reproduced without permission.*)

Preface

"Our English archers shot their shafts,
As thick as hayle in skye,
Ad many a foeman on the feelde,
That happy day did dye"
—A ballad of Agincourt, 1415 (anon.)

In *The Crooked Stick: A History of the Longbow*, a companion volume to this book, the slowly unfolding story of the weapon appeared—its development was traced from a Stone Age origin lost in time, through prehistory and early recorded history, first as the hunting weapon that gave humans mastery of their environment, then as a successful tool in warfare, and more recently to its use as an instrument for pleasure and recreation. With this knowledge at our backs, in this new book we will examine both in text and photographic detail the ins and outs of this most effective and charismatic of war weapons, its creation, and that of its companion arrow and its string.

From a master arrowsmith come some fascinating details of how replica arrowheads are hand forged today and of their awesome penetrative power when shot from a heavy draw-weight bow at both static and moving targets.

From a modern maker of war bows are illustrations of his processes as he crafts a yew bow, and through the skills of a master fletcher we are shown, by photograph and text, the skilful creation of a medieval arrow from a beginning as an unshaped stave of wood to a fully fletched conclusion.

To complement the work of these craftsmen, we will look at the English bowman who used and trained with these potent weapons and—in his heyday—the tactical use to which his military commanders put him. Of the many battles that drew upon his courage and tenacity of purpose we will examine four from the French wars, and from their outcome we may judge both the skills and the shortcomings of charismatic leaders.

Irrelevant to battle it has become, but the longbow retains a hold on the minds of Englishmen and others, quite disproportionate to the simplicity of its purpose. Those who kept faith with the war bow turned to it later for recreation and pleasure, and it is proper that we should look closely and carefully at its use, easing from it and its associated arrow those secrets so familiar to our bowman forebears.

Read on and enjoy.

Chapter
One

THE ENGLISH
WAR BOW

"The might of England standyth upon her archers"
—Sir John Fortescue (d. 1478)

There can have been no more awesome sight for those who sought to challenge the might of England upon the battlefield than to be faced by rank upon rank of stolid longbowmen. Cold-eyed professional fighters, arrogant and xenophobic to a man, they stood in silence, confident of their ability, deadly shafts notched on taut bowstrings, anticipating the sound of battle horn and drum, ready to loose their fearsome arrow storm to maim and kill all in its path, for the arrow is blind and no respecter of degree: lowly foot-slogging peasant or high-born man-at-arms, neither escaped its murderous point.

It was the task of these bowmen to dull the opposition. Disciplined at village butt on holy days to shoot strongly and to effect, they knew their worth, these free-born Englishmen and their Welsh companions, and they did their work well.

Of the many battles in which the longbow and those who used it were prominent, none has been so thoroughly described as Agincourt—fought on a late October day in 1415—a day dedicated to saints Crispin and Crispinian. While the lowly bowmen are given credit—how could it be otherwise—understandably, perhaps, official English accounts, of which there are many, emphasize the activities of the men-at-arms.

Then the French came pricking down as if to over-ride our men, but God and our archers made them stumble. Our archers shot no arrows off target; all caused death and brought to the ground both men and horses. For they were shooting that day for a wager. Our stakes made them fall over, each on top of the other so that they lay in heaps two spear's length in height. Our king with his company and men at arms always fought on for he battled with his own hands. When the archers ran out of arrows they laid on with stakes.[1]

Another source states:

The warlike bands of archers with their strong and numerous volleys darkened the air, shedding as a cloud laden with a shower, an intolerable multitude of piercing arrows, and inflicting wounds on the horses, either caused the French horsemen [who were intent upon overriding them and fighting the English from the rear] to fall to the ground, or forced them to retreat, and so defeated their dreadful purpose.[2]

With archery thus dismissed, the author reserves the more purple of his prose for a gory description of the battlefield.

O, deadly war, dreadful slaughter, mortal disaster, hunger for death, insatiable thirst for blood, insane attack, impetuous frenzy, violent insanity, cruel conflict, merciless vengeance, immense clash of lances, prating [aimlessness] of arrows, clashing of axes, brandishing of swords, breaking of arms, infliction of wounds, letting of blood, bringing on of death, hacking up of bodies, killing of nobles! The air thunders with dreadful crashes, clouds rain missiles, the earth absorbs blood, breath flies from bodies, half dead bodies roll in their own blood, the surface of the earth is covered with the corpses of the dead, this man charges, that man falls, this one attacks, that one dies, this one recovers, that one vomits forth his soul in blood . . . cruelty reigns, piety exults, the brave and the strong are crushed and mountains of corpses are piled up, a vast multitude is yielded up in death, princes and magnates are led off as captives.[3]

While English accounts of Agincourt adequately describe the ebb and flow of the day's events, it is to the French accounts that we turn for graphic illustration, in particular, the dress and explicit activity of the archers. Most of these men, we are told, were without armor, dressed in their doublets, their hose loose around their knees, having axes or swords and hatchets hanging from their belts. Many had bare heads and were without headgear although some had hunettes or cappe-lines of boiled leather and some of osier on which were bands of iron. It was also noted that some archers went barefoot.[4]

One account is particularly scathing of these bowmen and their appearance as they came ashore with Henry at Saint-Vaast-La-Hague.

> Young men from various lands, some Irish, all with bare feet and no shoes, dressed in scruffy doublets made out of old bedding, a poor skullcap of iron on their heads, a bow and a quiver of arrows in their hand and a sword hanging at their side. That was all the armour they had. There was also a large quantity of scum from several lands.[5]

No mention here of hose. The "scruffy doublets" so dismissively described were jacks, the fifteenth-century equivalent of the earlier gambeson. Where the gambeson was of knee length with sleeves, the jack was a shorter, thigh-length sleeveless garment made, not from old bedding as our French observer suggests, but from layers of fustian, a thick cloth padded out with other material and often quilted in a squared stitch pattern. Some archers included horn plates or even small pieces of metal at vulnerable points within their jacks. Hose (tight individual leggings) were attached to a waistcoat-type garment worn beneath the jack. A pair of pants and a codpiece completed the ensemble, although these latter seem to have been dispensed with at Agincourt for occasions when nature called.

The placing of the archers at Agincourt is not entirely clear, although from accounts, particularly those of the French, they were on both flanks, or wings, of the English army as well as in ambush within a field close to the French lines on the Tramecourt side.[6] These archers were seemingly accompanied by a group of mounted English men-at-arms,

Contemporary sketch of a fifteenth-century archer wearing a jack.

and between them, they significantly disrupted the initial French advance.

The original English position is said to have been between three and four bowshots, or some 800 yards, distant from the French (a bowshot is around 240 yards), and it was here that Henry assembled his army in readiness.[7]

It is unclear whether Henry expected his opponents to march that distance to engage with him, but after due time, when they had shown no sign of movement, he advanced his army toward them. There is some doubt from various accounts whether the archers withdrew their stakes and carried them to their fresh position, but because the French cavalry charge was ultimately repelled, it would seem that they did.

As was the pattern in contemporary warfare, there was a preliminary meeting between the two sides, during which overtures of peace were made.[8] Henry let it be known that if he were granted the duchy of Guienne, 500,000 francs, and the hand of Catherine (the French king's daughter) in marriage, he would release Harfleur, renounce his title to the kingdom of France, and depart forthwith.

Predictably, none of these conditions was acceptable to French pride; and when the heralds had returned, Sir Thomas Erpingham, commander of the archers, addressed the men in the king's name calling upon everyone to fight with vigor against the French. He concluded by throwing his baton into the air, calling for the trumpets to sound in readiness for what was to come. His final shout, described by the French as "nestroque" is believed to have been a call for the "menée stroke," a hunting call in readiness for action.[9] It was also a call in keeping with the fox's tail said to have been tied by Henry to his battle standard.

Battle then commenced to the sound of trumpets, accompanied by lusty shouts from the archers as they prepared to dispatch the first volley of the arrow storm.[10] It is believed that this was the oft-repeated hunting halloo "Hey, hey," a frightening sound when roared in rhythmic unison from the throats of 5,000 English bowmen.

As the dismounted French advanced, they are said to have bowed their heads so that the arrows would not penetrate the visors of their helmets, a comment that suggests point-blank or low-trajectory shooting at around 60 to 80 yards.

Earlier, an attempt had been made to break up the archers by a cavalry charge. This seems to have gone seriously wrong, however, and is a vivid reflection of the fear engendered by the war bow and its arrows. Prior to the conflict, the French battle plan had been to mount an initial charge to break up the flank archers and thus gain the rear of the English.[11] Once there they would attack in support of the advancing dismounted vanguard. Between 1,000 and 1,200 mounted horsemen had been detailed off for this purpose, to be equally divided against the left and right English flanks.

So far, so good. However, when the time came for preparations to activate the plan, only 800 men could be found; the remainder had discovered an urgent need to be elsewhere. Matters deteriorated still further when the order to charge was given. Just 120 joined with Sir Clignet de Brabant, who had

Detail from a well-known fifteenth-century illustration depicting the Battle of Agincourt.

the unenviable task of dealing with the Tramecourt flank, while Sir Guillaume de Saveuses had little better success on the Agincourt side, mounting an assault with 300 lances.

With the ambush an additional problem, Sir Clignet wisely reined in and returned to base without testing the bowmen at close range. Sir Guillaume, though, was less inclined to turn around, and he reached the archers' stakes. Once there, however, his horse was shot from under him, and he was set upon and immediately killed. Confirming discretion to be the better part of valor, those of his party who had survived the arrow storm turned tail and made for home. Thus ended the first element of the French battle plan in dismal failure.

Things now could only get worse, and they did. Unlike the English position, which was on unplowed land, the ground in front of the French had been newly sown, and the soil was fresh and muddy. Rain and the activities of those who had

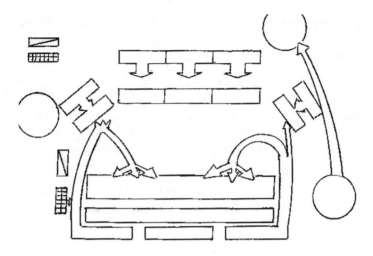

Battle of Agincourt, October 25, 1415, after French accounts. (*Author*)

exercised the horses during the evening and night had churned the earth until it became a quagmire. Squelching through this toward the English line in full body armor, it was then that the unhappy French men-at-arms met the English archers.

The archers had by now thrown down their bows and had emerged from behind their stakes armed with leaden mauls and whatever weapons they had or could pick up. Wherever they saw opportunity, they set upon groups of French, knocking them down, afterward either killing or disarming them and passing them back for potential ransom. It was said that as few as ten Englishmen pursued 100 Frenchmen and slaughtered them or herded them for capture like sheep. But we will leave Agincourt to history now, for it is time to consider the weapon that made such a victory possible.

Longbows that are designed for military use have necessarily to reflect their purpose. In the year 1252, when Henry III first included the weapon that we know today as the longbow in his Assize of Arms, he had in mind not the heavy draw weight bow that we are more familiar with, but a weapon appropriate to the style of warfare of the time.

We have no way of knowing for certain the character of these bows, but it would seem likely that they were little different from the bows used at that time for hunting. After all, hunting was an activity more common than warfare. We are, however, well served in the manner of the bow's use during early medieval times, since accounts of battles in which it featured abound, and in a later chapter we will discuss its tactical use in one or two. We are in some confusion though as to its form. Such drawings as exist, contemporary with the French wars, owe much to artistic license, often showing foreshortened weapons unsuited to lengthy war arrows or distance shooting, and this at a time when the war bow was prominent for its power.

There is an intriguing, if scanty, source of helpful knowledge in wall paintings depicting them.[12] These portray the martyrdom of Saint Edmund and are extant in certain English churches. Created perhaps by itinerant painters, there is little doubt that these vernacular drawings portray the fourteenth- and fifteenth-century bow as it was.

Three paintings represent the fourteenth-century bow. Let us see what detail we can glean. One from Weare Gifford in Devon depicts a rugged weapon, knobby of back but smooth of belly, suggesting yew, with evidence for self-nocks; in length it is a little shorter than the archer drawing it, but it is coming around in compass, as one would expect from a bow working fully in the hand. One shown at Troston in Suffolk is again a true arc, with smooth belly and rugged back but of relatively greater length; while the painting at Stoke Dry in Rutland is unique in including a dark mark at one bow end, which just might indicate a horn tip.

From Weare Gifford in Devon and Pickering in Yorkshire come fifteenth-century paintings. Here are bows contemporary with Agincourt. The one from Devon comes around in compass and comfortably exceeds the height of the archer drawing it. There is no evidence for tips of horn, and both back and belly are smooth. As with those from the earlier century,

Two vernacular representations of contemporary war bows. Top, a fourteenth-century wall painting depicting the martyrdom of Saint Eadmund, Weare Gifford Church, Devon. Note the apparent absence of protective sheaths (nocks) at limb ends and the curious positioning of arrow on string. Another of the same martyrdom, bottom, from the fifteenth century on a wall of Pickering Church, North Yorkshire. Note the presence of protective sheathes (nocks) on the limb terminals. (*Courtesy Anne Marshall*)

this is a substantial weapon, and one may readily guess its implied power. A curious feature of this painting is the presence of what may be an open-ended arrow bag carried from a belt in front of the archer.

From Pickering Church we have the most complete example of early fifteenth-century bowmen. Here the war bow has truly come of age. Of a man's height, these substantial weapons carry convincing evidence for both a recurved tip and a visible protecting horn nock. A little worrying however is the depiction of arrows carried head down behind the man; selection of these from an arrow case would have presented a difficulty if this was the method used in battle.

Earlier we noticed the dual-purpose weapon used for hunting and warfare where needed. With the passage of time, circumstances changed. As the fourteenth century drew to a close, England had become deeply involved with continental strife and continental military tactics. It had become necessary for the war bow to reflect its true purpose: to disrupt and embarrass an enemy cavalry formation as it approached the English lines.

And so the heavy draw weight medieval war bow had been conceived and born. Since it is primarily with this weapon that we are concerned, we will now examine its construction and its use in warfare.

The anonymous author of a late fifteenth-century French text concerning archery in general extols yew as the proper material for the manufacture of bows and details two kinds (both *Taxus baccata*).[13] One is white in color and the other has a redder tinge. The white, he writes, is from Portugal and is said to be soft and of open grain; the other redder wood is from Italy and is of straighter grain, giving a sharper cast and retaining its strength.[14] Italian yew, so it was said, was harder to work and broke more readily, but it was still considered superior to all other varieties. Yew was chosen for its better elastic modulus—its ability to return to shape—a feature that is more pronounced in yew than in other woods.

In addition to the above sources, yew logs, dark in color, were imported from the Baltic countries, Spain, the Pyrenees, and from southern Ireland. Logs were stored to season for a while before being split into staffs, or staves.

In 1574 bow staves of yew were imported from Salzburg via the rivers Rhine and Main. From this source they fetched between £15 and £16 for 100, or just 36 pence (about $1) each. At that time another source was Switzerland, where prices were rather cheaper at £12 to £13 for 100. A third but vastly inferior source was Poland and other eastern European countries, whose wood was said to be "hollow and full of sap" by reason of the coldness of the climate there. A fourth source was the renowned northern Italian yew, imported via Venice: "the finest and steadfastest wood by reason of the heat of the sun which drieth up the humidity and moisture of the sap."[15] We have already noticed the advantage Italian yew has over all others, and it is no surprise that it was widely sought.

Together with the multitude of staves brought into the country, on occasion completed bows were also obtained from abroad. In 1510 newly enthroned King Henry VIII applied to Venice to buy 40,000 completed bows (less their horn nocks), while in 1561 Queen Elizabeth bought others, again without horns, from Naples. These latter cost 3 pounds 10 shillings per hundred (purchased individually, 8 pence each). Since the cost in England of even the least marketable yew bow was 2 shillings 8 pence, if this price has been correctly reported, it is evident that these weapons were either of inferior wood or a remarkable bargain. The contemporary market price for a good yew bow was 3 shillings 4 pence.

In 1574 all imported staves were to be 3 fingers (2 1/2 inches) thick, squared, and 7 feet in length. It is unclear whether imported staves were fully seasoned, or even seasoned at all, although it is to be expected that bowyers would be told of their state and would act accordingly. If they were unseasoned, then one would expect each stave to have been waxed to prevent splitting as the wood dried.[16]

Bows could be made, and indeed were made, of other woods—"or othere wood of meane price," as our writer puts it. Wych hazel (a synonym for a type of elm); ash; laburnum; Brazil, or pernambuco, wood; and others served to make weapons.[17]

In the mid-sixteenth century, when yew became in short supply, bowyers were required by statute to make two bows of "elme wiche" for every bow of yew, and to guard against sharp practice by suppliers, dire penalties were promised for those selling bow staves in bundles. It was required that they be loose "so that each might be examined."[18]

The directive to make two bows of elm for every one of yew proved unpopular with bowyers. The English public knew a good bow when it saw one, and elm bows were being left on shelves unsold. In the face of opposition, the authorities relented, and in 1566 bowyers were excused from the statutory requirement. Matters did not go entirely their way, however, since they had now to be prepared to supply 50 bows of elm, wych hazel, or ash within 20 days.[19] It follows that the production rate in these woods was two and a half bows each day, since night work was specifically banned "by reason that bows cannot in manner be made as well or as profitably for the King and his people by night as by day."

The practical problems arising from inferior wood were foremost in a complaint by the Navy Council, addressed to Thomas Howard, Lord Admiral, aboard the *Mary Rose* in 1513.[20] Receiving a fresh supply of weaponry, he was taken to task for the number of broken bows that had been reported. In response he wrote:

> As touching the receiving of bows and arrows. I shall see them as little wasted as shall be possible. And where your lordships wrote that it is greatly marvelled where so great a number of bows and arrows be brought to so small a number, I have enquired the courses thereof: and as far as I can see, the greatest number were wych bows of whom few could abide the bending. But as for that was done before my time I cannot call again, but from henceforth, if

I do not the best I can to keep everything from waste, I am worthy [of] blame which I trust I shall not deserve.

One wonders idly whether the breakages were entirely due to chance or whether the honest English bowman, faced with inferior equipment, took matters into his own hands!

The situation was evidently corrected later, at least on paper, since the 1536 manifest for the recommissioned *Mary Rose* records "bowes of eugh—250," although current archaeology has revealed the presence on board of at least some bows of other wood.[21]

Penalties for poor workmanship were imposed by those responsible for quality within the various bowyer's guilds. These applied evenly throughout the country—the errant provincial bowyer was as severely dealt with as was his London cousin. The 1479 Ordinances of the Guild of Bowyers and Fletchers of Bristowe (Bristol) states:

It is ordeigned and assentid that every man of the said Craffte within the Fraunchise of Bristowe make and wirche [work] alle maner of stuff of the said Crafte as Bowes, Arowes and other tacles and stuff well and sufficiently of good and able Timbre and of no grene false ne disseivable tymbre, wherethrugh' the byar thereof in Anny wise may be deceyved or endammaged. And yef Anny of the saide Craffte do the Contrary and thereof be duly convicted shall restore and make Amendys to hym that be so endamaged be hit in Bowes or Arowes by the discretioun and Judgement of the Maire of Bristowe and Wardens of the saide Craffte . . . And also to pay iijs iiijd [3 shillings 4 pence]. That is to say xxd [20 pence] for the Chamber of the Toune and xxd for the Contribution of the saide Craffte.[22]

Much of the yew used by Bristol bowyers in those days would have come directly to the port from Youghal, a well-known early source in southern Ireland.

There are no contemporary descriptions of the manufacture of these early bows. No instruction sheet has survived—if indeed there ever was one. Skills were learned by example and each apprentice was bound by oath not to reveal his master's secrets. This oath he in turn extracted from his own apprentices in due course, and—as a matter of passing interest—it is the same oath sworn by me when elected a freeman of the London-based Worshipful Company of Bowyers in 2006. The master and apprentice system was not one that encouraged innovation, and it is unlikely that procedure altered much from century to century; however, much knowledge can be gleaned from various sources.

After initial preparation, the removal of bark and tidying the belly wood—perhaps with a side-axe and/or a float (a rough rasp), the belly was tapered, or pointed, crudely at first but with increasing care, using plane and draw knife and following the grain of the wood. The back was more carefully worked to preserve its tensile strength but in a similar fashion. Knots and pins, or warrants, on both back and belly were left raised, since to remove them would have been to disturb the integrity of the stave's tension and compression. Where it was deemed necessary by the master bowyer, pins might be removed and a Dutch plug inserted. In cases where the stave had warped or where one limb was crooked, the bowyer might straighten it by steaming. If perhaps there was a natural curve at one limb tip, then the other might be steamed for symmetry, although there is no direct evidence for this.

With tillering nocks cut into the limb tips, the stave would be finished with a scraper and tillered to come around in full compass, with occasional scraping to ease the process. When completed to the bowyer's satisfaction, the tips would be grooved for stringing or perhaps coned for horning, which is to say that protective horn sheaths would be attached and shaped. String grooves would then be cut into these—probably to their sides, since to our knowledge, side nocking was a matter of course. Finally the completed bow would be rubbed smooth and polished with a boar's tooth and an oilcloth.

Much is speculation, however, for here we meet a problem. No true medieval war bow exists, and we have to draw our limited practical knowledge from what is available, but we should recognize our good fortune. Just a quarter of a century ago, this arcane knowledge was confined to the examination of two bows recovered in the nineteenth century from the sunken warship *Mary Rose* by the diving Deane brothers, plus one or two other weapons of broadly similar date. However, from this same ship—recovered in 1982 from the Solent seabed—we now have almost a surfeit of sixteenth-century bows for comparison. From these we can draw informed, if speculative, conclusions about their earlier equivalents: those that a century before had so influenced the outcome at Agincourt.

We speak of heavy draw weights now, but what do we mean by this? Our comparisons are with today's recreational weaponry—bows with a style and limited power reflective of their modest purpose. A weight of between 50 and 60 pounds drawn with an arrow of 28 inches is more than adequate for their role at target and clout, and it is by comparison with these that we define our heavy bows. To accord with our modern archery custom, those bows available to us for examination have been assessed (by comparison with replicas) as being between 90 and 120 pounds in draw weight, and it is largely within that range that present-day tests with replicas have been carried out.

There is, however, no marking on a war bow to indicate its strength; the attribution of specific draw weight is a modern concept. There are no defining figures on either limb such as we are accustomed to seeing on nineteenth-century bows made by Aldred, Buchanan, Horsman or others, and this begs the question of how strength was determined in the past. We just do not know. It may have been by no more sophisticated a method than the judgment of the master bowyer in whose workshop it was produced.

The capability of a bow to cast diminishes exponentially with its mass, and we may fairly assume that the early and later medieval weapons were judged for their strength, and thus their effectiveness, by some reference to this. Although the sorting of bows recovered from the *Mary Rose* into "robust" and "fine" (the definition of archaeologists) may seem simplistic and unsophisticated, it is in fact a distinction most appropriate to their assessment and subsequent cataloging.

Let us now look more closely at these distinctions. The robust and, by definition, prospectively the heavier of the weapons are both longer (at an average of 77 1/2 inches) and of greater mass than their lighter companions. Of the 116 examined, they are also in the majority.

This is curious, since it is counter to perceived wisdom insofar as the recreational bow is concerned. Cross sections of war bows are greater in width than depth. The distinction is particularly marked when the two are set down side by side. The war bow might not in fact conform to the criteria of the British Long-Bow Society (the administrative body for the practice of traditional archery in the United Kingdom) for its recreational weapons, a fact that for reasons that will be explained is both acceptable and understandable in relation to its purpose.[23]

The theoretical advantages of a cross section of this shape in comparison with the deeper D section of the recreational bow were examined and set down by Paul E. Klopsteg, an American engineering physicist during 1931 and 1932, and it was through his seminal work that the flat-sectioned limbs common to all modern competition bows were introduced.[24] Klopsteg considered the relative properties of wood in tension and compression and recognized an imbalance between the two. To counteract this imbalance, he designed a section in which the compression factor occupied a mass greater than its tension counterpart.

As one might expect with yew as the medium, grain did not always run true, and to some extent this would have affected the section chosen by the medieval bowyer to prepare a particular stave. Equally it is entirely possible that, as today, individ-

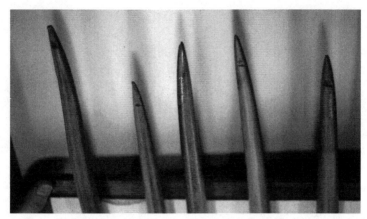

The terminal cones of sixteenth century war bows. Note the grooves caused when cutting theprotective horn sheath (nock) to create the side string groove. (*Author's photograph, with acknowledgement to the Mary Rose Trust*)

ual master bowyers used their knowledge and judgment to create weapons personalized to themselves.

This would seem borne out by observation. The section shape of sixteenth-century war bows, exemplified by those available to us for study, broadly ranged between variations of ogival (a shallow ellipsed back over a deeper ellipsed belly) and rectangular, with a considerable preponderance of the former. The rectangular-sectioned weapons, of which there are eight, are significantly more robust and longer than others, suggesting a specialized use, perhaps for delivering the heavier fire arrow, known to have been used on board ship. By comparison of relative mass, the draw weight of these formidable things has been assessed as significantly greater than the others. One of these eight examined by me showed evidence of squaring at the center, a shape that would have been most uncomfortable if held by hand, suggesting its use as a tiller bow: a weapon drawn and held on a tiller bar and shot in a way that shares some similarity with that of a crossbow.[25] Turning once more to the other weapons, variations in mass between robust and fine, expressed as overall weight, might seem slight at a maximum of 3 ounces, although it is arguable that this could affect draw weight.

Although distinction has been made by archaeologists between robust and fine bows—largely, it would seem, by the comparison of one box of bows with another—it is by no means certain that this distinction was either intended or has validity. It is equally arguable that the bowyer making the fine, or lighter, weapons was following his own design and not consciously creating a bow of less draw weight than his bow-making colleague—a suggestion equally applicable to the maker of the heavier (by mass) weapons. As those who work in the material know, there can be significant difference in strength between two yew staves that share the same nominal dimensions. The question whether bows were deliberately created lighter by design must remain unanswered, however intriguing its solution would be.

A significant number of bows recovered had marks pricked in various designs on their upper limbs, and their presence and purpose has led to some speculation. Although they may have no more significance than merely to draw the archer's attention to the upper limb, since they are invariably positioned there, they may perhaps have doubled up as advertising the master bowyer and his workshop. An early suggestion, correlating them to draw weights, seems unlikely; while what might seem to be an obvious purpose—identification of the arrow pass—is also improbable, since not all are in the appropriate position. Where no handle is indicated, as with a fully working self-bow, it would have been practice to balance the bow on the thumb to find the fulcrum and, by marking that position, thus to indicate the arrow pass. It is also understood from Roger Ascham's writing in *Toxophilus* to have been practice to smear the handle section with beeswax so that it might be readily found again.[26]

Although only one solitary horn tip sheath (nock) has been recovered from the *Mary Rose* archaeological site so far, there is indisputable evidence for presence of more, since bow limb ends have been cone shaped to receive them. Shallow cuts marking the presence of string grooves are apparent on the side of each cone, and these are indicative of a process known as "side nocking," where the cutting of the groove has gone through the horn into the wood. In explanation, where grooves to take the bowstring are today cut around the horn sheath (the "nock") and are deepest to the forward face (or back) of the bow, tapering out on either side toward the bow's belly, the grooves of side nocks are cut on alternate sides of upper and lower horn sheaths and do not extend further.

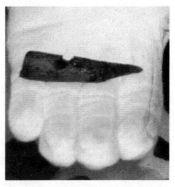

A solitary horn tip sheath (nock) recovered from the wreck of the Mary Rose. Evidence suggests that war bow limb tips were protected by horn sheaths from the fifteenth century onward. (*Author's photograph, with acknowledgement to the Mary Rose Trust*)

Since only one sixteenth-century side nock has been recovered, we do not know whether it is an upper or a lower example. Indeed, it is entirely possible that both nocks were the same. Such slight evidence as exists from artists' drawings and contemporary vernacular church wall paintings indicate protective tips but without explicit detail as to shape or size. Once again, we are in the realm of debate.

Some slight circumstantial evidence for there being no difference between the two nocks rests with the prick marks, which we believe indicate the upper limb. If there were distinguishing differences between upper and lower nocks, then it might be argued that the prick marks were superfluous. Or did they have another, as-yet-undisclosed, purpose?

As a side note, we learn from an early writer that "all horns should be fairly large where they fit on the bow so as to keep the string away from the wood, and the shorter they are the better it is, so long as the bow may be strung."[27] Short or long, shaped or otherwise, we do not know, but it is time to leave conjecture.

We will now travel half a millennium back in time to the position of the war bow in early English history. But before we do, we will glance momentarily at the record of warfare even longer ago, portrayed for us as a Neolithic rock painting from a cave in southern Spain; for depicted there is the forerunner of the historic warrior bowman. Here or nearby, two groups of archers joined in battle, each man using a bow for military purpose—surely prehistoric forerunners of the true war bow. How fascinating it would be to know whether this conflict, preserved for posterity, depicted the outcome of an important victory, or whether (since there is evidence from the painting to suggest that one side was unprepared) it merely served as an illustration of tactics. We shall never know.

Much is made of the power of the English medieval war bow, and rightly so, for its purpose was to embarrass the enemy on land at a distance. It was created for that purpose and it performed well. To see it as the sole representative of its genre, however, is to deny the purpose and achievement of its predecessor weapon, that used by the Anglo-Saxon ancestors of the English. Other situations—and here we should mention sea fighting—may be satisfactorily resolved by bows of lighter weight, and this does no discredit either to them or to their users.

To labor the point, the Anglo-Saxon butsecarl with his boga (bow) and his herestræl (war arrow) guarding coastal waters with the scipfyrd (sea soldiers, or marines) was no less well equipped for war than was his scion on the bloody field of Agincourt.

That the bow was held in awe by the early English is manifest in many ways. The Anglo-Saxon Exeter Riddle No. 23 makes little pretense of hiding its secret.

> *"Agof" is my name turned around*
> *I am a splendid creature created through struggle*
> *When I bend and from my bosom goes*

> *A deadly missile; I am prepared*
> *So that I sweep that life-bane far from me.*[28]

The heroic poem Beowulf is evocative of the now-dead lord's previous survival of an arrow storm.

> *Now shall the fire consume — the bright flame grow —*
> *the warrior's lord who often endured the iron-tipped*
> *shower*
> *when the arrow storm powered by bowstrings*
> *sped across the shield wall, the shaft held to its task;*
> *keen in its feathered flight, it followed the barb.*[29]

The expression "arrow storm" is intriguing, since it implies massed archery, and at an early period. How frustrating it is not to know where, and by whom, the arrow storm was delivered.

That the bow and arrow were not always used successfully in warfare is evident. From a thirteenth-century account of the preliminaries to the battle of Stamford Bridge we learn that initial attempts with bow and arrow to dislodge a single Norseman guarding the bridge were manifestly futile.[30] "Englisc mid anre flane ac hit nactes widstod." [Then one Englishman shot with an arrow, but it achieved nothing.]

Earlier we have seen the use of horn on bows. There is an enigmatic reference, again in Beowulf, to a hornbogan—literally "hornbow" in Anglo-Saxon—with which a man unwittingly slew his brother, and this merits some slight speculation. Clearly from the context in which it appears, the weapon was rather special, so was it a composite bow of horn? The origins of the poem are lost in time, but early Germanic weaponry did include composite bows, and the young nobleman who so sadly dispatched his brother may well have come by one.

Professor Gad Rausing in his book *The Bow* refers to High German literature that mentions the hornboge as a weapon of the heathens, although alternatively there may be a more mundane explanation.[31] Many, if not most, early English bows were self-nocked; that is, their string grooves were cut directly into the limb tips. Horning—a recognized expression used by later bowyers (that is, adding protective horns to the bow's tips)—was, as a general rule, a later development. The appropriate expression on completion would be a "horned bow." If this early weapon bore horn sheaths—possibly carved in the form of an animal face as later horn tips were carved—this would have made it a horned bow and thus distinctive, but we must leave it for others to debate the matter and return to reality.

Outmoded anachronism that it is in these days of sophisticated weaponry, the longbow continues to exercise its magic over British minds. It was in recognition of this fascination, and the wishes of those within the British Long-Bow Society who wished to test themselves against the weight and power of replicas of the old war bow, that the society introduced a first trial meeting in 1987.

The purpose of the meeting, the first of many annual gatherings as it proved, was to shoot for distance (required practice when the war bow ruled). Two goals were set: first, achievement of 11 score (220) yards, a statutory requirement for all men over 21 years of age in Tudor times; second, to reach 12 score (240) yards, the commonly accepted distance for a full "bow shot."

To allow fair comparison, a specification was produced for a Standard Arrow—a replica battle shaft based on run-of-the-mill livery arrows as recovered from the warship *Mary Rose*. This specification required all taking part to use a shaft, preferably of ash, 3/8 inch in diameter and 31 1/2 inches in length, its string groove protected by a horn nock-piece, and fletched with 6-inch-long feathers of triangular profile, not less than 3/4 inch high at their highest point. This shaft was to be armed with a military-style broadhead or an armor-penetrating bodkin point. The whole was to weigh no less than 52 grams.

No specification was set down for the bows initially, since profiles and sections of war bows recovered from the *Mary Rose* had yet to be released to England's bowyers by those

Since 1987, replica war bows have been constructed and tested. After nearly two decades of research and dedication, reliable approximations in both performance and design to the legendary medieval English war bow have been achieved. Here, Mark Stretton is at full draw while the author stands in the background with a measuring wheel. (*Author*)

responsible for the safeguarding of their secrets. In consequence, the bows used to deliver the Standard Arrow at early meetings differed in little but draw weight from the recreational weapons then in use.

As time passed, however, more became known, and bows that truly replicated their warlike predecessors began to appear. It became possible for modern archers able to draw these weapons to shoot a replica battle shaft with a replica war bow and thus to develop their skill.

Over the years technique improved, and with this came increased distance. Where a decade before, 9 score (180) yards was considered a fine, almost an optimum, achievement; today, 10 score (200) yards has become average for a good archer, and 11 score (220) yards—the statutory distance decreed by Henry Tudor for men over 21—is regularly made. Even bow shot, 12 score (240) yards and beyond to distances in excess of 300 yards (an almost impossible goal in the early days), is achieved with ease by a small but growing number today.

The following brief summary of carefully measured distances, made with replica war bows, relates the draw weight of the weapon to the distance that they achieved. When these data were recorded, weather conditions were not favorable to shooting, with a strong cross wind and inclining ground, but the summary will go some way to put fictitious claims into perspective. The minimum distance recorded is 200 yards, and the minimum draw weight is 80 pounds.

80 pounds draw weight = 200 yards.
80 pounds draw weight = 226 yards.
85 pounds draw weight = 227 yards.
90 pounds draw weight = 200 yards.
95 pounds draw weight = 226 yards.
100 pounds draw weight = 200 yards.
100 pounds draw weight = 201 yards.
110 pounds draw weight = 237 yards.
115 pounds draw weight = 209 yards.
120 pounds draw weight = 237 yards.
130 pounds draw weight = 224 yards.
130 pounds draw weight = 255 yards.
150 pounds draw weight = 265 yards.
150 pounds draw weight = 279 yards.

Of the 14 bows, seven were of self-yew; that is, one single piece of wood. The remainder varied in their combination of laminations of either hickory or yew backs with bellies of yew, recognizing that, through lack of good wood, towards the end of its days, the war bow was thus laminated or "backed."

To complete the picture, for comparison under similar conditions, distances achieved by heavy recreational bows while shooting the standard arrow were as follows:

60 pounds draw weight = 165 yards.
60 pounds draw weight = 168 yards.
60 pounds draw weight = 176 yards.
65 pounds draw weight = 164 yards.
65 pounds draw weight = 182 yards.
68 pounds draw weight = 169 yards.
68 pounds draw weight = 174 yards.
70 pounds draw weight = 164 yards.
70 pounds draw weight = 176 yards.
70 pounds draw weight = 177 yards.
70 pounds draw weight = 183 yards.

Variations in distance achieved both by war and recreational bows of nominally similar draw weight draw clear attention to three aspects of shooting, each as important today as when the war bow was used in battle: imperfections in technique, the quality of wood, and the skill of the bowyer fashioning the stave.

It is believed that the *Mary Rose* war bows range broadly between 90 and 130 pounds draw weight. The nine bows from those above that fall within that range averaged 221 yards. This equates to the statutory distance required of those practicing in the sixteenth century, and it is tempting to consider this, and the 50 yards between the shortest and the longest shot, to equate broadly with the distance and spread achieved in warfare by an average archer when using a livery arrow in battle conditions and poor weather.

We have looked so far largely at war bows made of yew. It is now time to consider another wood from which this genre were regularly made. Elm has a lower elastic modulus than has yew and is thus an inferior wood for achieving cast and therefore distance. It has the advantage, however, of being a native wood, more readily come by than yew and, in comparison with yew, more easily worked.

It is considered by many that heavy draw weight wych elm bows, made and used by the Welsh for ambush and warfare, were the pattern from which the great war bow evolved. Although they were no match for a yew weapon of equal poundage, the power of these Welsh weapons is not in dispute. Their place in the origin of the war bow may be fundamental, but there are some who point to the Saxon weapon of yew. The debate is sterile; bows of elm were made by statute and sold. Although, as we have seen, marketing them proved difficult. Some, more perhaps than we may guess, provided weaponry for the country's fighting men. An imposed choice for the best of reasons, since yew was becoming scarce, but it was not popular, and authority was often hard pressed to convince the public of elm's qualities. The English archer knew what made a good bow and was not about to be fobbed off with an inferior product to satisfy the whim of those in charge.

To conclude a chapter about the longbow in war without a mention of the Scottish war bow would leave it incomplete. Surrounded by a heady mix of heroic Celtic legend and hard fact, discovering the true Scottish weapon is not an easy task.

One such legendary bow, made, so we are told, of yew from Easragin in Lorn, features in the exploits of clan chief Donald "Dubh" MacAskill, the "Black Donald."[32] On one momentous occasion out of many, in defense of his lands, Donald shot from the beach and killed 12 MacDonald clansmen as they attempted to row their barge ashore on a raiding expedition. The feat was repeated by Neil MacInnes ("Neil of the Bow") who, at a clan gathering, proved the only man able to string and draw a mighty war bow, prized possession of the chief of the clan MacKinnon. With this, or one like it, Neil is reported to have slain a symbolic 12 MacLeod castle rustlers. Other adventures abounded!

Moving reluctantly from the misty world of legend to something approximating reality, let us consider the position and potency of the Scottish weapon. For no particular reason, other than the overriding appeal of different forms of activity (including, among others, football and golf), the Scottish male found archery largely unexciting.

In vain did King James I ordain in 1424 that "all men busk themselves to be archeres for they be twelve years of age," enjoining that "no man play at the futeball."[33] James could pass what laws he might; "futeball" and "goff" came naturally to the Scot; archery did not.

For all that, bow making, or bowing, was a regularly practiced activity, and bow makers (bowers, as they were known) were present in some numbers within all the major Scottish towns and cities. Edinburgh was particularly well served by them. Between 1445 and 1662—the year in which the war bow was dropped from military service in England—no fewer than 97 bowers are recorded in that city.[34] One at least came from elsewhere though. John Mores from Wales is recorded as an Englishman "once English, now Scots . . . To the Inglish boware for bowes to the king vj li [six Scottish pounds—a Scottish pound was worth 1/12 of an English equivalent]." Between 1530 and 1566, John Mores, transmogrified to "Inglish boware" provided bows made, one supposes, in the English style, to be used against his fellow countrymen, whoever they may have been.

For all the activity in Scotland, English bows were evidently in demand. Thomas Udwart, a general merchant who ended his days in Holland, requested the English authorities for permission to import four dozen bows and two cases of arrows to meet demand.

Sadly, we know more about the bow makers, or bowers, than we do about their bows, for the Scottish war bow is undocumented. It is probable that it was of yew by choice, although there is some circumstantial evidence for purchase of timber from inferior sources. It may have differed from its English counterpart in one important respect, however—its profile. Scotland has traditionally been influenced by Continental practice; Scottish troops formed a substantial part of the French army for many years. Where the English bow was largely straight of limb (and counterargument is duly noted), the Scottish weapon may have had recurved limbs in the fashion of the contemporary Burgundian bow.

This recurved style has become known by some as the McNaghton (or MacNaughton) bow, after a mercenary Scottish captain whose archers were customarily provided with it. It is perhaps significant, however, in the context of straight or recurved limb that when Alexander McNaghton was commissioned by Charles I to lead his men on an (abortive) expedition to relieve the Isle of Rhé, he was equipped with English weaponry for the occasion.[35]

Since Scottish archers were regularly outclassed and their bows outshot in conflict with the English, the suggestion must be that they were lighter in draw weight—a factor that recurved ends did not appear to counter. The haunting refrain of the Scottish lament "The Flowers of the Forest" tells of the virtual annihilation of the archers of Ettrickdale, sought out for special attention at Flodden in 1514 by their English counterparts.

Although the Scottish war bow was to continue in use by Scottish clans in battle until the end of the eighteenth century, it appears to have ceased to enjoy royal favor by the late sixteenth century.

Matters changed promptly however, following an engagement during which the royal troops seem to have come off decidedly second best. In 1595, during the latter years of the reign of Queen Elizabeth, James Ferguson, bow maker to King James VI of Scotland, was sent to England with a request to buy up to 10,000 bows and bow staves. Unfortunately for one reason or another, these were not available, and he was forced to go to the "East Countries" for them. The circumstances of the request as reported by James Ferguson are interesting. This is his explanation for the request:

[In 1595] certaine rebelles did rise there [Scotland] against the king who sent against them five hundred horsemen, well appointed. They, meeting three hundred of the Rebels bowe-men, encountered each with the othere where the Bowe-men slue two hundred and four-score of their hors-es, and killed, wounded and sore hurt most part of the king's men.

The report was contained in a complaint about a downturn in trade made to the Council of Aldermen by "decaied" bowyers.[36] Authority may have had something to do with the refusal to supply, however; the prospect of 10,000 English war bows in the hands of the old enemy may not have appealed in the least to those responsible for the security of the nation. In fact it is not improbable that England had a finger in the rebel's pie, since Francis Stewart, Earl of Bothwell, was subsi-dized by London for his punitive expeditions against King James.[37] It is also possible that the bowmen who wreaked such havoc in 1595 were themselves mercenary English archers, and the weapon that they used was the mighty English war bow.

It is now time to leave the old weapon, but before we do let us reflect upon the twist of fate that has provided such detailed knowledge of the late medieval war bow. For we have to thank the English weather and the vagaries of sixteenth-century sea-manship for the information we possess today. We should rec-ognize the foresight of those who sought, found, and planned the raising of the sunken ship, the *Mary Rose*, and the dedica-tion of the men and women divers who brought these weapons to the surface and the deft skills of those who conserved them for posterity. Through this unity of effort, skilled modern bowyers have been enabled to create authentic replicas, and today's bowmen may now savor the deadly power of the weapon that medieval English archers used to such effect.

After four hundred years of service, between the 1252 Assize of Arms when the bow was first officially recognized as a military weapon, and that of 1662, when it was omitted from the list of national weaponry, it is incredible that until today our knowledge of it has rested solely upon paintings, woodcuts, and etchings and from naive vernacular paintings on church walls that have survived by chance. Why, we may ask, do no traces of the many thousands of medieval weapons we know were made remain for us to study?

We may ask the question, but no answer is forthcoming. It is enough that through the caprice of fate we have Tudor samples to examine. Let us now turn to its modern manufacture as, in the following chapter, a master bowyer explains the creation of a replica war bow.

Chapter Two

THE DESIGN AND CONSTRUCTION OF THE WAR BOW

"Then bowes for England. Bowes we see, Doth bring home fame and victory For one gun shot they will shoot three"
—Ancient ballad

While the purpose of this chapter is to describe the war bow and its making, we will deviate a little and, risking the accusation of academic pedantry, open with a question. Do we speak of a long-bow, a long bow, or a longbow? The question is an interesting one, and really not at all bookish, since each of the three descriptions has a separate meaning.

The authoritative Oxford English Dictionary lends its portentous weight to "long-bow" and defines it as "The name given to the bow drawn by hand (and so distinguished from cross-bow)." But, hang on, surely many crossbows can be spanned by hand, even if subsequently released mechanically! The distinction in this respect is surely between the longbow, which is held and shot lengthwise, and the crossbow, which is held and shot cross-wise. Perhaps we should let that pass, but what about the second of the terms, the "long bow." This clearly implies a bow of more than average length—one thinks immediately of the Japanese Yumi or those of the Brazilian Indians.[1] Each of these is clearly a long bow, since each well exceeds the height of its user. In contrast, the famed Turkish flight bow is about 3 feet 6 inches in length, drawn by hand but clearly not a long bow by our understanding if one accepts the vernacular definition of the term.

It has to be said, of course, that prior to the mid-fifteenth century, the term "longbow," however spelled, was not in common use, if indeed it was in use at all. "Hand bow," "bend bow," "English bow," "noble bow," "trusty tree," or "crooked stick": each appear in early ballads and all refer to that weapon that we recognize today. With the term "longbow" now in common use and others discarded, let us see how sixteenth- and seventeenth-century writers refer to it.

The first of note is from Thomas Elyot, Knight, whose 1531 book *The Governour* set down benchmarks for behavior by men of consequence and their sons. He is absolute in his approval of archery—"none may be compared with shooting in the longe bowe"—and, it might be noted, is both perspicacious and forthright in his condemnation of football—"wherein is nothing but beastly furie and extreme violence." Curiously, the perceptive Sir Thomas writes "crossebowe" as one word.

Roger Ascham, our earliest author in English to write explicitly on the subject of archery, while dedicating his book *Toxophilus* to "All Gentlemen and Yomen of England," includes the paragraph "By this matter I meane shootinge in the longe bowe, for Englishe men."[2] No help there!

The *Boke for a Justice of Peace*, written in 1559, continues the use of "longe bowe."[3] Conversely, in 1583 Sir John Smythe's stolid defense of his favored weapon brought on his head the acrimonious wrath of dedicated but volatile harquebusier Humphrey Barwick, who wrote deprecatingly of it as the "Longbow."[4]

We move on to 1596, when the bowyers themselves, in a plea to authority to uphold statute law concerned with archery practice, refer equally to "Longe-Bowes" and "Englishe Bowes."[5] The description is perpetuated in 1628 by John Bartlet, patriotic author of *A New Invention of Shooting Fire-Shafts in Long-Bowes.*[6] Such arrangements included, as an off-the-cuff tidbit, shooting these at tethered bulls instead of baiting them with dogs.

In 1676 Thomas D'Urfey and his fellow Finsbury archer Robert Shotterell, in their poem "Archerie Reviv'd, or the Bow-Man's Excellence," refer to the "Long-Bow," and from then on, through the early and mid-eighteenth century, this term prevails; the hyphen finally disappeared as the late eighteenth and early nineteenth century revival got under way.[7]

Now it is de rigeur to call it anything but "longbow," and only the British Long-Bow Society clings to the archaic form. As a matter of some casual interest, one wonders how a fifteenth-century writer on the subject would describe the archer who used the bow—a "long bowman" perhaps?

Our diversion is done. We will move on to other matters and to the more detailed examination of the war bow, together with a summary of the construction of a replica by an English bow maker.

Although, as might be expected, the bow was used in sea warfare, and much testament for this exists in both history and legend, it would seem unlikely that a specific form was developed for the purpose. There is evidence, however, for the adaptation of arrows; in early times these were used to propel bags of lime and for incendiary purposes.

A well-documented account of sea warfare concerns the engagement at Sluys, off the Flanders coast, in 1340, between the navies of King Edward III and King Philip VI of France. Ranged against the English were four formidable divisions of French ships, including—and flaunted prominently in the first division—the *Christopher*, an English ship recently captured by the French and manned by a huge force of Genoese crossbowmen. Not unexpectedly, retaking this vessel was a matter of honor for the English, and the barrage of arrows put down by the archers quickly cleared the decks of opposition. With Genoese blood clogging the scuppers, English sailors swarmed aboard, and the ship *Christopher* took her rightful place with the rest of the English battle fleet. After a fiercely contested struggle that went on throughout the night, and during which many thousands of sailors and soldiers died or drowned, the French divisions slowly gave way, and resistance crumbled. In the light of early morning, those French vessels that had survived fled the scene. This hard-won victory gave Edward a much-needed command of the English Channel, which was to prove invaluable in later excursions against Philip of France.

The bow was an obvious weapon for sea-borne soldiers. Most medieval ships carried them as defense against attack and as an invaluable means of clearing enemy decks of sailors. Typical perhaps of small fifteenth-century vessels was the single-masted *Thomas*, a ship of 130 tons used largely for trading voyages but also impressed into royal service for Henry V when she formed part of the naval force carrying men to France in 1415, where they would conduct the campaign that ended at Agincourt.[8] We do not know her normal complement of archers, if indeed she carried any at all, or, for that matter, her regular inventory of weapons; but when the *Thomas* was disposed of in 1422 as a going concern, sold with her were just four bows, five sheaves of arrows, and three "pollaxes" (pole-axes).

The sea-borne soldier was seemingly greeted with some ambivalence in legend, although he always proved his worth.[9] A curious ballad of Robin Hood exemplifies, perhaps, a common sailor's view of his comrade soldier archer. Robin is so useless at sea that the ship's master threatens to throw him overboard. However, when a pirate ship appears upon the scene, Robin comes into his own. Tied firmly to the mast in order to keep him upright, with customary skill, he disposes of the opposition and is then hailed as hero.

This tall tale may have some tenuous basis in fact, however. During the reign of Henry VIII, a Scottish pirate, Sir Andrew

Barton, was making free with English shipping and had to be brought to heel. While this was successfully achieved under Admiral Lord Howard, enduring legend attributes to an archer, William Horseley, the shot that killed him.[10] From these and other more literal events we may deduce that archery at sea relied rather more upon individual accuracy than upon the arrow storm saturation shooting of set-piece land battles, and it would be logical to presume the importance of bearing, or personalized, shafts to achieve this accuracy. It might also be logical to presume the importance of good sea legs for the shipborne archer, perhaps suggesting his recruitment from the English maritime counties. Men accustomed to the sea might be preferred to those who were not.

Sadly we know little of the early war bows fifteenth-century archers used, beyond their stylized representation in woodcuts depicting battles, for of the many thousands that we know were made, none now exist within the public domain. Why none are present is unanswerable, but there is little real mystery here. The bow is essentially a stick, and a stick for which there is no further use is readily disposed of. Perhaps some survived to the death of their owner: cherished mementoes of past battles won, and even possibly for a generation or two beyond; but association grows dim with the passing of time, and eventually even these few evidently succumbed.

Thus it is that by a coupling of sad chance and great good fortune those war weapons available to us for examination are solely of the succeeding century and specifically from the decks and chests of the great Tudor warship *Mary Rose*, which foundered with such loss of life in July of 1545.

Built originally around 1510, and named, it is thought, after Henry's favorite sister, the *Mary Rose* was the pride of the king's navy, earning an enviable reputation as a fine warship that handled well. For many years she was principal among those warships owned by King Henry. Forming the core of England's naval sea-power, these Great Ships, as they were known, would be joined during hostilities by other vessels impressed into service.[11]

The *Mary Rose* was first refitted in 1536, when it is thought that her gun decks may have been strengthened to take the heavier ordnance then available. She was later to have had a second, and this had scarcely been completed before she was hastily made ready for service and sailed to Portsmouth to join the fleet assembled against the French threat of July 1545. Now one of England's first great broadside battleships, the latest refit had converted her from her original clinker build (overlapping planks) to a carvel one (abutting boards)—a major but necessary alteration to allow her gun ports to be properly closed.

The English had been at war with France intermittently since 1510, and a French fleet, including highly maneuverable galleys, now under the command of Admiral Claude D'Annebault, had sailed audaciously across the English Channel into the Solent to engage the English fleet in battle.

Initially becalmed, but with a light offshore breeze now springing up, the *Mary Rose* hoisted a full head of sail to catch what little wind there was and came about to counter the attentions of a French galley. She heeled as she turned, however, and her lower gun ports, open perhaps to engage the lower-built galley, took in water. Adding to her problems was significant overmanning, indifferent seamanship, and possibly guns that may not have been properly secured against sliding from port to starboard.[12] For whatever reason, she shipped water in greater quantity than either bilge or primitive pump could expect to manage and within minutes had foundered, coming to lie at rest upon her starboard side. The subsequent great loss of life was compounded by the anti-boarding netting, which prevented escape.

It is only natural for the French to have claimed responsibility for the loss of this Tudor naval icon, and this they did. Claude D'Annebault, French Admiral of the day, recounts his view of events:

Our galleys had all the advantages of working which we could desire to the great damage of the English who for

want of wind not being able to stir laid exposed to our
cannon and being so much higher and bulkier than our
galleys hardly a shot missed them whilst they, with the
help of their oars shifted at pleasure. Fortune favoured
our fleet in this manner for above an hour during which
time among other damages the English received, the *Mary
Rose*, one of their principal ships was sunk by our cannon
and of 5, or 600 men which were on board only 5 and 30
escaped.

Although nothing remained of her port side, when raised,
the *Mary Rose* revealed no damage by gunfire to her starboard
side, and D'Annebault's claim may therefore rest upon a pre-
sumption that the ship was maneuvering to bring the starboard guns on her orlop deck to bear upon a menacing galley
sitting low in the water. Such is conjecture, but let us return to
the bows and to the many questions that they pose.

One question that has exercised the thoughts and minds of
experienced bowyers today concerns the original profile of
those sixteenth-century bows recovered from the depths of the
Solent. Were they straight (or at least as straight as the
vagaries of grain would allow in a self-bow) or had they been
artificially enhanced to produce a recurved end?

It is appropriate here to explain the term. To recurve a bow
is to artificially curve the final 10 inches or so of each limb so
that when braced, the ends curve away from the archer. The
purpose is to improve the conversion of potential to kinetic
energy and maximize power.

Some tenuous circumstantial evidence exists that suggests
that two of the bows recovered might have been so shaped.
This exists in a drawing made of two bows recovered by the
Deane brothers who explored the wreck site in the early nineteenth century. The drawing shows an even curvature on each
limb, and this suggests to some that they had been artificially
enhanced. Sadly, neither of these two bows now exists; their
whereabouts are unknown, and we have only the drawing
from which to judge.

A second case is made by others who refer to the Cowdray Print illustrating the scene at Portsmouth on the occasion of the sinking of the *Mary Rose*. A number of the archers shown have bows with curved ends. The print is a stylized representation, however, and there is the distinct possibility of artistic license. Principal among the recurvists, as we may call the believers, was respected veteran bow maker Richard Galloway, who, with his detailed knowledge of the Scottish practice of steaming in curves, was convinced that completed bows were so treated—going so far as to say that in his opinion those boxed bows carried aboard were unfinished.[13] Advancing his claim, Galloway drew attention to the draw weight gained by curvature and assessed this as adding some 20 percent to cast when compared with a straight stave, a useful method of improving performance on a lighter bow. The question of why unfinished bows would be found upon a fighting warship is left unanswered.

While there is no more than the slightest evidence for curvature in those bows recovered, and now in the Mary Rose Trust's museum and store, it is nevertheless certain that its advantages were both known and appreciated, due to known contact between English and Burgundian archers.

Henry VIII was closely involved with Emperor Maximilian I; they had joined together in an adventure into France in 1513, which culminated in the set-piece battle known colloquially to archers and to the less staid of historians as the Battle of the Spurs and to academicians as the Siege of Therouanne.[14] English troops would therefore have had firsthand knowledge of Burgundian archers and of their heavily recurved bows. Further than that, Maximilian had employed English mercenary archers in his campaigns during 1511, and contemporary drawings show a number armed with the Burgundian weapon.

To develop the subject a little further, it would be unproductive to directly compare the English weapon with its Burgundian counterpart, for the latter differed significantly,

Detail of a painting in the Royal collection showing Henry VIII's fleet, including ships similar to the Mary Rose, off Dover.

not only in profile but also in cross section. The English war bow had an even taper from handle to limb end; the Continental weapon employed three separate sections, ranging between ogival below the handle (via thin, low-cambered, plano-convex limbs) to elliptical limb ends. It was a more sophisticated bow entirely, and one involving significantly more work than the basic English weapon.

A further significant difference concerned performance. An English war bow that came around in full compass employed one force curve. It would (and its replicas will) work effectively with an arrow between 29 and 31 inches in length. The recurved Burgundian war bow was a more complex weapon entirely. With a set back, nonworking handle, flexible limbs, and stiffer working limb ends, at full draw it provided two distinct force curves. It reached its fullest efficiency, however, when used with a longer arrow than that of the English weapon. Additionally, the construction allowed greater cast from a comparatively lower draw weight. I possess a modern example of this fascinating weapon and can confirm the sweetness of its shooting ability.

It is tempting to believe that returning English bowmen, convinced of the advantages of the Continental weapon, brought examples back and that examination of these persuaded some bowyers to add recurves to the limbs of their weapons. However, we are now deeply into the realms of speculation and must move on.

There have been past endeavors in modern times to recreate heavy draw weight war weapons. However, with little on which to base their construction, what have been fashioned have been recreational style bows with deep-cambered, planoconvex sections, differing significantly from those forms we now know to have been used by medieval bowyers.

English bowyer George Sorrel created a number of heavy draw weight bows for his unit of the Kent Home Guard during the early years of the Second World War; while the firm of Purle is known to have made one or two for export to Canada and the United States during the 1930s.

Perhaps the most accurate representation of a war bow in modern times was that made and tested in the early 1920s by Saxton Pope and described by him in his book *Bows and Arrows*.[15] His replica drew on the exact dimensions of one of the two Tudor bows recovered from the sunken warship *Mary Rose* and held in the Tower of London.

Pope used *Taxus brevifolia*, which had 40 growth rings to the inch and a 3/8-inch sapwood layer. To his surprise, this 6-foot-4-inch weapon gave a draw weight of just 72 pounds when drawn to 36 inches. Pope subsequently cut his bow down to 6 feet in length, which improved the draw weight somewhat, but it was still disappointingly low. He records, "These records are [a] distinct disappointment and are seemingly not the fault of the quality of the wood or of its construction."

As we have noted, veteran bow maker Richard Galloway believed the Tower bows to have been unfinished. Replicas made by himself he shortened and piked (tapered), thus greatly increasing their cast. We will later see that Roger Ascham,

A detail from a panel painted by Hans Memling in 1489 showing the recurved profile of a continental style bow. (*Memlingmuseum, Saint-Janshospitaal, Bruges*)

author of *Toxophilus*, has pertinent comment to make concerning new bows, and these will set Galloway's remarks in their proper context. We will take the matter further, for it will be constructive to see what Roger Ascham, a contemporary of those bows, has to say. He is explicit in his advice. However, it is directed (as are most of his comments) not at the bowyer or maker of the weapon, but at the archer who will shoot in it.

When his bowe is boughte and broughte home, afore he trust much upon it, let him trye and trimme it after this sort [in this way]. Take your bowe into the fielde, shoote in him, sincke him with dead, heavye shafts, look where he cometh moste, provide for that place betimes [mark it] least it pinche, and so freate [develop crysals]: when you have thus shotte in him, and perceyved good shootinge woode in him, you must have him againe to [take him to] a good, cunninge [skillful] and trusty workman, which shall cut him shorter, and pike [thin] him and dresse him fitter, make him come around in compasse every where, and whipping [taper] at the endes, but with discretion, lest he whippe in sunder, or els freete soner than he be ware of.[16]

If this was expert advice and regularly followed, then it is plain that bow maker Richard Galloway is vindicated and right to say that the boxed bows were unfinished. However, they had been tillered by the bowyer, and there is evidence that they had their horn nocks; so, even if not perfected, they were serviceable items, which might properly be described as shootable but perhaps without realization of their full capabilities. Honor is satisfied.

However Ascham tucks in an enigmatic, almost throw-away, remark a little later on—one with interesting connotations as we shall see: "And if he be flatte made, gather him rounde, and so shall he both shoote the faster, for farre shootinge, and also be surer for near prickinge."[17]

If by "flat," Ascham means "straight limbed" (and it seems that he may do), then what does "gather him rounde" mean? It is very tempting to see this as building a curve into the limbs; the creation in effect of a recurved bow, one that would, as we know today, give greater cast for "farre shootinge." Perhaps the owners of those Cowdray Print bows with curved ends had followed their mentor's advice? It has to be said, alternatively, that by "flat," Ascham may have meant "flat backed," in which case he is recommending changing the back to one rather more round. The remark remains enigmatic.

Beyond the knowledge that the vast majority of war bows were manufactured from yew staves (*Taxus baccata*), it is unlikely at this stage that dendrological science can determine the place of origin of those recovered from the sea bed. It has been said, correctly, that the quality of English-grown yew does not generally compare well with that grown in the harsh mountainous conditions and poor soil of Continental Europe, notably the central European countries, the Spanish Pyrenees, and the mountainous area of north Italy; and since trading

The European yew tree, *Taxus baccata*, showing its characteristic tangle of branches, leaves, and berries. Yew was the preferred wood for war bows. All parts of the yew plant are poisonous to humans.

arrangements existed with all, it would seem likely that staves from those areas were the origin of the *Mary Rose* bows.

With yew from these sources now unavailable, replica war bows today rely largely upon carefully selected native wood, some of which is of excellent quality, or upon hard-grown North American *Taxus brevifolia* from mountainous regions.

Occasionally small quantities of good-quality Italian yew does become available, and there is thus the opportunity to measure good *T. baccata* against good *T. brevifolia*. Such an opportunity occurred in 2005. The comparisons are revealing, and as I believe them to be of interest, they are set down accordingly.

Five replica war bows, each to similar specification, were compared for distance achieved. Two were of English yew (*T. baccata*), each of 120 pounds draw weight; two were of United States Oregon yew (*T. brevifolia*), one of 130 pounds and one of 150 pounds draw weight; and one was of Italian yew (*T. baccata*), of 100 pounds draw weight. The United

States and the Italian yew bows were crafted by professional bowyer Philip (Pip) Bickerstaffe, and the English yew bows were made by war bowyer Joseph (Joe) Gibbs. Three shafts of equal weight were shot from each bow. The weather conditions were not ideal but were deemed shootable: a cold but bright autumn afternoon following a heavy frost and a clearing mist.

The Italian yew bow (100 pounds draw weight) harvested from the sunless side of a dark northern Italian valley, achieved 225 yards with a 31-inch standard livery battle shaft weighing 68 grams and 270 yards with a lighter flight shaft of similar length but lower fletchings. The two English yew bows (120 pounds draw weight) each made 220 yards with battle shafts of similar weight and 270 yards with a flight shaft. Grown hard, from the mountains of Oregon, the heavier United States bow (150 pounds draw weight) made 255 yards with a 68-gram arrow and 300 with a flight shaft; while its lighter companion (130 pounds draw weight)—from the same tree—made 240 yards with the war arrow and 280 yards with the flight shaft.

It is apparent from these tests that for distance shooting, the lighter Italian bow was almost a match for an Oregon yew bow 30 pounds heavier in draw weight and equal to an English yew bow heavier by 20 pounds. Considering the greater length of this bow (84 inches as opposed to 76 inches), it is probable that if using a longer arrow, the Italian bow would actually have outshot its greater draw weight competitors.

It is of passing interest that while the average mass (weight) of the known sixteenth-century bows checked varies between 700 and 890 grams, the Italian yew bow shot weighs 1,085 grams, the heavy draw weight Oregon yew bow weighs 1,134 grams, and the English yew bows each weigh 1,028 grams. We should attribute little significance to this comparison, however, in view of the likely cellular degradation in those recovered from the depths of the sea, the greater length of the Italian yew bow, and other variables.

Comparison between the Oregon and English yew weapons suggests that good English *T. baccata* is almost a match for good *T. brevifolia*, but of course the latter species was not available to our medieval bowyer. However, results indicate that weight for weight, Italian *T. baccata* will outshoot both. These tests appear to show why Italian yew was prized above all other cultivars for the construction of war bows and indeed later for recreational weapons.

In the context of native yew, it might be appropriate at this point to comment on the deeply held belief that the ancient yew trees often to be found in older English churchyards were planted to provide a ready source of bow wood. Sadly this is almost certainly not the case. Often, in fact, the trees predate the church and were objects of veneration by our remote ancestors.[18] Additionally, yew leaves are toxic (hence the designation *taxus*) to cattle and are thus best enclosed. This is not to say that bough, or country, bows will not have been made from native trees, including on occasion those within church precincts, but bough bows are notoriously fickle and do not match the ability of those made from the trunk to create cast.

The lack of esteem with which English yew was held in the sixteenth century is evident from the cost of bows made from it. With sources of Spanish and Italian yew drying up, the best of yew wood was now imported from Poland and other East European countries, and this was reflected in their price.

Bows meet [suitable] for men's shooting being outlandish
[of foreign origin] Yew of the best sort, not over the price
of 6 shillings and 8 pence; bows meet for mens shooting
of the second sort, 3 shillings and 4 pence; bows for men,
of a courser sort [the bows, not the men!] called livery
bows, 2 shillings and 2 pence, bows being English Yew 2
shillings.[19]

Good wood was in such short supply that no person under the age of seventeen, "unless possessed of moveables worth forty marks, or the son of parents having an estate of ten pounds per annum," might shoot "in a yew bow."[20]

Unfortunate folk without these qualifications were relegated to inferior bows of elm, wych (witch) hazel, or ash. In Elizabeth I's reign, it was a symbol of a person's quality to be seen at the butts bearing a yew bow. One wonders whether the popular later nineteenth-century practice of staining inferior wood to look like yew had already begun. Perhaps a suspicious, sharp-eyed beadle, charged with the superintendence of the local butts, would occasionally look closely at a young man's bow before moving away muttering darkly to himself.

During the years between 1530 and 1560, England imported over half a million bow staves of yew from the forests of Nuremberg, Austria, and Poland. Understandably these sources eventually dried up, and during the last half of the century, supply diminished to a trickle and finally ceased altogether.

In 1598 London historian John Stowe was bemoaning the loss of the traditional practices of bowyery and fletching in London's Grub Street. "Of late years inhabited in the most part by bowyers, fletchers, bowstring makers and suchlike occupations, now little occupied; archery giving way to a number of bowling alleys and dining houses, which in all places are increased and too much frequented."[21] Despite the obvious problem of lack of good bow wood, Stowe was clear about one other important reason for the forsaking of archery by the populace at large: "for by the means of closing in the common grounds, our archers for want to shoot abroad [outside] creep into bowling alleys near home where they have room enough to hazard their money at unlawful games."[22]

The Englishman, however, has ever sought excuse for avoiding unwelcome effort, and archery practice was not to the taste of all. Although there were indeed some closures of common land, Finsbury Fields, with their roving marks, overseen and kept tidy by authority since 1498, were to remain open for shooting over the next 100 and more years until finally closed off in the early eighteenth century. There was clearly adequate opportunity for shooting in the yew longbow by those disposed to seek it out.

Although as yet we have no idea precisely when it occurred, at some point, with yew in short supply, the backed bow was introduced. Backing bows by removing the knotty sapwood and replacing it with a strip of better-quality wood was forced upon bowyers through the diminishing availability of good yew sapwood. We know that it was found early in the development of the recreational weapon and with certainty that it predates the nineteenth century, but the practice is believed to have begun toward the end of the sixteenth century and is said to have first originated with the Kelsal family of bowyers of Manchester.[23] The practice proved beneficial. As Thomas Roberts reports, "the experiment exceeded their expectations." Many archers now preferred a backed bow to a self-bow—a term that now appeared to distinguish one from the other. To what extent the backed bow was used in warfare is unknown, since none now exist; however, the weapon continued in an occasional secondary capacity well into the seventeenth century, and certain of those weapons known to have been used during the civil wars of the 1640s may well have been backed.[24]

But, we move too fast. It is now time to look at the late medieval bowyer's bench to see him at work. Some license is necessary here, for beyond the sketchiest of detail, we have no knowledge of the organizing of his day. We do know for certain that he was forbidden by statute law to work during the hours of darkness, and we also know something of the simple tools that he would have used.

As a relevant aside, because of the sumptuary laws, we also know that in early times he and his wife were required to dress according to their station. Those early dress codes were quite precise, though it will seem incredible to today's generation that seventeenth-century men and women had their clothing dictated to them. To perform his tasks, our bowyer would have been dressed in breeches of plain woolen cloth; would have worn a shirt of unbleached linen, white woolen hose, and low-heeled leather shoes. His wife would have been required to wear a cap or coif of white woolen yarn and a gray dress—unless her husband could prove himself a gentleman by descent, in which case she could indulge herself to some degree. His grandfather, as a bowyer or a fletcher, would have dressed even more simply in a knee-length skirted doublet but would have worn a rather fetching hat with an upturned castellated brim.[25]

As previously discussed, the bowyer's oath, taken at the end of his apprenticeship when, or if, he joined his guild, was explicit—as was that of the fletcher. He would reveal the "mysteries" of his trade to no one. That this was carried out to the letter explains the lack of written evidence for the early bowyer's craft. As recently as the 1950s, bowyer George Sorrel went to his grave with his lips tightly sealed. However, one ex-apprentice did set down the secrets of his craft in the early twentieth century, and thus we have an inkling of past practice.[26] Later in this chapter, we will examine these revelations and, employing a little literary license, consider how they might have been applied to sixteenth-century bows recovered from the *Mary Rose*, but first we will examine the bows themselves. We will look in detail at two.

Each is of good quality yew, and for convenience we will identify them as bow A and bow B. Overall length, length of cones, maximum girth, depth, width, and general profile of cross section will be considered individually. Where at all possible, dimensions are given in Imperial measure. Each bow's cross section conforms to the general criteria for sixteenth-century war bows established by examination of other bows recovered from the *Mary Rose*, in that width is invariably greater than depth.

Bow A: overall length, 77 inches; length between string nocks, 75 inches (determined by examination of cone grooves); length of each cone, 2 inches; width of bow at geometric center 1 1/2 inches (38 millimeters); depth at geometric center, 1 1/4 inches (32 millimeters); girth at geometric center, 4 1/2 inches (11.4 centimeters).

I had the opportunity of examining this weapon, and in the course of this, I checked the point of balance. This was established at a point 37 1/2 inches from the limb tips, or an inch from the geometric center. Considering a feature occurring at the geometric center—two raised humps on the back of the bow, their centers 4 inches apart and a depth at their apex of nearly 1 1/2 inches (37 millimeters)—this would seem to have been the optimum position for shooting a well-balanced weapon. Noting the relationship of the point of balance to the geometric center, there is no obvious lower limb, thus this bow could perhaps have been shot either way up. Still, concerning the two humps, it is possible that this bow would have been stiff in the hand and would perhaps not have worked through the center section as would other bows having an even taper. Comparison of dimensions along the stave will indicate the potential quality of this bow and the care with which it has been made. To determine the relation of back to side, 19 broadly ogival sections have been measured, each approximately 4 inches apart.

From one cone to the other, the width and depth (expressed in millimeters for convenience) are as follows:

At 4 inches, 21 millimeters wide and 18 millimeters deep.
At 8 inches, 26 millimeters wide and 21 millimeters deep.
At 12 inches, 28 millimeters wide and 24 millimeters deep.
At 16 inches, 31 millimeters wide and 26 millimeters deep.
At 20 inches, 35 millimeters wide and 28 millimeters deep.
At 24 inches, 36 millimeters wide and 31 millimeters deep.
At 28 inches, 37 millimeters wide and 31 millimeters deep.
At 32 inches, 36 millimeters wide and 30 millimeters deep.
At 36 inches, 37 millimeters wide and 31 millimeters deep.
At 40 inches, 38 millimeters wide and 33 millimeters deep.
At 44 inches, 38 millimeters wide and 30 millimeters deep.
At 48 inches, 38 millimeters wide and 31 millimeters deep.
At 52 inches, 37 millimeters wide and 32 millimeters deep.
At 56 inches, 35 millimeters wide and 31 millimeters deep.
At 60 inches, 32 millimeters wide and 29 millimeters deep.

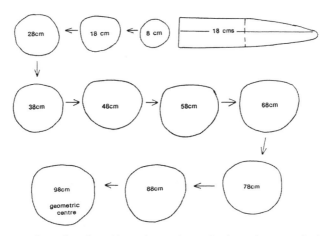

Cross sections plotted at 10 centimeter intervals along the upper limb of
"Bow A" recovered from the *Mary Rose*. (*With acknowledgements to the
Mary Rose Trust*)

At 64 inches, 29 millimeters wide and 25 millimeters deep.
At 68 inches, 28 millimeters wide and 23 millimeters deep.
At 72 inches, 26 millimeters wide and 20 millimeters deep.
At 76 inches, 14 millimeters wide and 16 millimeters deep.

The mass of this bow is not known, so it cannot therefore
be deemed either strong or light. However, its shorter length in
comparison with bow B below suggests a lighter weapon.
Having regard to the vagaries of grain and a dogleg in one
limb (between 24 and 28 inches), both the side and plan profiles show an even taper.

Bow B: overall length, 83 inches; assumed length between
string nocks, 81 inches (determined similarly to bow A); length
of each cone, 2 inches; bow width at geometric center, 1 5/8
inches (41 millimeters); depth at geometric center, 1 3/8 inches
(35 millimeters); girth, 5 1/4 inches (13.3 centimeters). As with
bow A, 20 well-proportioned but broadly ogival cross sections, each some 4 inches apart, have been measured from one
cone to the other, beginning at the nock groove and numbering
from one cone to the other. The width and depth (again in millimeters) at each point are as follows:

Stylized representation of the typical cross section of a war bow at its geometric center. Width, 38 millimeters (1.5 inches), depth 32 millimeters (1.25 inches). Limb tapering to 13 millimeters (.5 inch) at the base of the nock. Length of nock cone: 4 centimeters (1.5 inches). (*Author*)

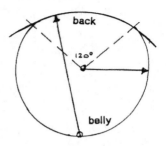

At 4 inches, 19 millimeters wide and 19 millimeters deep.
At 8 inches, 25 millimeters wide and 21 millimeters deep.
At 12 inches, 31 millimeters wide and 25 millimeters deep.
At 16 inches, 36 millimeters wide and 30 millimeters deep.
At 20 inches, 37 millimeters wide and 28 millimeters deep.
At 24 inches, 39 millimeters wide and 30 millimeters deep.
At 28 inches, 41 millimeters wide and 29 millimeters deep.
At 32 inches, 40 millimeters wide and 31 millimeters deep.
At 36 inches, 40 millimeters wide and 32 millimeters deep.
At 40 inches, 41 millimeters wide and 36 millimeters deep.
At 44 inches, 42 millimeters wide and 32 millimeters deep.
At 48 inches, 41 millimeters wide and 34 millimeters deep.
At 52 inches, 38 millimeters wide and 37 millimeters deep.
At 56 inches, 37 millimeters wide and 35 millimeters deep.
At 60 inches, 35 millimeters wide and 32 millimeters deep.
At 64 inches, 34 millimeters wide and 32 millimeters deep.
At 68 inches, 31 millimeters wide and 34 millimeters deep.
At 72 inches, 28 millimeters wide and 29 millimeters deep.
At 76 inches, 25 millimeters wide and 25 millimeters deep.
At 80 inches, 20 millimeters wide and 18 millimeters deep.

It would be inappropriate to do more than make casual comparison between these two weapons; however, while the cross sections on bow A show an invariably greater width than depth—in accord with the general criteria for all recovered bows—those for bow B show far less distinction between the two measurements.[27]

Bow A was recovered from the weather deck of the ship where, one may assume, it had been abandoned by its owner as he strove (sadly, probably without success) to escape from drowning. While the attractive and functional dip at the handle section may have been an original feature, it is tempting to think of it as a personal touch. The bow is certainly shorter, by some 6 inches, than its companion, bow B—again suggesting some personalizing.

Bow B, one of a number in a bow chest (or bow coffin, to name it correctly), is not without its interesting features. Besides its length—toward the upper limit of the range of those recovered—and its qualification as a more massive and thus a stronger weapon than bow A, the limb terminals show just a suggestion of forward positioning; and although this may be a natural feature, there are those who will point to this as evidence of artificial recurving.

Before leaving these examples of sixteenth-century weapons, it will be instructive to briefly compare dimensionally an example of a much older weapon: a longbow recovered in 1932 from an Irish crannog and in a tenth-century context. Originally 75 inches in overall length and straight, the Ballinderry bow is 1.6 inches in width, 1 1/4 inches deep at its geometric center, and a little over 4 1/4 inches in girth. It is of yew, with sap and heartwood in proportion, and is broadly plano-convex in section.[28]

This self-nocked bow differs only in degree from those recovered half a millennium later, for it compares favorably with bow B above. Known colloquially as the Viking bow, if this is truly typical of contemporary Viking weaponry, then the bows in use at Maldon in AD 991 are put into perspective, and doubt may be cast upon the belief that weapons of that period were inferior in draw weight to those of later times.

It is time now to look in some detail at the making of these fearsome weapons and, in passing, at those whose choice it was to exercise the skill of bowyery. Most are familiar with the great and still-powerful London livery companies, many of which are still in being, albeit in roles far removed from their original purpose. There were, however, many smaller equally

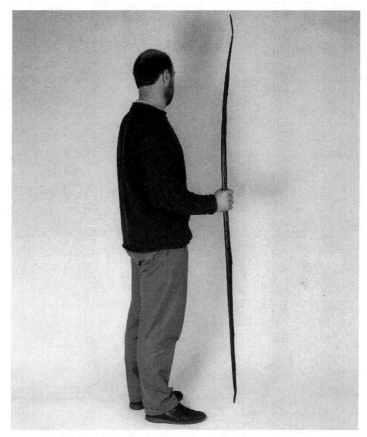

A Curator holding the Ballinderry carnnog Viking bow. Dating to the tenth century it is among the earliest intact longbows known. (Copyright, *National Museum of Ireland*)

formal gatherings in provincial cities, and one such existed for a short while in the west-country English City of Bristol.[29]

In 1479 a composite guild of bowyers and fletchers was formed here. Hitherto, the bowyers and fletchers had shared a guild with the hoopers, a trade in which artisans used many of the same tools. The guild would never have been large, and we do not know the names of those who founded it. Two wardens, one presumably from each skill, took responsibility for the smooth running of things, including the important control of quality.

Every man of the same Craft make and wirche [work] all manner of stuff of the said Craft as Bows, Arrows, and other tackle and stuff well and sufficiently, of good, able and dry Timber, and of no green, false nor deceivable timber wherethrough the buyer thereof in anywise may be deceived or endamaged.

Some indication of the relative size of this small guild is the amount of wine provided for them at feast days by the mayor, at his expense. They received just two gallons to share between them, where the hoopers received three. They were required, however, to collect this themselves "always purveyed [provided] that the saide persons of Craftes shall send their own servauntes and their own pottes for the seyd wine."

We may not know the names of those Bristol bowyers who plied their trade in 1479, but from the City's apprentice book for the sixteenth century, we have a fuller picture; and it is time now to introduce a leavening of supposition. The indulgence of literary license will be based upon historic detail and contemporary practical reconstruction as we examine the making of a sixteenth-century war bow such as may have appeared on the muster roll of Henry VIII's flagship, *Mary Rose*. Alongside our narrative we will look in photographic detail at the work of talented young bowyer Joe Gibbs as he creates a replica war bow from a stave of good-quality English yew.

The year is 1535. Standing awkwardly by the side of his father, a husbandman from Astley in Worcestershire, is young Richard Vykeris, a fourteen-year-old lad. He is to be apprenticed to bowyer John Powell and his wife Katherine for seven years to learn the craft of bow making. A keen and successful young archer at the village butts, his sights already set on the stronger of his father's bows, Richard is anxious to learn more about the war bow and how it is made. He will be a willing pupil.

It will not be long before he is shown the rudiments of bowyery and the tools that he will be taught to use, for John

Powell has just received a bundle of yew staves, unloaded at Bristol docks together with a consignment of Malmsey wine from Spain. Legislation passed many years ago required that imported wine must be accompanied by parcels of bow staves cut from the forests of the Spanish Pyrenees. Bowyer John is friendly with the local farmer of customs and now has the maximum stock allowed by law, 300 superb billets of the best yew. His companion bowyers, John Phillips, Robert Jurden, and John Mascall, fellow members of his small guild, have been equally fortunate, and each is now equipped to provide the king with good war bows.

When Richard has settled in and is standing by John's side, bowyer Powell begins his instruction.[30] Ordinarily he would use judgment gained over many years to select a stave, but he has to explain why he might reject one. He is looking for straight grain, and his criterion is the run of its rift and reed. He looks at the back of the stave he has selected and shows Richard that the line of the reed runs true. If it had run out to the side within 15 inches, it would have been discarded. He is at pains to point out the distinction between reed and the feather, or chamfer, of the grain. He then looks at the side of the stave. He is not too worried there, however, although he sees that the reed runs out in about 15 inches. This will not unduly affect the performance or the safety of the bow. Turning the stave on its end, he shows Richard the rift of the grain, the annular rings.

Taking a piece of charcoal, he marks the position of two small pins on the back of the bow; another at the edge he discounts. The first two are potential weaknesses and must be carefully left when he is taking down the back of the bow. The one at the side will almost vanish as he shapes the camber and is no problem. It would now be his usual practice to take his side axe and chop out the rough outline of his bow. Experience would tell him what waste to remove. However, he has an apprentice to instruct, so the process must slow a little. He takes a piece of planed soft wood of a little over the length of

Checking the yew log before splitting. The log is split to obtain a stave. Wedges of either wood or iron can be used. The rough stave after splitting. (*Joseph Gibbs*)

the bow when finished, and with a straight edge, he first marks a center line upon it. From the middle of the line, using his rule and with his charcoal, he marks 2 inches each way. He bisects these marks to create a rectangle 1 1/2 inches wide by 4 inches long. This will form the handle of the bow. At 6-inch intervals from the corners of this rectangle, he bisects the center line, tapering these bisections toward the end of each proto-limb. When he has joined the ends of his marks in four continuous lines, he shows Richard the ideal profile of a bow.

Drawing the datum line, or center line, of the bow. (*Joseph Gibbs*)

He is now ready to rough out the shape of his bow using his side axe. Watched closely by Richard, he carefully takes away the bye, or surplus, wood from the sides, stopping every now and again to check that he is not beyond the limits of his marks. As a right-handed man, he works in a way that allows him sight of his markings at all times. As he proceeds, he notices that there are one or two places where the axe is biting more deeply than others. He leaves these areas for the time; he will return with a float, or bowyer's rasp, to take this part of the surface down.

When he is near enough to his marked lines, he puts his axe down. He now takes a block plane and, with long sweeping

Removal of outer bark using a draw-knife. (*Joseph Gibbs*)

strokes, smoothes the sides of his stave, tapering them cleanly. He is satisfied with the proportion of sapwood to heartwood, and is ready now to smooth the back of his bow, calling Richard to his side to watch as he studies the rift, or feather, of the wood and carefully works around the pins. Having prepared the back to his satisfaction with his plane, he then chamfers 1/8 inch along each side edge of the back. This is the first stage toward preparing the sectional profile of the bow. With this done, and as Richard watches carefully, John marks a point with his charcoal 1 1/4 inch below the handle section, and from there, with a straight edge, he marks a tapered line to the end of each limb.

He has been fortunate with his stave: it is an excellent piece, and the grain runs straight and true. This will not

Initial shaping with a draw-knife. (*Joseph Gibbs*)

always be so; good yew wood will become more scarce as the years pass, and increasingly he will need to follow the grain on back, sides, and belly. His skill will be tested to the limit, for although truly tillered to come around in compass, his bows will reflect these vagaries of rift and reed in their profiles. Apprentice Richard has a great deal to learn. John is now ready to work on the belly of the bow. He favors a light bow (in modern draw weight terms, a little over 100 pounds), feeling that if well made, it may outshoot a stronger one. He will create a flattish low-cambered section, and drawing an outline of the section, he shows Richard the shape he intends. Anticipating Richard's question, John Powell explains the purpose of the shape: although it might not make as great a distance as one with a narrower back and deeper sides, a bow with more back than side will last longer, and for the purposes of war, the stability of a stave is important. Now, holding the stave firmly in a carpenter's horse, he works carefully, first with a draw knife, following the reed or grain, and then a toothing plane. Richard is quite unfamiliar with this tool, and his bowyer master takes a little time to show him its secrets. We will share in these.

Working on a side using a block plane. (*Joseph Gibbs*)

This small plane, one of the more important implements in professional bow making, has its cutting iron upright in the throat. Set very fine, it will scrape rather than cut, to create a perfectly smooth and clean surface from even the roughest or stringiest of yew wood. Modern bow makers use a cabinet maker's scraper, or even a piece of glass, but nothing can beat the toothing plane to create a professional finish.

When John is satisfied, notches must be created at the end of each limb to take the tillering string, for although the body of the bow is to bowyer Powell's liking, the task of bringing the limbs around in compass must now start.

Ordinarily he would use a wall-mounted tillering stand and a block and tackle for this purpose, but with Richard at his side, he turns to his workbench and to a hand-held tillering stick. Holding the center of the unfinished bow in its jaws with the belly toward him, John takes a bastard bowstring and

Removing bye wood using a draw-knife. (*Joseph Gibbs*)

loops it tightly at each limb end. With the bow flat on his
workbench, he then eases this taut tillering string slowly backward, then forward, and back again, gradually bending the
bow and moving carefully from notch to notch on the tillering
stick a little at a time, while noting the bow's curve. He marks
where a high spot causes an imbalance between limbs and
eases the surplus wood away. While carefully doing so, he
reminds his attentive apprentice that although he can take
wood off with no difficulty, he can never replace it! It is the
most important axiom that Richard will follow during his
seven-year apprenticeship.

With the bastard string now replaced by a bowstring that
sets the bow at bracing height, the master bowyer places the
weapon on the bench. With his charcoal, he now marks three
spots on the belly of each limb: at 15 inches, 18 inches, and 21
inches from the center and then measures the distance between
each and the string. He carefully scrapes the upper limb until
there is variation of 5/8 inch between measurements from the
middle mark to the string on the lower limb in comparison to

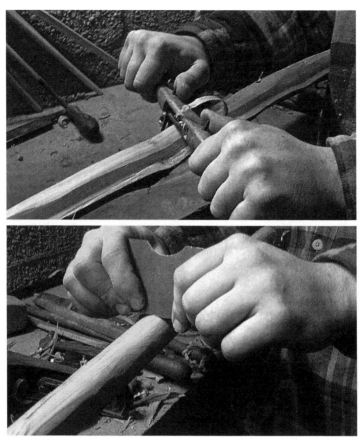

Preparing the belly using a shave (top). Finishing the back and the belly (bottom) using a specially shaped scraper. (*Joseph Gibbs*)

the upper. Curious to know why this should be, Richard asks the reason; the master explains that the lower limb is always made a little stronger than the upper to raise the arrow in its flight, and Richard must accept this. With the tillering process complete and bowyer Powell content with the curvature of his weapon, it is time to create stringing horns to protect the limb ends. These he will make from cow horn into which a taper of 2 inches long by 1/2 inch in diameter has been drilled. Into this taper he will temporarily glue a piece of bye wood, and he will then shape each horn. When these are roughly shaped to his

On the tillering stand. Drawn to full compass at 32 inches. The tillering stand is used to check the correct curvature on the limbs, with the object of making sure each limb is uniform with the other. (*Joseph Gibbs*)

satisfaction, he will remove them and turn his attention to the limb ends. These he will taper into cones closely suited to the horns, and when the fit is to his liking, he will brush the cones with glue and fix them into position. With the glue dried and cured, he will complete the shaping of the horns and will cut a string notch into each. With the back of the bow toward him, as in a stringing position, he will cut the upper string notch on the shaft-hand side, and on the lower, the bow-hand side. Looking quizzically now at Richard, the master asks him why he thinks that this should be. But Richard has the answer. He has had some experience of heavy draw weight bows and knows that to brace in this way is quick and easy; important in warfare. Accepting the answer, bowyer Powell adds that a side-notched horn needs a string with a tight loop in order to lie down the center of the bow limbs and a downward-formed groove to allow the string to find its proper place.

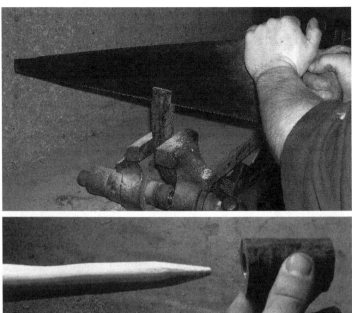

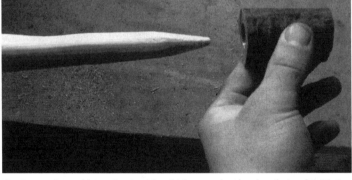

Sawing a piece of horn (top) with which to make the sheath (nock). Fitting the drilled horn sheath (below) to the bow cone (tip). (*Joseph Gibbs*)

After boning to compress the fibers, the bow is now complete, and apprentice Richard's first lesson is almost done. But, there is one more important step before the bow is truly ready. His master explains: if he needs the bow in battle, the warrior bowman should know readily which is the upper limb and which the lower. This will be indicated by peck marks on the upper limb. Handing Richard an awl and watching carefully, he guides his hand to mark five points in a steeple shape on the upper limb just above the balance point of the bow.

Our connection with Richard Vykeris is not yet done, however. After completion of his seven-year term in 1542, the ex-apprentice was accepted by his guild and became a qualified

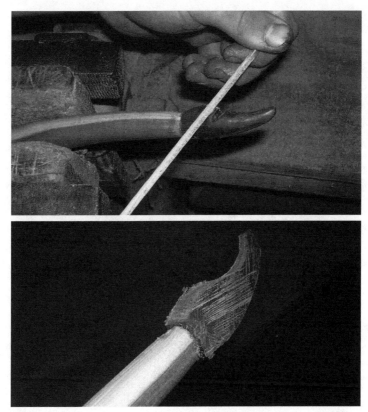

The horn sheath (nock) roughly shaped (top). Finishing the nock (below) with carborundum strip. (Joseph Gibbs)

bowyer in his own right. Starting in business a year later at the age of 23 and by now married to Isabella, Richard Vykeris, proud to call himself bowyer, took on his own apprentice. The circumstances are a little unusual; in 1543 John Powell, Richard's ex-master took on as apprentice young John Barns, son of one of the mayor of Bristol's sergeants at mace. For reasons that are not apparent, however, in the same year, he passed young John across to Richard for training, and it was with Richard that John completed his time.[31] It would seem that trust and harmony had developed between master and apprentice across the years.

We will draw this chapter to its close with two epigraphs, symbolic of dual facets of the mighty yew. One reputation as a dark, solemn, melancholy tree with its qualities and association with death is immortalized in poem and ballad.[32]

Old yew, which graspest at the stones
That name the underlying dead
Thy fibers net the dreamless head,
Thy roots are wrapped about the bones
—Alfred, Lord Tennyson

The other, firm and determined, without rival for its place in England's martial history, is likewise remembered.

The warlike yewgh, by which, more than the lance
The strong-armed English bowmen conquered France.
—Sir Thomas Browne (1605–1682)

So, we will leave this grim guardian of England's liberty to slumber in peace and turn to ash and aspen, companion sources of its partner, the murderous English battle shaft.

Chapter Three

BATTLE SHAFT

With Spanish yew so strong
Arrows a clothyard long,
That like to serpents stung,
Piercing the weather
—Sir Nicholas Harris Nicolas, *Battle of Agincourt*

Rich poetic hyperbole it may be, but it carries within it the seed of academic quibble, for the length of a clothyard shaft has yet to be settled satisfactorily by those concerned with mathematical accuracy.

There are some who are convinced by the linear yard of 36 inches; they have reason on their side, but they lack in practical knowledge, for they are not archers. Others there are who are more experienced and who think differently.

There is a clue. William Shakespeare, perhaps an archer himself in his younger days, supplies it in King Lear.[1] In this, the king says, "That fellow handles his bow like a crow keeper/ Draw me a clothyard shaft."

A crow keeper, or scarecrow, used to aiming at the airborne felons who menaced his crops, would draw to the chest—in Tudor parlance, "to the pap." A military archer would draw to the ear with a similar action to a clothier measuring out a piece of cloth. Holding one end at his ear, he would stretch out his hand for the required length. Since clothiers came in all shapes and sizes, it is possible that the term "clothyard" originally meant a piece of wood of a fixed length, used by all clothiers for common accuracy. Perhaps this yardstick was 36 inches in length, perhaps it was less; we do not know. But we do know the length of sixteenth-century military arrows, since over 2,000 have been recovered from the Tudor warship *Mary Rose*, and not one of them approaches 36 inches.

As an aside, through an incident of homicide that occurred in the thirteenth century, we do know something of at least one early medieval arrow. The detail comes from a Leicestershire coroner's report into the demise of one unfortunate fellow. Translated, it reads: "a barbed arrow with a head of iron and steel three inches long and two inches wide, and the shaft of the arrow was made of ash three quarters of an ell [assessed to be 33 3/4 inches] long and one inch in circumference, and feathered with peacock feathers." The circumference suggests a lengthier but lighter shaft of a diameter significantly less than that of later war arrows, and although fitted with a very substantial killing head, this may have been primarily a hunting shaft and not intended for war.

Before we leave the subject, let us note the advice given by the Sheriff of Nottingham to Robin Hood (as reported in the earliest recorded ballad) when our forest hero, masquerading as a potter, is about to take part in an archery contest.[2] "Draw to thine ear," exhorts the Sheriff, his advice suggesting that in those early days, this may not have been regular contemporary practice. But enough of this. We will allow the academics their prejudice, as we dig more deeply into the world of the English battle shaft.

I mentioned that no military arrow known to us reaches 36 inches in length. Since we have a host of these to study, it will be helpful to our understanding if, without preempting a forthcoming archaeological report by the Mary Rose Trust, we analyze and comment on some statistics.

Of the original 9,600 arrows believed from examining the Anthony Roll to have been on board, some 2,600 have been recovered. Many of these are in pieces, and although some inferences may be drawn from what remains, they are unsuited to a full examination. Analysis has therefore been confined to

Shaftments of sixteenth century battleshafts. Note evidence of binding of fletches into position and slits for protective horn "nock pieces." (*Author's photograph, with acknowledgement to the Mary Rose Trust*)

those complete steles that have been found. While a small number have been recovered from around the decks and have been included, the majority of those analyzed were contained in four storage chests, and it has been in the context of these that trial work has been carried out.

When created for penetrative and other related experimental purposes, replica battle shafts have largely measured 31 inches from base of nock (string groove) to shoulder of head (in practical terms, the shoulder of the cone onto which the arrowhead socket fits). But, how does this accord with those examined? Deducting the depth of the string groove, more or less constant at 1/4 inch, and assuming a draw to the end of the arrow socket (the shoulder of the cone), the effective draw length of the majority was between 28 inches and 30 inches.

Variations there were, however, and these are interesting. The shortest practical draw lengths were a little over 27 inches, and the longest, 33 inches, of which there were just nine. Were these longer shafts intended for special purpose? We can only speculate, but for practical reasons, certain special arrows did need to be longer. Were these perhaps intended for the propelling of fire, delivered by the few longer and heavier bows brought to the surface (a suggestion borne out by the associated presence of leather mittens for the left hand)?

What of the shorter draw length shafts? Speculation again, but Tudor bowmen came as they do today, in many shapes and sizes. A man 5 feet 6 inches high has by definition a shorter draw length than has a man of 5 feet 10 inches. While military policy may have been the production and supply of a one-size-fits-all livery shaft, it would seem reasonable that a shorter man would search out and welcome arrows more appropriate to his draw length if they were available, since a shaft that is not drawn to its full length will lose distance in comparison with one that is so drawn. If there were none, and authority and time were on his side, then he would perhaps take the opportunity to personalize what he could by reducing lengthy steles to a measure more suited to his draw.

In support of this hypothesis, Sir John Smyth, in the course of an acrimonious debate with Sir Humphrey Barwick about the relative advantages of bow versus harquebus, mentions that it was the usual practice for the soldiers to choose their first sheaf of arrows and to cut shorter the ones they found too long for their use.[3]

A curious indicator of what may have been past practice is recorded by eighteenth-century author and archer Thomas Roberts in a penciled note within his personal copy of *The English Bowman*.[4] Discussing arrow length, Roberts wrote, "If the arrow should be again used in war, then if instead of having them of different lengths according to the power of the shooter would it not be better to have them of one length, with the Bow suited to each man's strength."

The implication is interesting; we are reminded of the Sheriff of Nottingham's exhortation to Robin Hood to "draw to thine ear" and later still to William Shakespeare's line in Richard III when he has the king tell his bowmen, "Draw archers, draw your arrows to the head."[5] Thomas Roberts lived within three generations of those who last used the heavy draw weight bow, albeit for recreation, and his throwaway penciled note perhaps reflected past practice. In his grandfather's day, not all who handled a bow were able to draw it to its full extent.

There is some slight physical evidence for variations in arrow length, as we note from the findings of the Tudor shafts recovered from the *Mary Rose*, although whether they are intentional or not we cannot say. That shafts were personalized we may fairly assume; however, there is a balance to be struck. Although a shaft ideally should be drawn to its full length, a shortened version, while making distance, will lose effectiveness because of its lighter weight. The matter is worthy of examination. We will turn to Ascham for his succinct wisdom on the subject.

> It is better to have a shaft a little too short than over long; somewhat too light than over lumpish; a little too small [in diameter] than a great deal too big, which things are not only truly said of shooting, but in all other things that ever man goes about, as in eating, talking, and all other things.

With Ascham's homely philosophy to guide us, we will leave length and turn to profile.

Four types of profile are recognized today.

1. Barreled shafts taper from their greatest diameter at a roughly central point toward each end—nock and shoulder. The perceived virtue of this profile is in providing greater stability by reducing shaft vibration just beyond the point of release from the bow and, in so doing, effectively increasing distance.

2. Bobtailed shafts taper from shoulder to nock. These predominate among those arrows recovered from the *Mary Rose*, and they would seem to have two particular virtues. First, despite modern concepts that are in direct contradiction, they were believed to be better suited to distance shooting; second, by virtue of the greater diameter of their shoulders, they could carry a heavier arrowhead. As an aside, rather curiously, the appellation "bobtailed" was an early slang expression and a pejorative term (for example, the derogatory expression "rag, tag, and bobtail" to describe the gathering of a rabble). Another contemporary description for this arrow profile, not now used, was "rush grown."

3. Breasted (or to use an earlier alternative description, chested) shafts taper from shoulder to nock. Sixteenth-century wisdom saw these as best fitted for point-blank range. Roger Ascham writes, "It for him which shooteth right before him." In fairness to Ascham, he wrote largely of recreational archery and may not have had warfare in mind. It is problematical whether a breasted shaft would remain intact if shot at close range into plate armor.

4. Straight, or Parallel, are of equal diameter along their length and are of the profile most in use today for recreational archery.

A fifth profile, which may or may not have been intentional, concerns a doubly barreled shaft. To explain: On an otherwise barreled shaft, at broadly the point of balance, the diameter lessens and increases again on each side. Those examining the *Mary Rose* shafts have defined these as saddled, and the description is fitting. The purpose remains speculative, however. If deliberate and not the result of wood degradation across the centuries, the result of drying after lengthy immersion in seawater, or of inept profiling by the fletcher, then future experiment may show some aerodynamic advantage. It will be interesting to plan. Nothing must be dismissed on grounds of bias or prejudice, and it would seem significant that of the recognizable profiles, saddled was not numerically the least.

While it may now be time to look at the wood from which the shafts were made, before we do so, there are two vital parts of our arrow to be examined. They lie respectively at the heel and the foot of the arrow and are of course the nock, or string groove, and the cone to which the arrowhead is fitted.

The average depth of the string groove on those war shafts of which we have knowledge is 1/4 inch (6 millimeters), and this is indicative of a tightly woven (hemp) string. Since hemp was used for string making until comparatively recently, our knowledge of it as a string material is considerable, and many complete examples exist as testament to the tightness that can be achieved, particularly when the strands are held together with a water-based glue, as was regular practice.

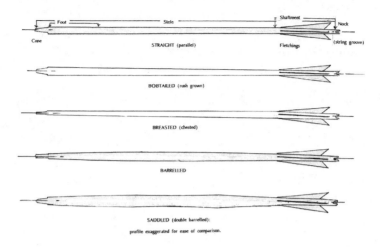

Identifiable profiles of arrow shafts. (*Author*)

That there is variation between nock depths is evident, and it is tempting to see this as a mere whim of the apprentice to whom responsibility for cutting them may have been delegated by a master fletcher. Like some other simple and seemingly elementary arrangements, however, there is more to the humble nock than meets the eye.

Ascham devotes some time to its description.[6] For convenience I have used modern spelling, but otherwise, the words are his.

The nock of the shaft is diversely [variously] made, for some be great and full, some handsome and little; some wide, some narrow, some deep, some shallow, some round, some long, some with one nock, some with double nock, whereof every one has its own property [character]. The great and full nock may be well felt [grasped], and [in] many ways they save a shaft from breaking. The handsome and little nock will go clean away from the hand. The wide nock is naughty [bad], both for the breaking of the shaft and for sudden[ly] slipping out of the string, when the narrow nock does avoid both [of] these harms. The deep and long nock is good in war for sure keeping in of the string. The shallow and round nock is best for our purpose in pricking [a form of target shooting] for clean deliverance of a shoot. And double nocking is used for double surety [safety] of the shaft.

Since the median of nocks on those war shafts known to us is 1/4 inch, this supposes that as Ascham has said, some were shallow and some were deep. Whether deliberately so or not, we have no way of knowing. We will not delay our examination further.

Ascham mentions double nocks, and this is enigmatic. What is, or was, a double nock? The question is taken up by Thomas Roberts, author and archer in 1802.[7] He supposes it to have been a cross nock and suggests that it was used in warfare to enable speed in shooting. It is fact that today those who shoot for speed do occasionally use two string grooves, one at right angles to the other, and this could be a simple explanation. However, the truth may be a little more complex; we must look at two sources to take our study forward. First, we look at a listing of arrows set down in 1422—the Arundel Inventory.[8] Here we find cross nocking in abundance. I quote briefly from a selection, using the compiler's now-archaic terms.

XV arrows of grey goose with duckbill heads crossnocked of a sort [all the same]

1 broad hooked arrow the head dagged [jagged?], feathered with peacock, cross-nocked, bound in iii places in gold

1 sheaf of XVII arrows of grey goose, crossnocked, V heads lack [five are without heads]

The purposes for which the many hundreds of arrow listed in the inventory were intended is a matter for conjecture. Many were decorated in red and gold (the actual word used is "powdered," a term thought to mean "spotted") and were seemingly used by, or on behalf of, a person of rank, probably for hunting. Others appeared more mundane, fletched with gray goose and armed with what seem to have been heads for war. There is mention of "byker" heads (used for initial skirmishing), while "duckbill," "hooked," and "broadhooked" heads suggest a dual military and hunting purpose. Others again seem more suited to recreation. However, it is not our task to define their purpose, much as it intrigues, it is with a possible explanation of these cross nocks that we are concerned.

For a potential interpretation, we may turn to a seventeenth-century source, Randle Holme's *Academy of Armory*, wherein we find reference among those terms used by fletchers to "slitting it" (putting the horn in for the "nick") and immediately following this, "a cross-slit" (making the nick of the arrow).[9]

The horn referred to is the protective piece some 2 inches in length that is slipped into the heel of the shaftment and glued into position as a protection against the power of the string immediately following release. These slits are a regular and fundamental feature of those arrows recovered from the *Mary Rose* and available for examination. As an aside, the use of horn pieces for this purpose was continued well within living memory, in particular by American arrow manufacturer Philip Rounsevelle.

With the deep cut, or slit, for the horn piece made and the horn glued in position, a cross slit at right angles was then cut for the string groove. Was it perhaps occasional practice for the horn slit to be left open at its top so that when the string groove was cut, a cross nock was formed? Is this the origin of Ascham's double nock and the earlier inventory descriptions? It is certainly a possibility, but both meaning and purpose are enigmatic and we must leave it there, for we now need to look in a little detail at the cone onto which the arrowhead is fixed. Ascham says little on the subject, confining his comments to heads being either "full on" or "close on." Full on is "when the wood is set hard up to the end or stopping of the head [the inside bottom of the socket]." Close on is "when there is left wood on every side [of] the shaft." To offer an explanation, which may be open to correction (since Ascham's description, no doubt perfectly understood in the sixteenth century, is imprecise today), apparently this means that the head is a tight fit but does not reach the shoulder of the cone.

In practice there appear to have been two forms of cone: one that has been prepared as one would sharpen a pencil and one that has a recognizable shoulder and is the result of a more complex cutting. The cone of a sixteenth-century arrow in my possession is 3/4 inch (19 millimeters) in length, 3/8 inch (9 millimeters) in diameter at the shoulder, and 7/16 inch (11 millimeters) at the shaft.

The average length of a cone is 7/8 inch (22 millimeters)—compare this with the one in my possession. This is indicative of considerable variation and perhaps explains Ascham's rather enigmatic description, since an arrowhead that fitted one cone would not necessarily fit another. As a relevant aside, tests have shown that on an ash shaft, the socket of a head that the cone does not fill will open if it strikes a hard surface such as plate armor, significantly reducing the effectiveness of impact. If fitted to an aspen shaft, the shaft will shatter.

What of the wood of which the arrow was made? While a number of woods appear to have been used in the making of sixteenth-century war arrows, predominant among them are poplar (aspen) and ash. It has been said that wood that will make a good bow will not make a good arrow, and if we turn to Ascham, we see that his recommended timber for bows is slim indeed. Yew is the only wood that he considers suitable. He is aware that Brazil wood (Pernambuco wood), elm, wych elm, and ash have all been used, but "experience does prove them to be but mean [poor] for bows."

Contrast this with the lengthy list of arrow woods commonly used in his time—"Brazil: Birch: Blackthorn: Turkey Wood: Ash: Beech: Fustic: Oak: Elder: Sugarchest: Servicetree: Aspen [poplar]: Hardbeam: Hulder: and Salow."

Ascham was writing rather more for the recreational archer than for the warrior bowman, and many of the arrow woods he names are more appropriate for peaceful use rather than for

The cone of a sixteenth century battleshaft. Note the ridged shoulder. (*Author's photograph, with acknowledgement to the Mary Rose Trust*)

warfare. Of the above, he dismisses "Turkey wood: Fustic: Sugar-chest" as making "dead, heavy, lumpish, shafts," while "Elder: Asp: and Salow" "either for their weakness or lightness, make hollow, starting, scudding, gadding shafts."

Birch, hardbeam, some oak, and some ash he feels are strong enough to "stand in a bow" and are light enough to fly far. His condemnation of aspen (poplar) is a little surprising in view of its choice for sixteenth-century war arrows, but in many ways, he plowed a lonely furrow.

The reference to "Turkey wood" is interesting. Geoffrey Chaucer refers to "turkie bows" in his prose poem "Romance of the Rose." The context identifies them as what we today call longbows, while among an inventory of Henry VIII's personal archery gear appears a "turqybowe" with six "boltes."[10] This entry is enigmatic, since it is associated with a box containing a "byrde of Arrabye" and may thus have referred to a Turkish-style bow, although equally it could have been a weapon constructed of turkey wood, but enough of such speculative diversions. We will return to the arrow and its wood.

There are few contemporary sources from which we may glean information, but one from France will help us in our search. It is *L'Art d'Archerie*, and it was published at the beginning of the sixteenth century.[11] Examination of the original French has suggested to some that it originated from the Picardy area, where archery was particularly strong. The writer tells us that since he has succumbed to illness and can no longer shoot, he is setting down his knowledge in order that it may help others.

Like Ascham he is primarily concerned with recreational archery, or perhaps more exactly, recreational practice for warfare, and prefers some woods to others. He does mention ash, although solely as a suitable wood for battle purpose. He describes it as appropriate only to prove armor, and for this he says, "Arrows should be large at the point [bobtailed] and reduced in feathers so as to withstand the impact." He likes aspen for target and butt shooting, and birch and cherry wood for distance.

Before we leave aspen entirely, however, we should note a controversy that arose in the early fifteenth century in England concerning the wood. Aspen was a wood well suited to the making of pattens, a form of overshoe, but they had become scarce because of the need of fletchers to meet requirements for the many thousands of arrows used in the French wars. A lengthy and tautologous complaint was made to authority by distressed patten makers demanding a fair crack of the whip. Conscious of the need to balance one important trade against another, a statutory regulation was passed permitting them (rather reasonably, one feels) to acquire "that part of the aspen tree not suitable for arrows," and this rule lasted until repealed a century later.[12]

It is time to turn now to fletching—the arrow's guidance system—and the platform on which it rests: the shaftment (or little shaft). The poetic term for a fletch, a term that has indeed come to mean the arrow itself, is the "'Grey Goose Wing," and this is at its heart, for as yew is the only wood suited to the mighty English war bow, so the feather of the goose is that most suited to guide the heavy battle shaft on its murderous journey.

Ascham debates whether there are other possibilities. He does not dismiss the suggestion out of hand, but points out that metal, wood, or horn are unsuited because they are inflexible; and cloth, paper, or parchment are inappropriate because unlike the feather, they are not flexible enough to retain their shape while en route to their destination. However, we might note here in passing that "sprights," or arrows fired from muskets, had vanes of leather (they cannot be called fletches) to withstand the heat of the explosion.

He questions whether the feather should be taken from an old goose or a gander, a young goose, or a fenny (wild) goose and decides that for best results, the matter rests between a stiff and strong primary feather taken from an old goose and a secondary pinion taken from a younger bird. The former is both stiff and strong and carries well in a wind, while the latter, says Ascham, is better for a swifter shaft. He adds a caveat, however; the younger feather should be cut to a higher profile, since it is prone to flatten in flight. This is an interesting observation and one with relevance to certain variations in distance achieved today with replica war arrows whose only difference is in the use of either primary or secondary pinions.

Detail of a portrait of Antony of Burgundy (c. 1430–1504) holding an arrow. The nock is bulbous to assist in the drawing of the arrow when shot, and it appears to be cross-nocked as well as pinned. (*Rogier van der Weyden, c. 1461; Musées Royaux des Beaux-Arts, Brussels*)

As all who fletch shafts know well, it is crucial to use feathers from the same wing. Ascham favors neither right nor left, although there are today those who favor the curl away from the bow limb of a left wing feather when preparing arrows for a right-handed archer, and traditionally, English fletchers use the left wing. He does make a curious point though, and one relevant to distance shooting. A cross wind, says Ascham, will drift the flight of a shaft if the feather is curled in the same direction as the wind. Thus, shafts should be carried fletched with either right or left wings to cater for this situation. To my knowledge, there has been no experimental work to confirm this interesting theory.

Preparing a feather for fletching is a task not to be undertaken lightly. There are two ways of removing the web from the quill: either by lifting the edge and stripping it by pulling or by carefully cutting it away with a round knife and grinding the edge. The first method is the quicker but is difficult to master, and with feathers not in particularly generous supply, is not recommended for the novice. It is far better to spend time and care to safeguard a scarce resource.

With the fletch now ready and rough cut to a rectangle, there is a decision to be made. What should be its length? The primary feather from an old goose will give a maximum of 10 inches, as will that from a peacock or a peahen. Of the fifteenth-century arrows included within the Arundel Inventory, just two have their fletching lengths listed.[13] Seven sheaves have peacock fletches 10 inches in length, while 11 shafts are fletched with peahen feathers 9 inches long. In passing, it is worthy of mention that besides goose and peacock/peahen, swan-fletched shafts also appear in the Inventory.

With the length decided, the fletching needs to be attached to the shaftment. But, before it is, it should be properly prepared, and here the fletcher would dampen it and press it in order to straighten it prior to gluing or, as was apparently an alternative, fastening it with waxed silk. Ascham says nothing about fastening, but our anonymous French writer does.[14] I quote:

> You must know that there are only two sorts of shaft, the glued and the waxed. Waxed arrow are of two kinds, of which one is feathered with the front wing feather (the primary) and is only good for butt shooting, and the other which is feathered with the hinder (secondary) wing feathers and is both good and favourable for target shooting. And understand that a good round waxed arrow should be feathered from the wing of a swan. Many arrows are

made and feathered from the wing of the goose but they are not so good and are only suitable for war arrows.

To what extent, if at all, fletches on English battle shafts were secured with wax is unknown. An experimental water-proof paste of 60% melted beeswax mixed with 40% turpentine (not white spirit) has been tried and found effective, although whether this was ever in general use is unknown. It was certainly invariable custom to bind fletchings to the shaftment, and what slight reference there is to the fastening method mentions glue: curiously, one made from—of all things—the common bluebell.

From John Gerard's sixteenth-century Herbal, we have:

The blew harebell [bluebell], or English jacinth [hyacinth] is very common throughout England. It hath long narrow leaves leaning towards the ground, amongst the which spring up naked or bare stalks laden with many hollow blue flowers of a strong sweet smell: after which comes the cods [balls] or round knobs containing a great quantity of small black shining seed. The root is bulbous and full of a slimie glewish juice which will serve to set feathers on insted of glew.[15]

Experiment has shown that boiled with a little water, the bulbs produce a glue strong enough to join two pieces of wood together effectively, and it is thus quite sufficient for Gerard's suggested purpose. However, while this is undoubtedly an effective adhesive, it has two serious drawbacks: it is water soluble and thus unsuited to military purpose, and the native English blue harebell, or bluebell, is a protected species. Glued or waxed, we will leave the fletches for a while and consider the shaftment and its preparation—but first, a word or two about this important part of the arrow and an element of confusion that has crept in, for the word itself has a specific definition. "Shaftment," as a length is precisely defined as half a Drusian foot, or some 6 1/2 inches. In vernacular terms, it is the width of the fist with thumb extended, a measurement incorrectly called "fistmele," (Old English fystmæl) or "fist measure," today and used to determine the proper distance from string to bow when a bow is braced.[16]

Enough of such arcane detail, let us return to examination of the shaftment of a sixteenth-century arrow. This reveals a green substance coloring the wood beneath the fletchings. What is this and what was its purpose? It is somewhat of a rhetorical question, for here we are in the realm of speculation. However, there has been some practical experiment, and I am indebted to a colleague for his account of work on a waterproof varnish/glue that might have been used on Tudor arrows.[17] This includes verdigris (copper sulfate), the green residue of copper, and may explain the presence of green coloring on shaftments of that period; a basic recipe for the production of this substance is to place scrap copper plate into a mass of grape skins and stems that have been left over after wine making and allowed to undergo acetous fermentation.

The researcher's experimental suggestion for this water-resistant varnish/adhesive consists of a mixture of 50% dammar resin (pitch), 45% beeswax, and 5% very fine verdigris. When heated and thoroughly mixed, this is applied to the shaftment and allowed to cool, when the fletchings are then positioned for binding with waxed thread. Once binding is complete, the varnish/glue is reactivated, and after straightening, the fletchings are secure.

Relevant to the matter is the recording during the inventory of Henry VIII's possessions of the following within the Crosbowe Chambre at Calais:

Packe threde: Glewe for bowes and arrowes: Petir Oyle di gallon: Salarmoniac oone lib di: Azafetida oone lib: Quick Silver iiij lb: Grene Coporas oone lib: Rosalgare iij lb: Camphere oone lb.

"Grene coporas" would seem to have been verdigris, while the presence of camphor suggests mothproofing. The contents of the Chambre remain something of a mystery, however. "Azafetida" was commonly known as "devil's dung" because of its overpowering smell (curiously, it also had—and in Indian cookery, still has—a culinary purpose!), and "Quick Silver" (mercury) is a poison. "Salarmoniac" (sal ammonia) is the main constituent of smelling salts, but besides its strong odor, when crystals are dissolved in water, ammonia and hydrochloric acid are formed, suggesting an alternative use as a cleansing agent. "Rosalgare" has so far defied identification, but "Petir Oyle" may perhaps have been a lubricant. If a purpose has to be ascribed to this odd collection, then one obvious suggestion is the preparation of fungicide and insect repellent. The presence of verdigris, a toxic substance, on shaftments and in direct contact with feathers was presumably intended to keep feathers free from infestation.

As an aside, I was once told by a long-since-departed fletcher that in the early years of last century, he was taught by a master arrow maker to dribble hot hoof and horn (carpenter's) glue down the quill of a fletch before placing it on the shaftment. Once it was positioned, he then blew gently on it to cool it; and once it was cooled, it held fast. Carpenter's glue is/was susceptible to damp, however, and its advantages were therefore limited.[18]

Having glued and bound the unshaped feathers, one must shear, or cut, them to profile. Fletching shapes are a combination of the practical and tradition. While today there are four—shield, parabolic, French curved, and dumpy—each serving an element of modern archery, in past times there were also four—swine backed, saddle backed, round, and triangular—serving butt practice, distance shooting, and warfare. Of these shapes, swine backed and saddle backed are explicit of the animal or object with which they share their name. Round (or to be more precise, half-round) and triangular present no difficulty either. Although swine-backed fletches are represented on certain medieval hunting scenes together with triangulars, scenes of longbow warfare invariably show triangular shapes, and it is probable, if not certain, that the sixteenth-century arrows that we have for study were fletched in that way.

So, how did they perform? Ascham is uncharacteristically brief.

> The swine backed fashion maketh the shaft deader [duller in flight] for it gathereth more air than the saddle backed and therefore the saddle back is surer for danger of weather [bad weather] and fitter for smooth flying. Again, to shear a shaft round as they are wont sometimes to do, or after the triangle fashion which is much used nowadays, both be good.

It is unfortunate that the fifteenth-century Arundel Inventory, while explicit about nocks, heads, and feathers, tells us nothing of the fletching shape. We may speculate that those with long feathers were triangular, yet because of decoration, we are in doubt of their purpose. There are clues as to fletching profiles on battle shafts, however, and we turn once again to the vernacular source of the early church wall painting at Pickering Church in England's North Yorkshire and the one at Weare Gifford Church, Devon. The one at Pickering Church depicts the martyrdom of Saint Edmund, an early English king killed by Viking invaders. The depiction is of archers in the style of the late fifteenth century, armed with ballock knife and longbow, and shooting heavily barbed broadhead armed arrows, quite clearly bearing long triangular fletchings. In contrast, it should be said that the similar, fourteenth-century representation of the martyrdom on the wall at Weare Gifford church shows the use of swine-backed profiles, although here the archers are using what seem to be short hunting bows!

A feature of arrow flight is the turn, or spin, of the shaft as it travels through the air. A feather has both a natural curl and a rough and smooth side, and it is a combination of these features that cause the arrow to turn as it flies. Spinning has both an advantage and a disadvantage, however. While the motion helps to stabilize the arrow in flight, at the same time, it produces drag that reduces velocity and thus optimum distance. It is a balance between these two effects that, across the years, fletchers have sought to achieve. We have no way of knowing

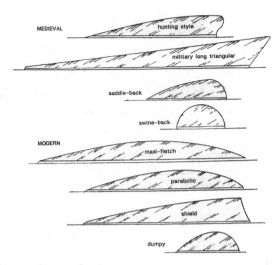

Fletching profiles (*Author*)

whether the lighter medieval war shafts shot for distance when an engagement opened were low fletched in comparison with their heavier companions, but today's practical knowledge suggests that they would have been.

The matter of fletch profile has been a recurrent theme for years by those concerned with the dynamics of wind resistance, or drag. Many are the inquiring minds that have pondered the question. In 1935 Royal Naval academicians and aerodynamicists Oliver Bellasis and B. P. Haigh pondered the optimum shape of shaft feathers.[19] While their inquiries ranged around the recreational arrow, the solution applied equally to the battle shaft. The point considered was whether the fletch should be cut with the deeper end first, as were certain early aircraft rudders; the answer: a height gradually increasing to the rear provides the greater steering potential with the minimum of drag (think of the modern design of aircraft tail-plane).

While no arrow is complete without its fletching guidance system, an interesting experiment by the United States Army Ordnance Department concerned the recreational stele. This experiment established that at an initial velocity of 200 feet per second, a 5/16-inch diameter, 26-inch-long shaft (three fletched with 2 1/2-inch feathers and a total area of 7 1/2 inches) gave a drag resistance equivalent to 0.039 pound. Unfletched, the same shaft showed a reduced resistance of just 0.016 pound. This confirms the drag factor to be a significant element in the calculation of the arrow's ballistic curve.

A recurring feature of recreational fletchings across the past 200 and more years has been helical fletching. We will not dwell overlong on the matter, but since it is possible that it was a feature of the war arrow, a paragraph or two may be helpful in understanding principles.

Helical fletching involves the setting on of feathers at an angle to the horizontal line of the shaftment. The reason, and thus the effect, is to induce more spin and, it is presumed, a more stable flight. The result, however, is to increase drag and thus decrease velocity. Distance is sacrificed for potentially greater accuracy. It is inappropriate in a chapter dealing with the battle shaft to do more that casually mention the furor over this form of feathering that erupted during the mid-nineteenth century, but such there was, and great names in the sporting world were drawn into the argument. It is sufficient to record its dismissal, for despite claims of advantage by those eminent in their field, helical fletching was consigned to the woodshed of history, where, with occasional forays into the light, it languishes to this day.

I have written at some length about the various aspects of the shaft; it is now time to see something of its performance and to consider the effect upon it of that most important and—unreasonably—arcane of archery circumstances: the paradox. What, you may reasonably say, is an archery paradox? The answer is complex and warrants some explanation. The term concerns the path of the arrow as it leaves the drawn bow. When the arrow is on the bowstring at full draw and the point is lined up to the target, be that the roundels of the straw butt or the breastplate of an advancing cavalryman, one might expect that it would fly straight and true toward its goal.

However, as the string is loosed and makes its way toward the center of the bow, vibrating as it does from the effect of fingers leaving the string, the arrow is carried off to the side of the bow limb. It no longer lines directly with the target but with a point at an angle several degrees to its left (we speak here of a right-handed archer holding the bow in his left hand). Paradoxically, however, it strikes the target, and this it does because of the whippiness of the arrow. Driven by the release of kinetic energy, it bends around the bow at the arrow pass as it leaves the bow limb, and now stabilized by the fletchings, it flies straight and true. This is an excessively simple explanation of a complex series of events, for a moment's thought will recognize that the arrow is bending on both horizontal and vertical planes while revolving at the same time.

The whippiness, or spinning, of the arrow is measured today against a moderated scale, and shafts are carefully matched to the draw weight of the bow to eliminate mechanical error as far as possible. Thus, an arrow that is too whippy will deflect to the right of the target, where one that is too stiff will fly to its left.

Although the relationship of arrow to bow was known in medieval times, no such sophisticated matching was practiced. The whippiness—or as we should properly call it, the elastic modulus—of various arrow woods was recognized, however, and reflected in the diameter of shafts made from them. Thus aspen shafts were generally greater in diameter than their denser counterparts of ash. General-purpose sheaf, or livery, shafts generally stood stiff in a bow, and since bow draw weights would not have greatly varied, they probably served their archers well enough in situations where the blanket cover of an arrow storm was appropriate. Certain shafts were carefully selected however for their ability to fly straight, and these bearing arrows, as they were known, were employed where accuracy was necessary. Suffice to say that the profile of an arrow has a direct effect upon its performance when leaving the bow, and experiment to determine parameters is ongoing.

We have earlier seen that the bobtailed shaft, with its heavier forward end, was considered most suitable for distance; and we have noted that in more modern times, the emphasis has changed, with the lesser forward diameter of the breasted shaft now preferred. How and why did this change occur?

We may look to the East for the solution.[20] Distances achieved by Turkish archers are legendary, and the reason given is interesting, so we will examine it. It related largely to the balance of the arrow, to the relationship of the geometric center of the arrow to its center of gravity and the center of pressure, or the point at which all upward forces may be considered to act. The traditional relationship was for the center of gravity to be somewhat forward of the geometric center, depending upon the type of head fitted—a feature it shared with the English late medieval battle shaft.

The center of pressure on a Turkish war arrow was affected by the area of the fletchings but was considered to be between 2 and 3 inches behind the geometric center and some 4 to 6 inches to the rear of the center of gravity. The distance between the center of gravity and the center of pressure was critical, since it gave what was termed the "righting moment," enabling the axis of the arrow to remain parallel to the flight path without yawing or deviating and thus potentially losing distance. However, if the center of pressure were to be moved closer to the center of gravity by reducing the fletching area, then the righting moment was reduced and, in this way, a gliding effect was produced; the parabola, or normal ballistic curve, of a conventionally fletched Turkish war arrow was not followed, and distance was increased. It has to be said that there are those today who are skeptical of the principle, but it is known that with the short, powerful, heavily recurved Turkish bow, war and flight arrows were shot over immense distances.

Another aspect of arrow shafts is starting to be considered to account for variations in flight distance: that of the resonance or natural frequency of the wood of which an arrow

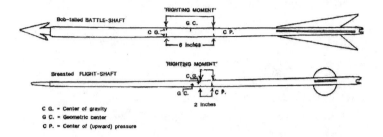

C G. = Center of gravity
G C. = Geometric center
C P. = Center of (upward) pressure

In calm air an arrow will normally achieve its greatest range when shot at an angle of 43 1/2 degrees, to strike the ground at an angle of about 54 degrees. But arrows behave differently. A bob-tailed battleshaft has its center of gravity (CG) some 3 inches in from of its geometric center (GC). As with all missiles, it has a center of pressure (CP), a point through which all upward forces are concentrated. Because of drag imposed by the area of fletching of a war arrow this CP is some 3 inches behind the GC. The distance between the CG and the CP is called the "righting moment," and as this is long, approximately 6 inches, the axis of the arrow remains constant to the ballistic parabola (the flight path). As velocity decays during flight and gravitational pull increases, the arrow moves, or "pitches," at a rate which exactly follows the change in curve of the flight path. A chested flight arrow is constructed differently. The CG is fractionally behind the GC and because of reduce fletching size the CP is advanced to lie closer to the CG. The righting moment and thus the axis of the arrow is significantly shortened, approximately 2 inches, and in consequence the pitching rate is slower than the change in the curve of the flight path. Although gravitational pull is still exerted, the arrow does not follow the expected flight path. In this way a "gliding effect" is achieved from the apogee of the ballistic parabola, the reason why Turkish flight arrows achieved such distances. (*Author*)

shaft is made. It is known that given two wooden arrows seemingly identical in every respect, one will travel farther than another. The resonance of the wood, or harmonic frequency of the wood, when the arrow is shot is believed to be a factor, but further research must be conducted to bear this out.

Before we turn to the making of a replica English battle shaft, let us briefly consider a specific repair that was occasionally carried out, perhaps on a particularly prized bearing shaft. This was footing, or to use an archaic term, "piecing," the forward end of the arrow. Footing involved fish-tail splicing a piece of timber, some 6 inches in length, into the foot of the shaft. Often, but not always, this was of denser material than the stele itself. As Michael Drayton (1563–1631) commented, "Their arrows finely paired for timber and for feather,/ With birch and brazil pieced to fly in any weather." Later in this chapter, we will note how that repair is carried out.

Ascham adds nothing to our knowledge of tools but is quite exact about the wood best suited for warfare.

Yet, as concerning sheaf-arrows for war, as I suppose it were better to make them of good ash, and not of asp [poplar] as they are nowadays. For of all other woods that ever I proved, ash being big, is swiftest and again heavy to give a great stroke, which asp will not do, What heaviness does in a stroke, every man by experience can tell; therefore ash, being both swifter and heavier is more fit for sheaf arrows than asp.[21]

He continues:

The stele must be well seasoned, to prevent it casting [warping] and should be made as the grain lies or it will never fly clean . . . a knotty stele may be suffered in a large [thick] shaft but is not fit for a small one. A stele which is hard [stiff] to stand in a bow, without knot and straight—naturally straight as it grows—is the best to make a shaft of.

It would seem that Ascham's condemnation of contemporary practice was founded on fact, for a substantial proportion of the 2,500 arrows recovered from the *Mary Rose* are of aspen. Matters had not greatly changed by 1625, when the "trewe invytorye" of Richard Hollyester, a fletcher from Bristowe, included (among other things) "xij [twelve] sheafe of Rowe Aspe [rough aspen] undrawen [unworked] at ij [twopence] per sheafe."[22]

From a seventeenth-century source we learn of the first four stages in the making of a stele.[23] This involved creating a

Preparation of arrow staves from an ash plank. Note side-axe for initial splitting and roughing out of staves. (*Christopher Jury*)

staff by first "cleaving out the timber," then "pointing of it out" (a first cutting of it round with a knife) out of the rough, "ripping it" (to give it the first round), and "shaving" (rounding with a hollow shave). These activities were followed by smoothing the rounded stele with a fish skin.

And so to today. In order to make an arrow, you will need a small block plane with its cutting edge well forward, a shuting board, a doweling plane (or a concave sandpaper-covered doweling block), a hand saw, a pair of calipers, a doweling plate, and ideally a plank of dressed (planed) ash or other dense wood that is straight and about 3 feet in length by 1 inch thick. This you will cut into lengths of approximately 1/2-inch square. These are your staffs. How you cut them is up to you—by hand saw if you are feeling traditional or band saw if you are not.

Your shuting board is an essential piece of equipment and is easily made. Take two 3-foot lengths of dressed pine plank 2 inches wide by 1 inch deep. Plane the edge of each to create a V that is 1/4 inch deep and 1/4 inch wide when the planed edges are placed together. Glue and clamp the two. Against one end, secure a stopping piece, its upper edge level with the face of the plank. This is your shuting board.

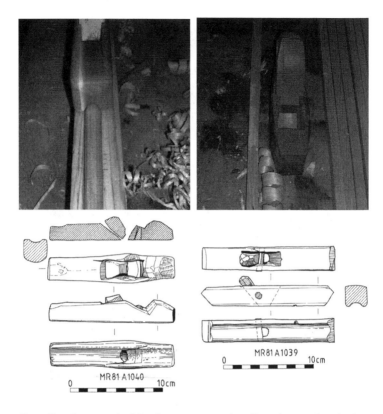

Rounding the stave (stele) using a concave doweling plane and a shuting board (top). (Christopher Jury) Plan drawings of two doweling planes recovered from the wreck of the *Mary Rose*. (*Copyright Mary Rose Trust, may not be reproduced.*)

Now, to avoid damage to your hand in the event of breakage of the completed arrow, ensure that the reed of your staff runs away from and not toward you. Place the squared staff in the V groove of your shuting board, its end against the stopping piece, and with your block plane, its cutting edge sharp and with a fine setting, take off each corner. Let the weight of the plane do the work. Continue this until your staff is rounded. Discipline yourself to plane from center to ends, not from ends to center, to ensure a shaft of even thickness. Not to do this may result in a dowel that is thinner in the middle (recall the saddle profile of the *Mary Rose* shafts).

The finished staves (steles). (*Christopher Jury*)

Complete the rounding process with either your doweling plane, again set finely and handled lightly, or a concave sanding block using a medium- to coarse-grit sandpaper. From time to time, try the diameter, either with calipers or, preferably, against the doweling plate. This is not difficult to make and is a most useful addition to your kit. If you have access to a blacksmith or possess the wherewithal yourself, take a piece of 1-millimeter or 1 1/2-millimeter mild steel plate and drill through it holes of three diameters: one 1/2 inch, one 7/16 inch, and one 3/8 inch. Screw this plate to a piece of hardwood 4 inches long by 3 inches wide by 1 inch thick and drill through three equivalent holes. This is your doweling plate; it serves the same function as the hole drilled by the Neolithic arrow maker into sandstone. There is nothing really new in the fletcher's art.

When you are satisfied with the chosen diameter of your shaft, polish it with fine sandpaper, and although there is still work to do at the shaftment, you now have a parallel profiled dowel.

Having mastered the basic shaft, you can now move to breasted and bobtailed profiles. The breasted is generally a lighter arrow, and modern recreational examples taper evenly from shaftment to the shoulder of the foreshaft. What evidence we have for the medieval breasted battle shaft suggests that the taper commenced at a point toward the geometric center of the stele, increasing slightly some 4 inches from the shoulder. With a variation of little more than 1 millimeter along its length, the breasted shaft will offer a profile distinctly different to its modern recreational counterpart.

Creating it is a matter of careful work with your doweling plane or, for the hypercautious, your concave sanding block, with regular checks with calipers or against the 7/16-inch hole of your doweling plate. Again, you will have work to complete at the shaftment. Check the point of balance from time to time. When completed, this should be between 3 and 4 inches either forward of or behind the geometric center of your shaft. The bobtailed profile provides the greatest taper, varying evenly between 12 millimeters at the shoulder and 10 millimeters at the shaftment. Here, if you are converting a parallel dowel, you may wish to use your butt plane to carefully shave off flats before finally rounding with your sanding block, again checking with calipers as you go. Work first an inch or so from each end, gradually moving back to ensure an even taper. The point of balance of a barreled shaft will not greatly differ from that of the parallel profile and will be a little forward of the geometric center. The barreled stele is at its greatest diameter some 12 inches from the shoulder, thickening from 11 millimeters to 12 millimeters and tapering to 9 millimeters at the shaftment. Should you choose to construct a doubly barreled shaft (that strange sixteenth-century profile that may or may not be genuine), then you will need to taper back 8 inches from 12 millimeters at the shoulder to below 11 millimeters at 10 inches, then increase once more to 11 millimeters at 16 inches before flattening off at 20 inches, reducing slightly in diameter to 24 inches before tapering the remaining 7 inches of shaftment to 10 millimeters at the nock.

With the five profiles satisfactorily mastered, you are ready to turn to the heel, or nock end, of the shaft to form the string groove with its protective horn sliver and to the foot to form the cone to accept the socket of the arrowhead.

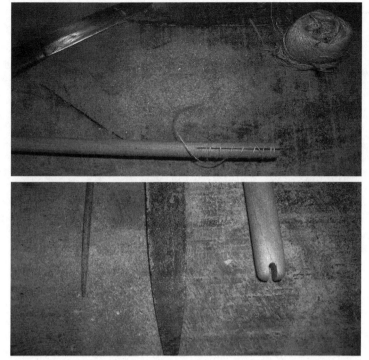

Glueing and securing the protective horn "nock piece" into position. The string groove (nock) prepared. Note broad and rat tail files used. (*Christopher Jury*)

Prepare your protective nock piece by sawing a slice of horn 2 inches long by 1/2 inch in width and 1/8 inch thick. For ease of subsequent insertion, taper the bottom with a warding file and file it slightly concave. Now, bisect the shaftment end of your arrow stele with a penciled mark, running it with, not across, the grain. Continue this line down each side of your shaftment for 2 inches.

To cut your 1/8-inch-wide horn insert slit, you will need a saw blade of that thickness. An industrial hacksaw blade will be most suitable, but two domestic hacksaw blades fastened together are adequate for the purpose. Clean the cut and glue the horn insert in place; its top should be level with your shaftment end.

When all is dry, you are now ready to prepare your string groove. Mark the line of your intended cut with a sharp pencil; this cut will be at right angles to the rift of the grain, to a suggested width of 3/16 inch and a depth of 1/4 inch. Following an initial saw cut, a rounded rattail file or a circular warding file is very suitable to complete this. The groove should bell out toward the base of the groove, terminating in a width of 1/4 inch to hold it closely to the string. When finished, file the base convex to accommodate the string angle while the bow is at full draw and tidy the ends into neat curves.

Turn now to the foot of the stele to prepare the cone to take the head. The internal diameter of the sockets of medieval arrowheads varies around 3/8 inch, while the socket depth appears to vary with the type of head. Bodkin-pointed heads, for penetrating heavy mail and plate armor, may have sockets well in excess of 1 inch in depth; lighter broadheads, around 3/4 inch. Those sixteenth-century arrows of which we have knowledge have cones that are around 7/8 inch in depth—the wood of the example in my possession has degraded, however, and thus measures a little less.

Remembering Ascham's advice on filling the socket, we will settle on 7/8 inch as the depth of our cone, and we will now prepare to cut it. With a pencil or fine pen, mark a line around the diameter of the stele 7/8 inch from the end. Taking a sharp blade, carefully cut a 1-millimeter-deep groove around its perimeter. Following your marked line, measure and mark a second line 1/2 inch from the end; and with your blade or paring knife, meticulously slice toward the groove to create a shoulder. Now, mark a point at the center of the end of your stele and slice down toward the tip until you have a blunt point centered on your mark. Then with a fine warding file, finish off the cone, slipping the socket of the head on to it from time to time to ensure a tight fit.

With your cone and string groove complete, you are ready to prepare the feathers to fletch your shaftment. Ideally these will be natural primary or secondary pinions from either the

Removing surplus rachie (quill), top. Preparing turkey feathers by trimming the web, bottom. (Christopher Jury)

left or right wing of a greylag goose: gray for the cock (leading) feather, white for the remaining two shaft feathers. Peacock or turkey feathers are strong, however, and equally suitable.

Using a sharp blade, or a round knife if one is available, split three quills for as far toward the end of the web as is practical. We will settle on 6-inch-long fletchings, so cut a strong piece 7 1/2 inches long. A good primary feather should provide a usable length of over 9 inches. Roughly trim the excess web, leaving at least 3/8 inch standing. Holding the web firmly in a clamp, rub it on some coarse grit paper to remove

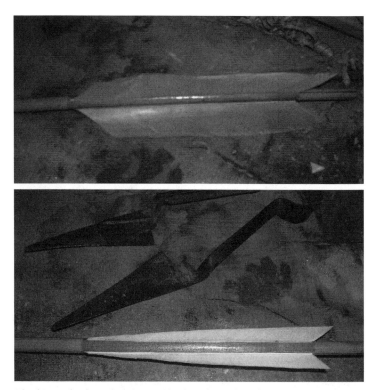

Fletchings glued in place (top). Fletches sheared to shape and bound. Note shaftment painted with liquid containing verdigris to waterproof and protect from infestation. (*Christopher Jury*)

most of the rachis, leaving sufficient in position to secure the fletch to the shaftment. Now take each prepared fletching and place in a damp cloth under light pressure to straighten the rachis.

Meanwhile, you can mark your shaftment to receive the feathers; these will be positioned 120 degrees apart. Your cock, or leading, feather will be aligned at right angles to the string groove, so you must now draw a line extending from 1 inch below the base of the groove for 7 inches parallel to the shaftment. Establish the circumference of your stele (which should be about 1 inch), draw a line of this length on a piece of paper, and on it mark three equidistant points. Align one to

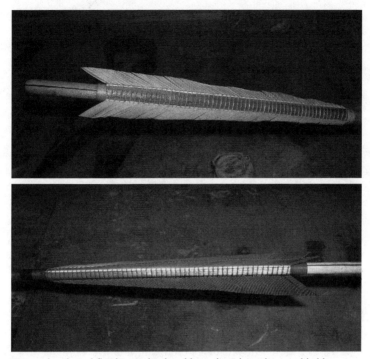

Triangular shaped fletchings glued and bound, with verdigris added between feathers (top). Note protective horn nock piece in position. The completed fletchings. (*Christopher Jury*)

your cock feather datum line and mark the other two points. From each mark, draw a parallel line along the shaftment, and you have the positions for all three fletches.

Take each fletching and remove the barbs for 1/4 inch from each end of the rachis. At this point you may wish to roughly shape your fletch, and to accord with tradition, you will perhaps want to use a triangular format. If you possess a sharp-bladed round knife, place a template cut from metal or thin hardwood hard against the web, its point at the forward end of the web, and roll the knife to carefully cut the barbs. If you have no such knife, then be prepared to shear the fletch in situ.

We will depart a little from tradition here, for after smearing on a good contact adhesive and using round-headed pins through the protruding rachis ends to secure it, carefully place your fletchings, their barbs angled toward the string groove, along your datum lines and hold them in position for a minute or two. When firmly affixed, mark each feather 1/2 inch above the shaftment then, with the longest and sharpest shears you have, and drawing a deep breath, carefully cut from the nock end, endeavoring to complete in one cut.

To finish the arrow, taper the lower excess rachis level with the shaft. Take a length of silk thread, bind it for several turns over the bare rachis, and secure it with a drop of glue or liquid beeswax if you prefer. Then, holding the arrow steady, part the barbs carefully at approximately 1/4-inch intervals and bind upward toward the nock, taking care not to crush the base of the web as you go. You should achieve about 24 turns before encircling the bare upper rachis, tying off, and securing with glue. Any ruffled barbs can be restored by running through finger and thumb.

Finally, identify your arrow with your personal mark. Then with an arrowhead forged to master arrow smith Mark Stretton's instructions firmly attached and a bow made following bowyer Joe Gibbs advice, you are ready to heed a call to arms!

Now that you have made a shaft, let us imagine that after you have shot it and it has performed exactly as you wish, when you withdraw it from its resting place, you discover, horror of horrors, that it has hit a rock and the end has snapped off 3 inches from the shoulder. But, all is not lost, for you can repair your broken shaft by footing it. Recover the point and head for the workbench. Tidy up the broken end, making sure that the stele is not split along the reeve of the grain.

Mark a circle around the circumference of the shaft 4 inches from the broken end and, from this, draw a line toward the end parallel to the shaft. Draw another exactly opposite. Now, keeping these datum lines in view, plane carefully toward the shoulder to produce an even taper terminating about 1 mil-

A selection of shafts armed with replica, hand forged military style arrow heads. Note five armor piercing bodkin points, and one lightly barbed broadhead for skirmishing. (*Christopher Jury*)

limeter thick.

Take a piece of staff long enough to complete your stele and, bisecting its length with a central pencil mark, cut along this a 1-millimeter central groove 4 inches in depth. With a clamp at the base of your saw cut to prevent splitting, force the taper into the cut once or twice to open it. When it is finally fully in, withdraw it, glue the taper, and push it home. True up both footing and stele and clamp in position. When all is dry, dowel your new end to the diameter of your stele, tidy up the taper with a fine-grit sanding block, and cut a new shoulder. Replace the head and look for a friendlier, rock-free environment in which to shoot next time!

Chapter
Four

THE DEVELOPMENT
AND MANUFACTURE
OF MILITARY
ARROWHEADS

Mark Stretton

"We must beat the iron whilst it is hot,
but we may polish it at leisure"
—John Dryden (1631–1700)

An arrow fitted with a large barbed broadhead—an almost iconic image, instantly recognizable to the viewer—is probably what the average person would think of if asked to describe a medieval arrow. Over time, depictions of this image have varied, from classical sculptures and medieval paintings to modern photographs and book illustrations; yet they all convey the same message to the eye: the viewer instantly knows that what they are looking at is an arrow, purposely designed to be shot from a bow into a target or into flesh.

The head also suggests that the arrow will be hard to extract, as the barbs will dig into the flesh while some poor unfortunate tries to remove the shaft. The larger the barbs, the more powerful is the image to the viewer, who is left with no doubt in his mind that this is something of which one would not wish to be on the receiving end.

The broadhead arrow image persists in modern directional signs, pointing people in the right direction.

Medieval paintings and carvings nearly always show large swallowtail-type heads fitted to the archer's arrows—sometimes grossly overexaggerated and out of all proportion to the rest of the scene. Some have concave cutting edges, which give the head a rather cruel appearance, while others are more stylized, with graceful, convex edges. I have noticed in churches stone carvings of archers drawing their bows, and the barbed heads depicted are enormous. Had the heads really been that size, they would have been too heavy for the arrow to fly properly when shot, resulting in it dropping very quickly.

These representations raise certain questions. Why were the heads so exaggerated if they were not really made that large? Why are other types of head rarely shown in contemporary depictions of archers in battle? Were barbed broadheads perhaps the common military head?

To answer these questions, we must look at the way the medieval artist/craftsman worked. Nearly all contemporary works of art relating a story to the viewer make the important features the largest. The king, for example, is usually the largest man on the scene and often, in relation to certain battles, central to the painting. When set-piece battles are depicted, the opposing sides are invariably shown as being just a few feet apart—no doubt because the artist wished to show all notable people together on one canvas. The same is probably true when he depicted archers; arrowheads were made to look large and cruel, thus reinforcing the formidable nature of a nobleman with archers among his men. Had bodkin-pointed arrows been shown, the dramatic effect would have been lessened and the statement weakened.

I have seen a church misericord carving showing an archer drawing a bow with an apparently headless arrow. My first reaction was that the head had been broken, but after studying the grain of the wood it was clear that all was intact and the arrow was as originally carved. I believe this meant the scene was of an archer shooting a bodkin-tipped arrow. The carving was perhaps historically correct for a military archer but my initial impression was that something was not as it should be.

There are many contemporary paintings and carvings of archers in hunting scenes, and these invariably show the use of large broadheads. Hunting was often portrayed in order to demonstrate wealth and power—what better way to reinforce a statement than through large, stylized arrowheads?

One medieval French statute required the distance between the barbs of a hunting broad head to be 4 fingers. Thus the heads may have been between 3 and 4 inches in width; very large and impressive. However, hunting heads of this type were made just for the privileged who were allowed to hunt; I think it unlikely that this type was mass produced on the scale of that of military heads.

So, was the broadhead the most common military arrow used in warfare? Before attempting an answer, we should consider how the bow and its arrow developed from a hunting tool into a decisive military weapon and examine the place in society of the people who used them.

The first people to use bows and arrows to overcome their limited physical ability to hunt for food were the Neolithic hunter-gatherers over 6,000 years ago. While they were possibly used as weapons for defense against attack from a rival tribe, the arrow's primary use was to kill animals for food. The Neolithic period was a time when creativity was awakened, as people learned how to make sharp cutting tools from hard material such as flint and obsidian. The discovery in Europe by archaeologists of delicately made barbed flint broadheads is evidence enough that humans had improved upon the fire-hardened pointed stick used by their predecessors. The sharper cutting edge of worked flint readily penetrated thick hides, while the barbs prevented the head from falling out, causing the animal to die quickly by bleeding.

Fig. 1 shows an extremely well made Neolithic flint arrowhead found by a field walker in England's North Yorkshire. It was made by a process known as knapping, where the hard stone was chipped into a flake or shard by striking it with another stone. Then, to produce a sharp cutting edge, a deer's tine was pressed against the edge of the shard, held in a leather pad. This process—known as pressure flaking—produces the sharp serrated edge that can be seen in the photograph. This edge would make the cutting action more effective.

Fig. 1. A tanged Neolithic flint arrowhead found in North Yorkshire. (*Mark Stretton*)

On completion, the head was inserted into a slot cut in the shaft, bound with nettle fibers and secured with glue, the chief ingredient of which was birch sap. While the head profile could have been of a leaf shape, the tang of a barbed head would have permitted its tighter binding to the shaft, with plenty of cutting edge exposed.

Let us now move many thousands of years into the age of bronze. A new and superior material—something we now call metal—had been discovered and was being developed to produce cutting tools. The human ability to cast arrowheads in molds meant that delicate, intricate, and identical heads, superior to those achieved by knapping flint, could now be created. Once mold making was mastered, heads could be readily mass produced, and it is here that the arrow was transformed. With the discovery of bronze, the bow and arrow became more than just personal hunting tools; they were now weapons suitable for the purposes of war, utilized by the Greeks and other great nations.

The next important discovery came in the Iron Age. Iron was found to be harder than bronze and a superior material for the manufacture of cutting weapons. Many Northern European civilizations mastered the working of iron and found the range of what could be done with this new material amazing. While bronze may be forged to shape by hammering, its structure hardens under impact and so is prone to crack; casting to shape was almost certainly the preferred option. Iron, however, could be worked either by casting or forging— although in the case of arrowheads, they usually appear to have been forged.

Although the early British were skilled in iron working, it was the Romans who took the mass production of iron weaponry to a higher level. Many Roman sites excavated by archaeologists have revealed tools and weapons made of iron, particularly swords and heads of spears. What I find most interesting is the discovery of some arrowheads made in a shape suggestive of hunting, while I have seen others with shapes clearly designed for the single purpose of warfare— shapes purposely made to penetrate types of armor rather than animal flesh. Triangular, conical, and square points (similar in character to the much later medieval bodkin heads) were all used against mail and other simpler forms of protection such as boiled leather.

The Roman war machine was magnificent, its strategies based on sheer size. The Romans were famous for their legions of foot soldiers equipped with sword, spear, and shield, supported by cavalry. Although archers were believed to be present on the battlefield, they were not as yet a supreme force in their own right. Consequently although Roman arrowheads were made for military use, we still need to move forward in time to find evidence of mass production in order to discover the most common type of head used on the battlefield.

The migrations of northern European tribes of Angles, Saxons, and Franks brought their great skills of iron working to new countries. This influx, combined with the collapse of

Roman rule, meant that England assumed a changed population identity. This new Anglo-Saxon race was very skilled and ingenious, especially with iron working. The very complex method of making laminated blades out of different types of iron and steel (known as pattern welding, or Damascus steel) is often attributed to the Asian and Japanese bladesmiths of the Middle Ages, but in truth the Franks and the Anglo-Saxons had pioneered this method centuries before in the Dark Ages.

The bow was an essential weapon to the Saxon people, especially for hunting. However, since the Anglo-Saxons were farmers and craftspeople as well as warriors, the bow was used to defend farms and homesteads from attackers as well as for providing food.

What I find interesting is that the majority of Saxon arrowheads recovered by archaeologists are of a flat, leaf-type blade—a classic shape for hunting. There is little evidence to suggest that the Saxons made arrowheads for the specific purpose of war. The leaf shape tends to have the same cross section at the front of the blade as do some barbed heads, and it produces a similar type of cutting action on flesh; but without barbs to hold it into a body, the arrow will drop out of the wound more easily. When hunting small game such as hares or rabbits, or even birds, the impact of the arrow and the trauma it produces is sufficient to kill the quarry. The bigger barbed heads are for larger game, and in the next chapter we shall look at the way these work on flesh.

Archaeological evidence for purpose-made military-style arrowheads is lacking, so when the bow was present in battle at this time, hunting-type heads were most probably used, and I believe these would have been quite effective against the type of protective armor worn by the enemy. Mail was in use at this time, but it was high-status armor with a main purpose of protecting against sword cuts. The individual links of mail were not designed to withstand point-load impact, and modern experiment shows them to be tested to the limit by arrows.

Lower-status warriors would have made the best of what they had for protection, consisting perhaps of layers of wool, linen, or leather. My belief is that these would also have been tested to their limit by arrows, and the leaf-shape head probably worked well. The style of Saxon warfare is well documented and is believed to be similar to that used by the Romans, utilizing shield and spear, but with the addition of skilled axe-men wielding huge two-handed axes behind a tightly packed defensive shield wall.

Evidence suggesting that archers were scarce in Saxon battle tactics comes from the Bayeux tapestry, which documents the defeat of Saxon King Harold at Hastings in 1066 by the army of Duke William the Bastard of Normandy. Here just one Saxon archer can be seen, against over 20 depicted in the Norman forces; it seems ironic that Harold was supposedly brought down by an arrow in the eye!

In the year of Hastings, Saxon kingdoms were under threat from an old enemy, one that had invaded the shores of England for over a hundred years: an enemy that had brought with it a new strategy of warfare. These Norsemen, or Vikings, came from across Scandinavia. They shared many Saxon characteristics but differed in one aspect that set them apart for, while farmers and peaceful craftspeople at home, they were— as the Romans before them—ruthless fighters when they moved overseas to find and conquer new lands. Their ferocious fighting method, using sword, spear, shield, and axe was backed up by numbers of dedicated archers shooting in ranks; and it is here perhaps for the first time that archers were used as a principal fighting force with bows dedicated to military purpose—the weapon that in time would evolve into the mighty longbow.

As with Saxon sites, Viking archaeological excavations have revealed hunting arrowheads, but then these people also needed to hunt for food. Also found, however, have been heads with shapes specific to warfare, not so efficient for the hunting of large game. Many long, pointed bodkin-style arrowheads have been found, designed to pierce mail and other types of early armor. These would have first split the links of mail then driven through any padded underclothing into the wearer's body. Others found have been leaf-type arrowheads with a strengthened rib forged into the center of the blade, giving great strength to the head when impacting upon protective armor. These improvements of shape design, while of no particular advantage against animal or human flesh, would, when striking a harder surface, have stopped the blade from rolling up its tip, preventing penetration. This I think is evidence for purpose-made military arrowheads.

The Normans were descendants of those Vikings who populated northern France—the name is derived from the term "North-men." They were great military tacticians who used cavalry to its maximum advantage. With the passage of time, the strategies learned by their Viking ancestors altered; the progress of military archery stagnated, while the use of mounted men-at-arms developed as an early form of the medieval knight. Although the use by Normans of archers in warfare is well known, they may have been regarded as low class and so used in a limited way. In Norman ideology the mounted knight ruled supreme and was of high status.[1]

Arrowheads found dating from early Norman times are usually flat-leaf blades or simple bodkin points, showing no evidence of development from the earlier Viking form—an indication perhaps of the use of low-status ceorls (peasants) as archers, with arrowheads matching their rank in Norman society? Funding for military campaigns seems often to have been lavished on armament for those of high status, leaving whatever remained to be spread thinly among the lower ranks.

It seems strange that the Saxons did not follow their Norman enemy's lead with specific tactical formations of archers, yet the Normans, while creating their knights, failed to build upon earlier military prowess.

Fig. 2 shows three heads from my personal collection of original arrowheads. The larger, leaf-shaped hunting head on the left is of typical Saxon type and is quite well preserved. Delicately made, with its wide cutting shape, it would have been ideal against human flesh but probably too weak for boar or deer, and it has no barbs to hold it in. The socket is forged with no overlap of the edges and has an external diameter of 3/8 inch where it would meet the shaft. The head in the middle is of the style of a typical Viking military bodkin head and it is well made. The tip has been broken off, but it was a long, thin bodkin point. Again, the socket has no overlap on its edges. It also has an external diameter of 3/8 inch, although the front portion is much stronger in build. The point has been forged into a cruciform section as it widens back toward the socket, finishing in a neatly formed shoulder where the socket taper starts.

The purpose of the cruciform shape is to produce four cutting edges that will work with great effect once the point has penetrated. I believe this to have been designed on purpose to pierce armor, probably mail, since the cutting edges would easily cut into and split open riveted links. I do not believe this head to have been sufficiently efficient in creating a gaping wound for the hunting of large game. Both heads show evidence of being riveted to the shaft with a small pin, a practice that appears common to heads recovered from the Viking and Saxon periods. It was also common practice in medieval times to pin hunting heads to shafts.

The smaller leaf-shaped head on the right is typically Norman and shares the same socket dimensions as the other two. It too has no overlap on its socket, and this is indicative perhaps that all socketed heads from this period were simple in their construction. The small leaf shape would be effective for small game but would not cause enough of a wound on deer or boar. The socket of this head is not pierced to take a pin, which means that it is probably not of Scandinavian or other Germanic origin. I think it fair to say that all three arrowheads would be effective if shot at a lightly armored enemy, but I believe that only the Viking type was specifically designed for a military arrow.

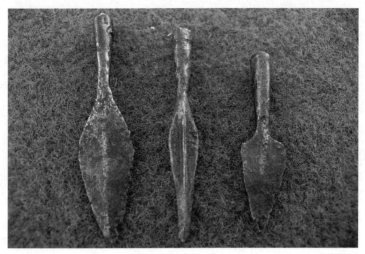

Fig. 2. Three early medieval arrowheads. From left to right: leaf-shaped Saxon-style hunting head, Scandinavian type military bodkin—note cruciform shape, Norman leaf-shaped head. Note also evidence of riveting on the Saxon and Scandinavian heads. (*Mark Stretton*)

Before I go on to the development of the military arrowhead, I would like to explain the importance of the socket in dating arrowheads from British archaeological excavations. Until the Vikings came to Britain, virtually all arrowheads made by the indigenous population—Neolithic, Romano-British, and Saxon alike—had a tang behind the blade portion to fit it to the shaft. The development of the socket meant that the head was both easier to fit to the shaft and much stronger. Although tanged heads were common across Europe during the medieval period, it is widely believed that socketed heads found in Britain date from the Viking period and onward; an example of the adoption of Scandinavian military experience in the forging of arrowheads, even though the tactical use of archers had been neglected by the Saxons and their worth disregarded by the Normans in favor of the mounted knight.

Let us move forward to a time when the Norman influence had grown in England, well established by William the Conqueror's descendants. Norman kings and nobles had developed military tactics to a high level, creating that important strategic element: the castle. The knight still reigned supreme upon the battlefield, but the importance of the archer was being realized, and as castles became strongholds that knights alone could not defend, he was used to advantage, his worth apparent to the nobility.

It was quickly realized that archers needed good equipment and that crossbowmen needed stocks of good quality bolts to defend castles effectively. It is from this time that the mass production of military heads for use with both arrow and bolt is thought to have begun. Dedicated workshops were set up where many thousands of heads were produced for arrow and bolt by arrow smiths. One place well known to historians and archaeologists was established close to St. Briavels Castle on the western edge of the Forest of Dean in Gloucestershire. It is well documented that crossbow quarrels were made here in vast quantities and sent, packed in barrels, to other English strongholds for use against Welsh uprisings. "Quarrel" derives from the Latin quadrus, meaning "square," and usually refers to crossbow bolts; but in the context of arrowheads, bodkins generally have four faces, so it may have been a general term for military-type heads simply grouped together by the medieval record keepers, regardless of their use with either bow or crossbow.

Records mention that quarrels were to be made for different strengths of crossbow under the supervision of John Malemort at St. Briavels in the time of King Henry III. John was a king's quarreller, and he was contracted in 1232 to produce 100 quarrels a day, for which he was paid a daily wage of 10 1/2 pence. This was a very good wage, although if he was working on his own, this would have meant at least a 16-hour day, producing one head every ten minutes without break. His money would have been well earned.[2] There is no specific mention of arrowheads in Malemort's orders, but it seems hard to believe that these would not have been manufactured as well at such an important place, especially when the bow was known to have been used against the Welsh rebels nearby.

We shall now move forward to the time of King Edward I and his late thirteenth-century wars with both Welsh and Scottish rebels. It is generally agreed that after suffering many losses of English soldiers from Welsh bowmen using guerrilla ambush tactics, Edward I was the first king to properly use specific units of trained archers tactically in his campaigns. He was a shrewd man and offered the Welsh rebels 3 pence a day to enlist with his army as trained archers. This was a successful incentive, since the average foot soldier received 2 pence a day and, during medieval times, the Welsh became among the best archers on the battlefield. The archer was now no longer viewed as a peasant, he was drawn from the type of middle class later to be known as yeoman, and his pay reflected his status.

What of the arrowheads in use at the time of Edward I? Once again both the military-type bodkin and barbed broadhead have been found by archaeologists at sites dated to this period. The armor at this time was still mail based, although the very rich had begun to wear the beginnings of simple plate armor. Bodkin heads have been found from this period with long, thin points similar to the Viking head we looked at earlier; and there are also records of four sided heads of quarrel type, correctly proportioned for use with arrows.

Armor was constantly being improved over time, and by the fourteenth century, the kind worn by those of higher status had become much more effective at protecting the wearer. Certain amounts of plate armor were now being worn in conjunction with mail, meaning that the weight of armor could be adjusted. I believe plate armor to have been developed to reduce the amount of weight, thus to make it less fatiguing for the knight to fight, as well as deflecting sword cuts more efficiently than mail. I do not think that plate armor was initially designed to prevent arrows from penetrating, although this may have been a later consideration as improvements were made.

Armor for those of lower status was also developed, but produced to a much lower budget. Layers of cloth were used, stitched into jackets to form a type of padded armor, and this also proved effective against sword cuts. However, both types of armor were tested to their limit when faced with arrows, especially those armed with bodkin points. We shall examine this in more detail in the next chapter.

It was not only armor that developed through time, arrow technology improved also. The head itself was altered to defeat armor, in a sort of medieval arms race; this can be seen in the subtle changes of design apparent on original examples. While the principle of the bodkin point remained much the same as earlier, the length and profile of the point altered to improve its efficiency at penetrating and cutting through armor as it became more advanced. Quarrel-shaped arrowheads become much more common as time progressed, their sockets showing evidence that they were being made with edges overlapping each other to make a stronger, cone-type shape. The reason is not difficult to find. As a military tactician, if enemy crossbow quarrels were defeating the armor worn by your soldiers, you would not be long in adopting the quarrel-shaped arrowheads for your own archers.

By the time of the Hundred Years' War, English archers were well and truly defined as a supreme fighting force, and many are the battles that might have been lost were it not for their deployment. The longbow and its arrow are often thought to have been the decisive weapon of the English armies against French cavalry, and it is here that on both sides, many of the principles of armor and arrowhead technology were learned. It would seem that arrowhead technology particularly was already at a high state of development, since military heads recovered from the later Wars of the Roses period are not that different in shape, although size and weight had increased, an indication that arrows were now made heavier. I believe this was because armor in general, and plate armor in particular, was by then vastly improved in quality, and both the bow and its arrow were developed to defeat it. Arrow smiths, it seems, had evolved a winning design and had stayed with it, improving it from time to time as necessary.

The military bodkin-style arrowheads show more evidence of development than do barbed broadheads, manufactured well into the late Tudor period, toward the end of the tactical use of the war bow. Differences in the barbed broadheads, visible through archaeological evidence, is improvement in the quality of manufacture. The general shape changes little from early medieval times to late Tudor times. Some heads have large, wide-open barbs and others have smaller barbs lying close to the socket, but they are all variants on the same theme. An interesting question here is that if armor changed and improved with time but the barbed broadhead remained the same, was this type of head used on the battlefield at all? To throw light on the question, we must look at how the bodkin and the broadhead may have been made by the medieval arrow smith and what materials were used. This should then shed light on the earlier question of what was the most common head used in battle?

As I mentioned above, the medieval arrow smiths were producing arrowheads by the thousands, on a scale that was breathtaking, even by today's standards of mass production. We know that specific workshops such as those at St. Briavels were set up to make large volumes of the arrowheads needed to supply the huge demand for arrows required for military campaigns abroad.

Remember, a hunter needs only a few good arrows, for he would hope to retrieve a head from the animal's carcass once it was dead. This could then be reused on another shaft if the old arrow was broken during the hunt. The military archer would expect to shoot each arrow only once—unless he was lucky enough to be able to retrieve some after (or during) a battle. His frame of mind was similar to that of a modern soldier who shoots his rifle and knows that the bullet has gone forever. However both the modern soldier and the medieval archer would need, and expect, their ammunition to be of the highest quality to perform its intended task. So, with that in mind, let us look at the type of metal used by the medieval smith to make arrowheads.

The majority of original hunting-type arrowheads that I have seen are made from iron, which shows a layer pattern when it degrades by rusting. This looks just like the grain in a piece of wood. Iron is good enough for cutting through flesh and bone—all that a good hunting head needs to do—and iron is much cheaper to manufacture than steel. I have seen early military bodkin-type arrowheads with a grain pattern, and these may also have been made from iron. However, later bodkin heads that I have seen show evidence of being made in a different way. They usually have no defined grain pattern and are often in a better state of preservation. This could be either because they were made from hardened steel, which is slightly more resistant to corrosion than iron is, or that the iron had a carbon-enriched surface to make it harder and better able to cut through steel armor. This is a process called case hardening, which involves heating the head in a carbon—rich medium, such as bone meal, or scraps of leather, until it is red hot and carbon is absorbed into the surface of the iron. The head can then be hardened to a surface that is very wear resistant but that has a softer, more cushioning type of core to prevent shattering on impact, as an overhardened steel head might. It would be possible for this process to be performed on a very large scale with many heads being treated together, a process well within the capability of medieval smiths. There is specific mention of heads being specially heat treated in certain medieval bills of sale. This could be evidence for carbon enrichment and a reason perhaps why the heads were listed at a higher price.

There is also evidence that specific types of metallic objects were recycled for use in arrowhead production. Edward III required anchor flukes to be salvaged to produce arrowheads for the wars with France. Unfortunately the statute does not explain why this particular source was chosen, and it has to be assumed that anchor flukes were made from some superior metal, possibly a form of steel. Now we know what material was probably used for arrowheads, let us look at the most likely tools.

The blacksmith's smithy, with its hearth fire for heat and its anvil and hammer with which to forge the metal, has remained unchanged for centuries. In fact, the only major modern change is the help of electricity to run the grind stones and perhaps a fan motor to force air into the fire to keep it at working temperature. The medieval arrow smith was most likely also the village blacksmith, and his smithy would have probably shared many similarities with that of the modern smith. It is known that charcoal was used to fuel fires at the St. Briavels smithies, and modern replica hearths have been constructed from descriptions given in medieval records. They had a wooden frame with a protective layer of sand in the bottom, and charcoal was used for the heat source. The hearth had its air supply forced into the fire through leather bellows, and the operation was controlled by the speed with which the smith worked the manual lever connected to the bellows. Charcoal works well, since it is a clean-burning fuel that provides sufficient heat to get the metal to the correct temperature without overheating the hearth.

The tools used by the medieval arrow smith would probably have consisted of differently shaped hammers with which to forge the metal together and specially shaped tongs with which to grip the socket without distorting it. The anvil would probably have looked much the same as a modern one, although it need not have been as large. It would probably have had a square hole—like a modern anvil—to take specially shaped tools known as stakes. These have been used in blacksmithing for centuries when a specific shape needed to be formed that could not be made by hammer and anvil alone.

I would like to suggest the methods a medieval arrow smith perhaps used to make arrowheads and to compare the relative time and cost between manufacturing hunting and military heads. The procedures that I will be explaining are based upon methods I have developed myself. There are of course other ways of making heads, but after discussions with other arrow smiths, I find that the basics are shared by all. Yet we each have our own techniques, so each smith's arrowheads are distinctive, a feature we may well share with medieval smiths. The special tools I shall be describing were developed to make the process of arrowhead production more efficient, and were made by myself. They are not copies of medieval tools, but they will nevertheless demonstrate principles that a medieval arrow smith might have used and give a good idea of how arrowheads may have been made.

The first technique is for making a short bodkin arrowhead (a shape listed in the London Museum Catalogue of arrowheads as Type 10). It has an external diameter where socket meets shaft of 1/2 inch and is based upon a genuine medieval bodkin head in my collection. Mild steel will be used for the making of this type of head, since it forges well without splitting, as can happen with some poor-quality iron.

To start making the head, a 12-inch-long piece of 3/8-inch diameter mild steel bar is heated at one end in the hearth fire until it glows first red, then yellow, from the tip to about 3/4 inch back along its length. When it is bright yellow in color (not white and sparking), it is laid flat on the anvil or forging stake. While still at the yellow stage, it is forged into the beginning of a flat spoon shape using a heavy ball-peen hammer (see Fig. 3 in gallery following page 126).

As it is worked, the metal cools and changes color from bright red to cherry red and spreads out quickly, meaning that it must be forged out equally on both edges as it spreads. The bar must not be allowed to cool too much at this stage, so it must be reheated to yellow again and the process repeated until the flattened socket blank is of a thin and uniform section. Because the socket will be a neatly tapered cone shape when it is finished, it is important that the socket blank is made large enough to provide the correct outside diameter where it will fit onto the cone of the arrow shaft. This particular type of head has an overlapped join on the socket, so slightly more metal must be allowed on the developed socket blank. A template is used to help forge the correct flattened shape, and this helps when heads are to be made in a large batch. The template is made by preparing a flat shape three and a half times the diameter of any given point on a formed socket profile. Then it is cut out of sheet metal that will not be burned through when the hot bar is laid upon it.

The edges of the socket blank must next be thinned to a feather edge, since this makes a neater overlap without a big step in it. Great care needs to be taken when the bar is reheated at this stage, since the metal is much thinner and can overheat and burn back at the edges. Now the socket blank is reheated to an even brighter red color and is placed over the concave section of the forging stake. A cross-wedge hammer is used to form the blank into a U shape (see Fig. 4). The bar is reheated, placed on the flat face of the forging stake, and a light ball-peen hammer is used to begin the formation of the socket. The far side of the U shape is gently tapped to curl it inward, then the near side is worked so that it curls over the other side to begin the start of the overlap (see Fig. 5). I prefer to work in this way, since I can see the first side roll into its desired shape more easily, making it simpler to form the socket when the second side is rolled across its top.

Some modern arrowsmiths work the opposite way, and I believe this to be a source of misunderstanding by archaeologists about medieval arrow smithing. There is a plausible theory that the way a socket is wrapped denotes a left- or right-handed smith. However, I believe it impossible to tell this unless all smiths forged in the same way. A right-and a left-handed smith who each wrapped opposite ways would produce overlaps that looked the same.

To resume, the area from which the socket is to be formed is carefully reheated until it is bright red in color, then the bar is placed flat on the forging stake. The overlap of the socket is gently tapped while the bar is turned slowly. This starts to tighten the socket and form it properly. Particular attention is paid to making the socket blend into the bar, with no cracks appearing where the socket taper and the overlap begin. At this stage it does not matter if the socket is smaller than the required diameter, since this can be rectified later.

The reheated socket is next placed on the flat face of the forging stake with the bar over its edge. The bar is then turned while the socket area is gently tapped to form the taper and also produce the beginning of a shoulder where the overlap meets the parent bar. After again reheating, the bar is positioned so that the taper of the socket is below the edge of the forging stake. The whole bar is then rolled along the edge and gently tapped with a hammer to form the shoulder properly (see Fig. 6). While in the same heat, each of the previous two stages is repeated several times until the bar loses its red color and appears black. This is known as black heat and is a stage at which the metal is still very hot, though it does not glow red in daylight. This stage is useful to a smith, as the metal may still be worked but will not stretch as easily as when red hot. This means that the socket taper and shoulder may be neatly formed and the hammer marks planished out.

With the socket placed over a tapered mandrel on the forging stake, the end of the socket is trued to an even circle. If the socket diameter is not correct, this can be simply rectified on the mandrel by reheating and gently tapping the outside of the taper. If the outside diameter needs to be decreased, the bar is turned following the direction of the wrap, which will tighten it. Conversely, if the outside diameter needs to be increased, then the bar is turned against the wrap. If the socket is now a bottle shape, then the earlier procedure for forming the taper and shoulder must be repeated. It is important to note that if the socket blank is not forged initially to a uniform thickness, then the finished socket will have one area thicker than another. This could lead to misshaped taper, difficult to fit properly to an arrow shaft, and a point of potential weakness.

The bar is now marked about 1/2 inch back from the shoulder and cut off at this point A saw, or more traditionally a blacksmith's hardie, which is fitted into the square hole on the anvil, may be used. The hardie has a flat chisel-shaped blade that will cut red-hot metal when placed on it and hammered.

The socket is now held in a pair of specially shaped tongs with matching tapered concave and convex sides, which hold it firmly without distorting its shape. The tip of the parent bar (but not the socket part) is heated until it is bright yellow. It is then placed on the flat face of the forging stake, near its edge and, with the hammer held at an angle to the face of the stake, is forged out. The head is turned through 90 degrees, and the process is continued. By repeating this process a square sectioned point will begin forming. The tip is once more reheated and is now drawn out until it has reached the desired length (see Fig. 7). The finished head is held against a light background to check that the point and the socket are in line. If not, this can be corrected by placing it flat on the forging stake and straightening by tapping with a hammer.

This method of manufacture is very efficient, since no material is wasted and the head needs little grinding unless a diamond-section point is required, although with practice, this can be included in the forging as easily as can a square point. The time taken to make this head is between ten and 15 minutes, depending upon the finish required and any problems encountered during the various processes. I believe this to be one of the easiest heads to make, so as a military arrowhead, it would lend itself to mass production on an enormous scale.

Now to the making of one of the most difficult arrowheads, the barbed broadhead. All arrowheads with barbs pointing back from the tip are made by one of two different processes: either in one piece or in two pieces. I will explain how a barbed broadhead is made using my own preferred method of one-piece construction, which may be compared to the process above, for forging a short bodkin point (London Museum Catalogue Type 10).

The amount of material necessary to make a barbed broadhead is greater than that for a bodkin head, especially if the construction is in one piece, since more metal needs to be moved into correct areas for the forging of the shape required. To make this type of head, a 12-inch-long piece of 1/2-inch diameter steel bar is heated at one end in the hearth fire until the bar glows bright yellow from the tip to about 3/8 inch along its length. This length is less than that for a bodkin, since the process differs. The hot end is then placed squarely against the face of the arrow stake and the cold end of the bar is hit hard with a hammer. This will mushroom out the hot end, and the process is repeated until the end of the bar is one and half times its original diameter. The end of the bar is then reheated, laid flat on the stake, and the swollen end is forged out into a flattened section. This must be done evenly and drawn out until it is about 1/8 inch thick on the end. While maintaining the thickness of the end, the sides of the flat section are worked to produce a symmetrical, elongated spoonlike shape (see Fig. 8).

It is imperative that the correct shape is arrived at now, since failure to do so will result in there being insufficient metal in the correct area for later on, when the barbed shape emerges. Unfortunately, only experience and many attempts will achieve the required shape.

Next, two lines are marked out on the flat piece with engineers' chalk. The middle area should be twice as wide as each of the side portions. The lines indicate where the flat section will be split with a chisel. Later, the middle portion will become the socket, the sides will form the barbs. The flat end is heated to a dull red (the chalk is still just visible at this temperature) and is then gently marked along the lines with a cold chisel tapped lightly with a hammer. The end is then reheated to a bright yellow color and split into three sections with the cold chisel while still hot (see Fig. 9). The forging stake is now changed for another of a different shape entirely. This has an undercut on one side that produces a sharp edge on the flat face. This is specifically used in the next procedure and is a most useful tool.

The bar is heated to a bright red color, and one of the outer parts of the flat section is placed on the sharp edge of the forging stake. The end of the bar is tapped down toward the stake with a hammer while the bar itself is levered up. This action opens out the side portion—later to become one of the barbs—while the undercut of the forging stake prevents the middle portion from becoming distorted by the process. The bar is then reheated, and the other side is opened up using the same method. When both split sides of the flat section are opened out at right angles to the bar, they are then forged into long square sectional points. This is done by placing the side portion on the flat face of the forging stake, while the middle portion is pressed close to the sharp edge. Then, with a hammer, the side portions are drawn out with a technique similar to that of drawing the point on a bodkin (see Fig. 10).

The middle portion of the flat section is then forged into the socket by using the same technique as described to make the socket of the short bodkin, However, there is no shoulder to neatly tighten the socket (which also leaves no gap in the overlap of the taper). The head must therefore be placed on the sharp edge of the forging stake, and using a cross-wedge hammer, the socket is neatly shaped where it meets the barbs, while the bar is slowly turned (see Fig. 11). This operation must commence when the socket area is bright red in color and continue as the head cools to black heat. This will tighten up the socket without over stretching it. Obviously the barbs must be kept at right angles to allow the socket to be turned and worked with the hammer.

The barb area is now reheated to a bright red color, with special care taken not to overheat the socket and burn it away. It is then fitted on to the tip of the socket mandrel on the forging stake, positioned in such a way that the mandrel tip supports the socket where it is joined by the barbs. The higher barb is gently tapped back to its final position, and when this is complete, the process is repeated for the other barb. The head is now starting to look like its intended shape. After reheating, the head is placed flat on the forging stake, positioned with the edge of the barb level with the edge of the stake. The head is then worked to flatten out the barb and produce a tapered knife-edge shape.

When a curved cutting edge is required, then the side is left to curve naturally as the edge is worked. Curves develop because the outside edge is thinner in section than the inside edge and thus will stretch as they are forged into shape.

If the head is to be made with straight cutting edges, the sides are tapped into line and the edges are thinned out again. If really long swallowtail cutting edges are wanted, then the sides are worked in a series of drawing and flattening processes that must be done equally on each side. I find the rounded back of my forging stake allows the bar to be pushed up to the stake, enabling the barbs to be flattened easily without distorting the socket or the head in the process.

The head is forged to a rough blank, which must have sufficient material allowed for it to be finished to the overall required size. When the barbs are flattened and worked into cutting edges, it is easier to achieve the final shape while the rough blank is still attached to the parent bar, since it can be held more firmly.

Since the head will be taken to its final shape by grinding, the rough blank should not be forged down to a fine edge, because if too thin, it can distort with the heat. However, the blank should not be left as a huge forged lump either, since this would take too long to grind into shape. It is quicker and easier to forge the head to approximately its finished size and then lightly grind it to its final shape. It is worth remembering that the medieval arrowsmith would probably have ground his heads on a sandstone wheel, manually cranked (an arduous task, even with an apprentice to turn the wheel), and a busy smith would have wished to keep such a task to a minimum.

The head now needs to be cut from the parent bar. The position where it is to be cut is marked with a piece of chalk, leaving enough of the parent bar on the head to forge forward from the edges to create a point. The head is then cut from the bar with the hardie or a metal saw as described earlier. With the socket held in the specially shaped tongs, the head is reheated for the last time. When it is bright red, it is laid flat on the forging stake, and the tip is drawn forward from the blank to form a square-sectioned point. It is then placed on the edge and worked into a blade shape (see Fig. 12).

A light grinding to shape should remove the hammer marks and will sharpen the cutting edges. As before, the head is held against a light background to check that the point and socket are in line, any corrections being made by straightening the head on the flat surface of the forging stake.

This type of head, as I said, is difficult to make; it can take up to 45 minutes to properly produce a big swallowtail, which is why I think these were probably made specifically for hunting. When the two manufacturing processes are compared, it is obvious that the bodkin lends itself to high-volume production of munitions-grade arrowheads, as mentioned in the record books for St. Briavels. The barbed broadhead was more likely to have been made in smaller batches for those nobles and others privileged to hunt large game.

It is worth noting that Henry V and the English army are recorded as having taken 1 1/2 million arrows to France for the campaign that ended at Agincourt. It was a tremendous feat of logistics in itself and even more impressive if one considers the time taken to make the heads. Let us theorize. Assuming all arrows to be fitted with bodkin heads, it would have taken a staggering 375,000 hours to make the heads alone; the equivalent of 100 arrow smiths each making 100 heads a day for 150 days. If broadheads had been fitted to all, then the time taken would be astronomical, with those 100 arrow smiths making 33 heads a day for 450 days. To the cost of labor would need to be added the cost of iron and wood for the fletcher to make the shafts. It would have been a truly enormous undertaking, both financially and logistically, which indicates to me that for war, the bodkin would have been more commonly produced.

Arrow spacers from the Tudor warship *Mary Rose* also suggest that the only practical heads would have been small enough to push through the spacers. Although certain barbed broadheads may have been used for warfare, they can quickly get locked together when bunched, making their use slow and difficult. My belief is that during medieval times, these expensively made and often overromanticized heads were used mainly for hunting. It is for you, the reader, to decide.[3]

The following chapter will deal with the effect of these heads on plate, mail, and other protective material as well as on flesh.

Fig. 3.
Forming a flat
spoon shape using
a heavy ball-pein
hammer.
(*Mark Stretton*)

Fig. 4.
Forming a U shape
using a cross-wedge
hammer.
(*Mark Stretton*)

Fig. 5.
Commencing the
overlapping process
to complete the
socket. (*Mark
Stretton*)

Fig. 6.
Forming the
Shoulder.
(*Mark Stretton*)

Fig. 7.
The bodkin head,
drawing out the
tip.
(*Mark Stretton*)

Fig. 8.
Commencing the
broadhead. The
finished symmetri-
cal spoonlike
shape.
(*Mark Stretton*)

Fig. 9.
Splitting away sections to form the barbs using a cold chisel.
(*Mark Stretton*)

Fig. 10.
Drawing out side sections to form barbs.
(*Mark Stretton*)

Fig. 11.
Shaping of socket terminal.
(*Mark Stretton*)

Fig. 12.
Shaping of socket terminal.
(*Mark Stretton*)

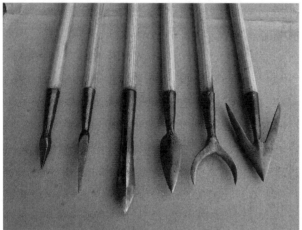
Fig 13.
Below, six arrow-head types, from left to right: short bodkin, long bodkin, heavy quarrel type bodkin, leaf shape head, crescent shaped blade (forker), barbed broadhead shaped blade.
(*Mark Stretton*)

Fig. 14.
Test arrows entering shoulder of a pig's carcass.
(*Mark Stretton*)

Fig. 15.
Heavy quarrel type bodkin head penetrating metal breastplate and carcass.
(*Mark Stretton*)

Fig. 16.
Fatal depth achieved. Full depth penetration with broadhead.
(*Mark Stretton*)

Fig. 17.
Penetration of unprotected ribs with severance of spinal column using crescent broadhead (forker).
(*Mark Stretton*)

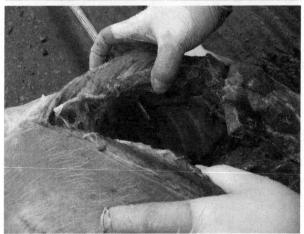

Fig. 18.
Penetration of mail by bodkin and swallowtailed broadhead (horse-head)(*Mark Stretton*)

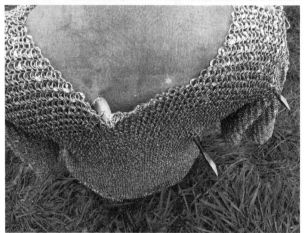

Fig. 19.
Full penetration of body and mail, front and back, by heavy bodkin.
(*Mark Stretton*)

Fig. 20.
Penetration of brigandine by heavy bodkin head. Exernal view.
(*Mark Stretton*)

Fig. 21.
Penetration of brig-
andine by heavy
bodkin head.
Internal view.
(*Mark Stretton*)

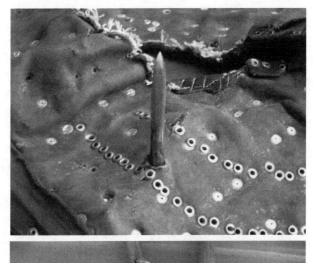

Fig. 22.
Damage to long
bodkin head and
crescent head (fork-
er) after striking
plate armor. Note
break at shoulder
of shafts.
(*Mark Stretton*)

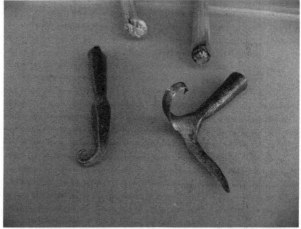

Fig. 23.
Decapitation of
dead goose using
crescent head (fork-
er).
(*Mark Stretton*)

Fig. 24. Shooting at a breastplate (top) affixed to a moving target, now five yards distant, traveling at approximately 20 miles per hour, the speed of a charging horse.

Fig. 25. Shooting of an incendiary arrow. (*Mark Stretton*)

Chapter
Five

EXPERIMENTAL TESTS WITH DIFFERENT TYPES OF MEDIEVAL ARROWHEADS

Mark Stretton

In the previous chapter, we looked at the development of the most common military head, which from its origins in the dark ages, evolved throughout the medieval period—especially during the French wars—to become part of an effective and decisive weapon that turned the tables on French nobility, allowing the flower of French chivalry to be defeated, largely by the deployment of lower-status English archers.

Although the bodkin-shaped heads may well have been the most common type of medieval arrowhead, it would be wrong to assume that other types were not used to great effect on the battlefield. Many differently shaped arrowheads from the medieval period have been found during archaeological excavation, used perhaps for specific purposes other than just warfare. These possibilities can be explored by testing a selection of different type heads against various forms of armor and comparing the result to see which head is most effective against each piece of armor.

Of the various strangely shaped medieval arrowheads recovered by archaeologists, some are developments from a much earlier time—similar to Roman or Viking-style heads, yet with evidence of redesign and improvement to suit the larger, medieval-style arrow. The use of these differently shaped heads is often the focus of debate, with some theories based more on fantasy than practicality. The descriptions of the results of certain practical tests that I performed with several known types of medieval head will, I hope, shed light on their exact use.

For the tests I chose the large barbed broadhead (sometimes called a swallowtail); the crescent-shaped head, or forker; the leaf-shaped blade of the earlier Saxons; the heavy lozenge-shaped, or quarrel-type, head; and the long- and short-type bodkin heads. I chose these differently shaped heads because among them were some possibly used for hunting, while others were definitely made for use in warfare. I find it interesting that some may have been used for both purposes, although it is only through practical experiment that the truth will hopefully emerge.

Fig. 13 (in preceding color gallery) shows the six different types of head, each fitted to an identical shaft of ash, measuring 31 1/2 inches from the nock to the shoulder of the socket. The shafts were 1/2 inch in diameter at the shoulder and were parallel for 20 inches; the last 11 1/2 inches were tapered (bobtailed) to 3/8 inch at the nock. Each was fletched with turkey feathers cut triangular and measuring 7 1/2 inches by 3/4 inch high. I chose to fletch with turkey feathers rather than goose, since I needed to shoot the arrows many times, and turkey feathers are more durable. The use of the more authentic goose feathers would have had no effect on the results.

The individual weights of the complete arrows were as follows:

Short bodkin = 82 grams (1,269 grains)

Long bodkin = 86 grams (1,324 grains)

Quarrel-type bodkin = 125 grams (1,925 grains)

Leaf-shape blade = 86 grams (1,324 grains)

Crescent-shape blade = 86 grams (1,324 grains)

Barbed broadhead blade = 92 grams (1,417 grains)

During experiments, each arrow was shot manually from a self-yew replica war bow with a draw weight of 144 pounds at 32 inches. This is not the fastest or the heaviest bow I have, but it shoots well and gives consistent results. One would expect an exceptional bow to provide exceptional test results and thus be unrepresentative of the average, or livery, medieval weapon.

What varies the penetration of an arrow into any given target is a combination of the speed at which the arrow travels and its physical weight. The way in which a head reacts to the surface at which it is shot will also make a significant difference to the penetration of the arrow into the target. Arrow weights are known, but to determine the kinetic energy value, the arrow speed must also be measured.

I therefore shot the six test arrows over a chronograph and recorded their speeds in feet per second. The short and the long bodkins, the leaf- and the crescent-shaped blades, and the barbed broadhead all achieved similar speeds of between 155 and 157 feet per second. The quarrel-type bodkin achieved a slower speed of 134 feet per second. It is, however, kinetic energy expressed as a value that is relevant to the penetrative ability of an arrow shot against difficult types of armor. This value is measured by the use of the formula mass (weight in grains) times velocity squared (feet per second) divided by a constant of 450,130 = feet per pound (kinetic) energy.

When the kinetic energy formula was applied to the test arrows, these were the results.

Short bodkin = 67.73 feet per pound

Long bodkin, leaf shape, and crescent shape = 70.66 feet per pound

Barbed broadhead = 77.59 feet per pound

Quarrel-type bodkin = 76.00 feet per pound

The arrows all have similar kinetic energy values to each other, since the velocity measurement in the formula is squared. This means that it is necessary for the mass of a slower-moving arrow to be greater than that of a lighter and faster arrow in order for it to be equal in kinetic energy. Therefore, the energy value of the heavy quarrel-type bodkin is similar to the rest of the test arrows. Momentum as well as physical mass also plays a part in the arrow's ability to penetrate, and we will look at that next.

If the majority of the arrows are similar in weight and they leave the bow at the same velocity, then the question is how far will each travel and does the head have an effect on arrow flight? I shot the six test arrows on a clear, crisp, and bright sunny day with a moderate tail wind. All three bodkin-headed arrows and the leaf-shaped blade arrow flew straight, and their flight was unaffected by the wind. The barbed broadhead and the crescent-headed arrows also flew straight without drifting off to one side. Both types of head experienced turbulence as they traveled forward, caused I believe by the wind acting against the natural spin of the arrow. This may have resulted in the arrow becoming unstable until restabilized by continued forward momentum. This was fine until the velocity reduced further, when the arrow once more became unstable, and turbulence began again. It is notable that a strong side wind will cause large-bladed arrows to plane to one side considerably.

The leaf-shaped blade and the short and long bodkin-headed arrows all made over 220 yards, the barbed broadhead and the crescent-shaped heads each made 215 yards, and the heavy bodkin type made a good 200 yards.

To me this indicates that the action of the wind on the two wide-bladed arrows, which caused them to fly with turbulence, affected their distance more than a slight increase in weight would have done. They were actually five yards short of the main group, showing how important it is for an arrow to fly smoothly. It is interesting to note that although the quarrel-type bodkin was 45 percent heavier than the average weight of the other test arrows, it had only traveled 10 percent less distance than the average distance of the group. I believe this to indicate that weight increase does not affect the distance an arrow will travel in a ballistic curve. Once the arrow is moving, the heavier projectile will have more momentum, making it harder to stop than one that is lighter. So, if this heavier arrow type is harder to stop than is a lighter version, would it have had a more devastating effect on the flesh of a real live body?

This is often debated by those interested in the war arrow and its potential, and is a question that can be properly answered only by shooting at a living body. I have worked with flesh-simulating putties and have shot into objects having the same density as muscle, but these results cannot be as definitive as that which is achieved with an arrow shot into something alive. To hunt with a bow is now illegal in England, and we are no longer at war with France. Not wishing to write this chapter while in prison charged with murder, I decided to test shoot my arrows into the body of a newly dead pig.

I obtained the carcass of a dead pig from a farmer friend. I will say quite clearly that it had died of natural causes, not having been slain with an arrow! I had previously arranged with the farmer that if one of his pigs died, he would let me know immediately. This would mean the pig would still be warm—an important consideration, as the flesh of a recently dead body will react in a similar way to that of a live body. This is the reason why a butcher will cut meat only after several days of refrigerated hanging; the meat will be firmer and more easily cut.

The muscle density and body characteristics of a pig are very similar to that of a human being, which is why I wanted to use a pig with similar muscle mass and proportions to that of a well-built man. This would then simulate a person without breaking any laws. The pig was placed in an upright position and secured to a post driven into the ground.

Fig. 14 quite clearly shows the six test arrows shot into the pig's left shoulder. The knife blade is there to indicate where the barbed broadhead has cut a gaping wound (note the similar wound on the left caused by the crescent-shaped head). The short bodkin to the right of the knife shows no gap; in fact, the skin has closed tightly around the arrow shaft.

The question now was to what extent would armor have prevented penetration? Before opening up the carcass to examine internal injuries, I removed the test arrows and fitted the pig with an old 16 standard wire gauge (1.6 millimeter) reenactment-quality breastplate (at which I had shot many times before in other demonstrations). This proved an excellent fit and added to the realism of my simulation.

I first shot the heavy, quarrel-type bodkin headed arrow at the breastplate, as I knew that this type of head had pierced it many times before. Fig. 15 shows what happened. The arrow pierced the armor and stuck into the flesh. However, when I examined the arrow within the plate, it seemed not to have penetrated the body to the depth I had expected—almost as though the head had been pushed backward after its initial impact.

After removing the armor from the carcass, I reinserted the arrow into the breastplate hole, when the true depth of the penetration was evident. The head had cut through the plate and had reached 3 inches of depth before the socket had finally wedged into the metal. I then found that when the arrow was placed in the corresponding wound, it could be pushed right into the chest with no resistance felt. In fact, the head could be pushed in as far as the beginning of the wooden shaft.

When I opened up the carcass I found that if the arrow were inserted to its full depth, it penetrated through into vital organs within the chest cavity. Fig 16. clearly shows the fatal depth, and I am certain that no one could have survived such a wound. However, I feel that the springing effect of the plate had pulled the arrow back slightly, giving a misleading initial impression of actual penetration.

When the wounds from the earlier test without armor were examined, I found that each arrow had inflicted enormous damage and associated trauma. The arrows had sunk deep into the carcass, and the heavy quarrel-type bodkin had been particularly devastating. It had passed through both the shoulder and ribs of the nearside, smashing the ribs around the wound. Having shattered the ribs, it had passed through the shoulder of the far side of the body and was protruding an inch beyond the flesh.

When the carcass was opened along its backbone, it could be seen that the barbed broadhead had severed the vertebrae, with the crescent-shaped head also breaking the spine, it being stopped from further penetration by the backbone itself (Fig 17). A final note on this part of the tests concerns removal of the heads. The crescent head could be readily removed by pulling hard on the arrow shaft, whereas the barbed broadhead had to be cut from the body, since its barbs dug so firmly into the flesh it could not be removed by pulling on the shaft.

When the angle of entry of the crescent shaped and barbed broadheads was traced and examined, it was possible to see from their final resting places that they had rotated slightly after entry. This would have greatly increased damage and hemorrhaging, adding to the trauma of a dreadful wound.

While the quarrel-type bodkin had defeated mild steel plate conclusively, plate was not the only type of armor worn on the battlefield, which leads to the question of what other types of armor were used in medieval warfare and would some arrowheads perform better against it than others?

With my first tests complete, for my next I visited Mr. Roy King, a well-known armorer from the village of Horam in East Sussex, southern England. I traveled to his excellent workshop and facilities where he had prepared two important pieces of armor for me to test. One was a shirt of authentically riveted mail and the other a very high quality Brigandine.

The Brigandine was constructed from a leather jerkin-style carcass onto which individually overlapping 18–16 standard wire gauge (1.2–1.4 millimeters) metal plates had been riveted, similar to tiles fixed to a roof. The outer surface of the plates was covered with fine-quality velvet secured in place by decoratively headed rivets. This type of armor is much lighter than mail and infinitely more flexible than plate. I was particularly interested to experiment with this expensive piece of reproduction armor, as I was uncertain about the outcome. There may have been penetration tests on a Brigandine in the past using a heavy draw weight war bow, but if so I do not know of them and have never seen results.

We set the mail up first. This was fitted over a tailor's dummy fastened to two wooden props against an earthen bank that supported the dummy and formed a backstop for stray arrows. I shot the six test arrows into the mail shirt, and examination showed that each of them, including the crescent-shaped and barbed broadheads, had penetrated this and entered the dummy (see Fig. 18).

Each of the bodkin-type heads had burst open the riveted links in their passage, which was my expectation. This result supports theories advanced by historians and academics on the use of bodkin points against mail in warfare. The blade-type arrows behaved quite differently, however, from the usual school of thought, and their results were a surprise. It is often said that the larger-bladed arrowheads would be stopped by riveted links of mail, yet in these tests, the leaf-shaped, crescent-shaped, and barbed broadheads each cut easily through the individual links. In fact, the leaf-shaped head had penetrated the dummy as had the bodkin points. All were protruding from the back of the mail shirt. The quarrel-type bodkin had penetrated the furthest to protrude from the back by some 3 1/2 inches (see Fig. 19). All arrows had survived the test with just slight nicks to the cutting edges of the bladed heads.

We then set the Brigandine upon the dummy, fastening it tightly with four leather straps and buckles riveted to the armor. The props were replaced against the earth bank, and I prepared once more to shoot the six test arrows. It was decided at this point to shoot at both the front and the back of the Brigandine to determine any weak spots. The results were quite different from expectations. Each of the bodkin points appeared simply to bounce off, including the heavy quarrel head. The crescent head remained but, on investigation, was found merely to have snagged within the velvet.

When the barbed broadhead struck the front of the Brigandine, it appeared to pass through the armor. On close inspection, however, it was found to have passed between the overlap and had sliced off the strap and buckle. It was not a true test of the armor, although the result would have meant death for the wearer. During further attempts with the barbed broadhead, it repeatedly bounced off. The sole reliable penetration of the Brigandine was with the leaf-shaped blade. This was only possible because the narrow, thinner blade could slide up and between the riveted plates.

When the Brigandine was removed from the dummy and the inside of the armor inspected, it was found that the leaf-shaped blade had indeed penetrated, protruding through the leather by about 1/2 inch; probably insufficient to cause death by hemorrhaging. Close examination showed that although it appeared to have bounced off, the heavy quarrel head had in fact penetrated a plate, putting a cross-shaped cut in the leather carcass. The armor enveloping the head had absorbed the power of the impact to some degree.

It would be wrong to say that the wearer would have escaped uninjured, but this armor worked well against each of the six test heads, stopping the arrows from penetrating to a fatal depth. The shock of impact would have been considerable, however, with this alone causing serious and perhaps fatal trauma. The effect of blunt trauma will be discussed later in this chapter, showing how deadly a military arrow would have been.

After inspection of the six test arrows (the shafts to which the short and quarrel-style bodkins and the leaf- and barbed-blade shapes were fitted), I found that each had survived unharmed. None of the six test heads had snapped off the shafts, showing clearly the absorption property of this ingenious system of armor. The long bodkin and the crescent-shaped blade head had been slightly damaged, however; each of their points had curled, rather like the tip of a Turkish slipper.

I returned home and thought about how the heads had fared against the Brigandine, in particular the way that the heavy quarrel-type bodkin head had cut the inside of the leather yet had not penetrated the body of the dummy. It was then that I decided to look at other versions of this head, to see whether subtle changes in shape would enable a penetration of the Brigandine.

I looked at known historical examples and noticed that some were slightly narrower in certain sections while still maintaining those angles critical to their shape. This would allow them to cut hard surfaces without disturbing the point and preventing the proper penetration of the head. At the same time, a good friend, Mr. Gwyn Zucca, a maker himself of excellent quality heads, was working on a shape based upon a historical example that he had seen. We compared notes, and I then forged a head that I thought might work well on the Brigandine while also being effective on thicker or harder plate armor.

The new head and the quarrel head shared similar dimensions in their sockets and overall lengths; the principal difference being a slimmer section at the widest point of the front of the new head than at the corresponding point on the heavy quarrel head. The angles of the cutting faces at the point are critical; they must be sufficiently oblique not to roll the point on impact, yet be sufficiently acute to cut and allow its passage through.

The process of piercing is performed in two separate and distinct stages, although they happen so quickly that they appear to be performed as one. First, the point must dig in and cut the surface; this will absorb much of the arrow's kinetic energy. Second, whatever energy remains is expended on curling away the cut surface to allow the head through—and this is where the success of the head shape hangs. If it is too wide at its largest section, then the amount of energy needed to punch through is immense, especially if the material to be pierced is hard and thick. The arrow appears to bounce off, even though a hole has been cut.

By reducing the cross section at its widest part, yet maintaining the critical angles of the cutting edges at the tip, it would seem that the amount of energy needed to punch through is less. Whatever energy remains after the head has penetrated will drive the arrow through and into the body of the wearer.

Anxious to test this theory with the new head, I fitted it to a fletched shaft identical in dimension to the original six test arrows and returned to Roy King's workshop. We set up the Brigandine once more, on this occasion, fastened to a bag of dried beans (these have sufficient density to support but do not have the harsh resistance of sand). The Brigandine was set on a table and secured to an archery target to catch any stray arrow.

I then shot at the Brigandine, and the arrow sank into the end of the socket at a point left of the center join. It had penetrated the armored part and appeared from an external view to have pierced two overlapping plates (see Fig. 20).

When I shot at the armor this time, I was struck by how little movement there was as the arrow slammed into the target, accounting, I believe, for a successful penetration. I opened up the Brigandine and, after removing it from the bean bag, measured the depth of penetration. Fig. 21 shows the head projecting through the armor to the impressive depth of 3 1/2 inches. When the head was removed, it could clearly be seen that the altered shape head had indeed cut through two overlapping plates curling them back onto the leather carcass and riveting them together. This had locked them into a rigid piece, and in consequence there was little enveloping around the head on immediate impact, explaining perhaps why there was greater penetration and no bounce as earlier with the bigger heavy quarrel head.

The test with the new head I consider to have been a complete success but of no detriment to those who had developed the Brigandine. I know that if I needed protection from arrows, I would choose to wear this form of armor.

During the Wars of the Roses, the Brigandine was worn by many soldiers and is often mentioned as specific to archers. Could this be because it was relatively light and flexible, but more importantly gave the wearer the best protection from enemy arrows? It is true that certain arrows would have defeated the Brigandine, but it undoubtedly offered better protection than mail. It was also cheaper to manufacture and less restrictive than full plate armor—essential for an archer drawing his bow.

For the next test, I returned to plate armor, as I wished to try each of the different shaped heads against a breastplate. I chose plate made from steel of slightly higher carbon content than that used on the pig's carcass. I performed this test last, since although I knew that the heavier quarrel-type bodkin could defeat certain plate armor I did not know how the other heads would react. I was expecting, however, to take heavy casualties among the other test arrows.

The plate was fastened around a bag of dried beans similar to that used for the Brigandine testing and was tied back to a stake driven into the ground.

On the first shot, the quarrel-type bodkin pierced as before, although moving back slightly after impact. This indicated to me that the dried beans were behaving in a similar action to flesh in their resistance to impact. The short bodkin also pierced the plate and remained stuck fast. I believe this happened because this type of head punches a small square hole, allowing the round taper of the socket to wedge itself into the plate. The depth of penetration would probably have been fatal.

The remaining three arrows—the long bodkin, the leaf-shape, and the crescent-shape heads—did exactly what I would have expected against plate armor. The long bodkin slammed into the plate, scoring deeply into the surface while, as with the test on the Brigandine, its point curled. This time, however, the head had snapped from the shaft and spun off to the side. The leaf-shaped bodkin did the same; the shaft shattering into many pieces.

The crescent-shaped head gave the most spectacular display, snapping from its shaft and spinning high up into the air. On close inspection, it was seen to have opened out (see Fig. 22). I then shot the barbed broadhead, expecting it to behave in the same way upon impact as had the other blade-type heads (having its point curl and the head snap from the shaft), but I was wrong! When it hit the plate, it certainly bounced, but the shaft did not snap. On inspection I found that the head had cut through the plate but had been stopped from further penetration by the barbs. I repeated this test, achieving the same outcome. These results surprised me, since the forward section of this head is similar to that of the leaf-shaped blade.

This head had greater mass than other blade-type heads, and it is possible that this extra weight, together with a subtle change in angles around the center rib, had prevented the head from destroying itself as the leaf-shaped and crescent heads had done.

The final head tested was the new, improved lozenge-shape that had been so successful on the Brigandine. As expected, this punched right through the breastplate, jamming into the toughened steel halfway up the socket. I counted this a complete success and felt that this must be one of perhaps many reasons why this type of lozenge-shape bodkin head appears so commonly among arrowheads of fifteenth-century origin recovered by archaeologists. It is notable however that, as mentioned earlier, similar examples dating from the thirteenth century have been recovered from places such as St. Briavels.

To me these tests indicate that there is a harsh, intense impact on the hard, smooth surface of plate armor, and overcoming it needs a specially shaped head. It does not envelop the energy of the impact as does the Brigandine. If some of those arrows that did not break had been shot at a glancing angle they may have shattered as well. The one head that really copes with angled surfaces is the lozenge-shaped bodkin, and in this area it truly excels. When I shot at special trials elsewhere, it took an angle of 40 degrees and a 14 standard wire gauge (2 millimeters) thickness of plate before it was defeated.

The question now is "Can this lozenge shape be further improved?" In my opinion this shape is at about its most efficient and is unlikely to be improved without creating a shape that has no historic precedent on which it might be based. However, there is a way in which the penetration of an arrow into armor can be increased without altering either arrow or draw weight and performance of the bow. The answer lies in the condition in which the target receives the impact of the arrow. This is something in penetration tests that is either overlooked or not considered but has an obvious solution: have the target move toward the archer, thus multiplying the effect of impact.

All tests that I have observed, or in which I have taken part, have been against static armor set against some support. What I now wanted to do was to research the penetration of an arrow shot at armor moving toward me at the speed of a knight on horseback at full charge.

I needed to know how fast a medieval war horse could gallop, assuming the ground to be favorable and long enough to get to full speed. I therefore contacted Dr. Tobias Capwell, curator of Arms and Armour at Glasgow museum. He is most knowledgeable about medieval armor and, in addition, is an authority on medieval horsemanship. We discussed my intended experiment and he expressed interest. He had not heard of any tests of this nature and wanted to hear of the results. Dr Capwell told me that a medieval war horse, a destrier, would stand at 15 to 15 1/2 hands in height. Given good conditions, it would be capable of moving from a canter to a full gallop (sustained over 200 yards of ground) at a speed approaching 20 to 25 miles per hour. My test therefore was simple. I would devise some way of moving the breast plate at about 20 miles per hour toward me from a point as far away as possible and then shoot at it. To describe the making of the test apparatus would require a chapter to itself! What follows therefore are the results in brief of many days of testing.

A wooden cradle was made to house a standard archery target in order to catch stray arrows. In front I placed a platform and on it a breastplate similar to that used on the static tests, strapped once more to a bag of dried beans. The whole rig was positioned to run down an aerial ropeway set on a gentle slope between two trees 100 yards apart. The apparatus, controlled by a hand-operated winch, was timed between the two trees and by great good fortune was found to run at a constant 20 miles per hour. Everything was set. All I needed to do was to shoot at the moving breastplate to see to what degree penetration was increased by compounding impact velocities.

I decided to have a team of helpers with this experiment and invited four good friends—Alan Edwards, Joe Gibbs, Jim Hughes, and Gwyn Zucca—to assist. It would be important to work as a team, since we were using a range of bows spanning the accepted draw weights of the medieval military weapon. We could also shoot more arrows at each run of the rig, saving time and providing a better average of results.

The basic tests consisted of three archers shooting at the breastplate from different distances with the penetration subsequently measured to establish what gain if any there was from the movement of the armor at speed toward the archer. Following from these initial tests, I hoped to find how many shots could be taken at one pass of the test rig during its effective run of 80 yards at 20 miles per hour.

The day dawned. The rig was released and quickly reached its optimum speed. Our first shots were taken very close at just 15 yards, the distance I had used during previous static tests. All arrows struck the breastplate simultaneously and penetrated the heart area with a loud noise of steel against steel. It was instantly recognized that each arrow had penetrated much further than if the target had been static. When the plate was removed and penetration measured, it was found that depth had increased by 1 inch. We were all delighted. My theory appeared to work, but we needed to shoot at varying distances to complete the tests and to obtain an overall conclusion.

I wanted to see how close an archer would have allowed a mounted knight, bearing down at full gallop, to be before taking a shot (while leaving sufficient time to avoid the horse). We therefore each took it in turn to see how close we might let the rig get before shooting and moving smartly out of the way.

It proved an exciting experiment. Fig. 24 shows me shooting at the breastplate from about 5 yards. The arrow has hit the breastplate smack in its center, and I am starting to jump away as the rig thunders by. The other arrows on the plate are from shots made by members of the team at different distances as the rig moved on its way.

It was found that 5 yards was the closest at which an archer could realistically aim a shot and move away from the rig. Any lesser distance and the arrow would not have straightened from the bow sufficiently to hit the target squarely. This we thought would have adversely affected the concentration of kinetic energy at the point of the arrowhead, with a glancing blow probably shattering the arrow. Additionally, and of greater importance, in conditions of battle, if a lance had been aimed at the archer from a distance of 5 yards, jumping from its path would have been extremely hazardous.

Finally, we tested how many shots could be achieved by one archer in one pass of the rig. This proved difficult. The rig was running at 20 miles per hour, equivalent to 30 feet per second, or 10 yards per second, providing a sensation similar to that of an approaching express train. In conditions of stress it also takes an average of 7 seconds to loose an arrow already notched on the string, then select, nock, draw, and loose a second arrow from a heavy war bow.

It must be understood that to shoot a powerful military draw weight bow takes time. Very quick cyclic rates have been recorded by those who speed shoot, but these are invariably performed with lighter weight, recreational bows with shorter arrows not always drawn to the head. These are in no way representative of the war bow. As I mentioned earlier, the effective run of the rig at full speed was across 80 yards; in the 7 seconds it had taken to draw and shoot the first, then prepare and shoot the second arrow, the rig had moved 70 yards toward the shooting line, meaning that it was effectively just 1 second away when the second arrow was loosed, giving virtually no margin for error.

We found that to get a second aimed shot away easily, the first arrow had to be loosed as soon as the rig began to move. There was then an opportunity to take a second shot without being unduly rushed; however, all action had to be slick and precise. The conclusion we drew from our experimenting was that with a military war bow of realistic draw weight, no more than two shots could be achieved during a head-on charge over 80 yards by an armored mounted knight on a galloping horse. As medieval archers, we would have been very grateful for the protection offered by our stakes.

It was found by analysis of all the tests that the compounding effect of a moving target had increased penetration by well over 1 inch and in some cases as much as 2 inches, depending on the distance at which the shot was made. Although there are many variables to consider, such as arrowhead shape, armor thickness, and even weather, I felt that in general the tests were conclusive. A moving target was harder to hit—especially at long distance—but a well-placed arrow would be catastrophic for a wearer of armor galloping his horse hard at a line of archers.

So far in this chapter, I have concentrated upon penetration. Now I feel another question must be asked and answered. Does an arrow actually need to penetrate the body to kill someone or something? To answer the question we must first consider a condition known as blunt trauma, and with this, the amount of energy necessary to kill if force is exerted on a vital area. For example, if a cricketer were to be hit on the head or chest by a fast-moving cricket ball, it would be potentially more serious than a hit on the knee or arm.

I posed this question to a specialist in the field of ballistics and body armor, one whose work was concerned with blunt trauma on modern, bullet proof vests. I contacted Dr. Paul Bourke at England's Cranfield University, and he told me that a Health and Safety document entitled "Controlling Risks around Explosives Store" advised that if a fragment or a missile were to strike a vital area with a kinetic energy of 80 joules or more, then it would be considered a fatal blow. The figure is understood to have been developed originally by the French army, their first experiments being with lead balls fired from guns.

Kinetic energy in joules is calculated by taking the mass (in kilograms) times the velocity squared (meters per second) and halving the result. Using this formula, I calculated that an arrow fitted with the improved quarrel-type bodkin head, having a total weight of 102 grams and moving at 47.23 meters per second had 113.76 joules of kinetic energy. This is substantially over the fatal figure. In fact, each of the test arrows had a kinetic energy value in joules substantially more than the fatal limit, leading me to believe that those heads that appeared to fail on different armors may still have given a mortal blow. Any shot hitting hard but shattering an arrow or bouncing off could potentially create an excruciatingly painful trauma that might well prove fatal.

Let us turn for a moment to hunting and the difference between it and warfare. A hunter requires his quarry to die quickly so that the body can be promptly found. A prime reason for the barbs on a broadheaded arrow is to prevent the wound from closing and to induce faster hemorrhaging. In addition, a faster death closer by allows the recovery of a valuable arrow or a head if the shaft has snapped.

In warfare the situation is different. An arrow shot is an arrow spent; the chance of its recovery is slim. If the arrow has found its mark, then it is not desirable for the victim to die quickly. Someone of low rank screaming in agony and dying slowly will induce fear and demoralize his comrades. Wounding someone of higher rank could involve necessary removal to a place of safety, accounting for valuable resources, also demoralizing and disorganizing his followers.

I have demonstrated earlier that a crescent-shaped arrowhead, or forker, to give it its vernacular name, can inflict horrific wounds to bare flesh. It will cut through mail, and although it destroyed itself on plate armor and the Brigandine, it might have been instrumental in producing death by blunt trauma. There are a number of theories as to the actual purpose of this strange head, and I would now like to explore some of these to establish, if possible, some fact from fantasy.

It has been suggested that its use in medieval times was for poaching large game, by causing maximum hemorrhage while not remaining firmly stuck and thus incriminating its owner if by chance the animal escaped. This is plausible for deer and boar, but could this type of head have also been used on feathered game?

Just before the wild fowling season ended, I asked a local sportsman if he could supply me with a large goose. He promptly brought me a large dead Canada goose, setting me on course to try a few theories of my own.

I had often wondered whether the crescent-shaped head would perform better on feathers than a swallowtail head would and whether the convex edge of the barbed broadhead blade might skip over the quills of the feathers if shot at an angle. I thought that the leading points of the crescent head might perhaps turn the head into the body rather than allowing it to skip away.

I set up the goose on a wooden cradle, with its neck stretched upright. I then set up to shoot at the bird from a distance of 15 yards. What followed was not what I had expected! When I shot at oblique angles with the barbed broadhead, the arrow passed through the bird up to its fletchings. When I shot the crescent-shape, it struck hard, but bounced off. From whatever angle I shot the bird using the barbed head, it sliced through. When I shot the crescent head squarely at the body, it jumped the bird up the cradle, cutting several wing feathers and breaking the wing bones. Even a direct shot at the breast left only a cloud of feathers and an arrow on the ground.

I began to realize that these results were down to the way that the different heads cut. The barbed head cut through by the point piercing first, with the convex blades parting the feathers. The crescent shape works in the opposite way; the points dig in but the concave profile bunches the feathers and thus prevents the blade from cutting. This would cause great trauma but would not skip off as a blunt end might. It would also not unduly slice the carcass, desirable if one wanted the meat.

I had heard tales of the Roman Emperor Commodus shooting crescent-shaped heads at large birds in the Circus Maximus and wondered just how much was pure fantasy. Rupert Matthews in his book *The Age of the Gladiators* writes of a chronicler who recorded:

His marksmanship with a bow was generally agreed to be astonishing, on one occasion he used some arrows with Crescent-shaped heads to shoot at Ostriches. Comodus decapitated the birds at the top of their necks so that they went running around as though they had not been touched.

I decided to see whether this strange display of marksmanship was possible and so, with a forker, I shot directly at the neck, just below the head. My first four attempts missed, although I noticed that the fletchings were brushing the neck in passing. When I retrieved my arrows from the target backstop, I noticed that the arrowhead had entered with the blade vertical. I knew from tests with the pig carcass that the crescent head had spun as it flew. I then realized that I was at the wrong distance. I therefore moved back two paces, to 17 yards from the goose, and tried again.

With my fifth attempt, the head was severed from the neck. Examining the angle of the cut showed that the blade had spun a little more over those additional 2 yards and had been horizontal when it struck, meaning that the crescent-shaped blade had focused on the neck, concentrating its cutting force on that one spot (see Fig. 23). Although it may be true that Commodus slew ostriches in such a bizarre manner, how well he could have judged distance to correctly spin the crescent head while the bird was moving is the stuff of legends!

When I skinned the carcass, I found that the barbed broadhead had cut the flesh to ribbons. The crescent head had delivered enormous trauma to the body and had also broken internal bones. However, it had not cut the flesh as had the broadhead, leading me to believe that if a goose or similar-sized large bird was swimming or waddling past, a bow hunter could shoot it with a crescent-shaped head without the head skipping off the feathers. The bird would die quickly, and damage to the meat would be minimal; just perfect for a noble feast in medieval times (I will just add that I removed the meat after the tests to feast myself!).

I have also heard it said that crescent-shaped heads were used to cut sails and rigging in naval battles, although there seems not to be any factual evidence in support of such apocryphal tales. So where do these heroic myths of sails sliced and ropes cut come from? We shall probably never know, but can these heads actually perform this stuff of legends? After discussing ideas about sail and rope cutting with armorer Roy King, I decided to experiment to see whether the myths were true.

I took a large piece of heavy canvas and nailed it to a square-sectioned plank of wood. I then fastened this to a telegraph pole in a field and secured the corners of the sheet with ropes, pegged to the ground. This nicely represented a square sail, and as the wind tightened it, it gave it a realistic billowing shape.

My first shot was square to the sail at 15 to 20 yards and went straight through leaving only a small cut. I then moved around and shot again, at 45 degrees to the sail; however, the same thing occurred. Finally I stood so that the arrow hit the canvas at such a shallow angle it would be almost a glancing shot. The arrow hit the sail and ran along the fabric perfectly, creating a 12-inch tear. I repeated the shot with a barbed broadheaded arrow from the same position, and it went cleanly through with only a small cut, and no tear.

This leads me to believe that the gathering effect of the crescent head when striking the goose feathers was repeated on the fabric, causing it to snag and tear the canvas along its weave. If several archers had shot with this type of head at a sail, it would soon be ripped to shreds, especially if the wind were strong and tears increased as the sail flapped to an fro. If sails may be cut, then what about ropes? Sir Arthur Conan Doyle mentions this in his novel *The White Company*, but is this pure fantasy? I determined to find out.

I obtained a piece of hemp rope over 3/4 inch in diameter and secured it to a block of steel weighing 220 pounds. I then asked my neighbor to help me with his forklift truck. With the rope tied to the forks of the machine, it was lifted until the steel block left the ground. Once again I placed my target boss behind to catch stray arrows. I stood at about 17 yards as I had done to shoot at the neck of the goose, and I hoped that the crescent-shaped head would be horizontal when it hit the rope. My first attempt was close but missed. My second shot found its mark, and there was the sound of a great "twang." The weight dropped to the ground, and the rope leapt into the air. It was over in a flash, but it could not now be denied that a crescent-shaped head was capable of cutting rope. It had worked in the same manner as when it had severed the neck of the goose. Obviously there are other thicker ropes on ships, and if the rope had been slack, the result would have been different. However, it does not matter how much these tales grow or are exaggerated in books, on film, or on television, I now know there to be a small, but real, grain of truth in them all.

There is one last strange medieval arrowhead that I will mention briefly. It is a subject almost warranting a chapter to itself: the fire arrow. Nothing captures the imagination more in a film than the sight of a flaming arrow with a comet-like path, blazing toward its destination, setting all around it on fire and creating an inferno on its landing. It might look real on modern film, but is this portrayal simply a product of myth and fantasy?

It is true that incendiary arrows were recorded by Roman chroniclers and were used in warfare, but how successfully is difficult to say. I have seen some oddly shaped heads supposedly for use with medieval fire arrows, and experiment shows that these actually work if used with the correct combustible material. However, there is a type that I feel has been overlooked as a military incendiary head, and I will explain why.

While I was working with Roy King on my tests, we had discussed the topic of fire arrows, and he told me of some of his experiments. Unfortunately they had been only partially successful. They had involved pushing a bag of gunpowder over a bodkin-pointed arrow and tying it off with a leather thong. The whole head was then coated in rosin and allowed to cool. Roy told me that the bag shortened the draw length of the arrow and made it very heavy. Also, the gunpowder burned through the shaft quickly, and if the head was not riveted to the shaft, it fell off when the heat melted the glue. Thinking about the problem, I realized that I had seen the solution before, on an original medieval bodkin arrowhead.

I had often thought it strange that some original examples of bodkin heads had spikes that were almost ridiculously long—at least 6 inches—and very thin in section. I know from my tests on armor that a short bodkin point is sufficient to penetrate mail and that long bodkins often curled when striking a hard surface. These extra-long heads had always puzzled me, but here perhaps was the answer. If an extra-long bodkin was used, the draw length of the arrow would not be shortened if the bag containing the incendiary material was pushed over just the spike. Also, if the spike was narrow, then a thinner and lighter bag of incendiary material could be used.

The completed arrows could be stored easily and safely with the rosin coating keeping away damp and stray sparks from an untended camp fire. In addition, without combustible material, they could be used effectively as normal bodkin points. It would be difficult to use specially shaped incendiary heads for any other purpose.

I looked at photographs of original examples in books and, to my delight, found some showing rivet holes, evidence that they had been riveted to a shaft. Although they may have been of Dark Age origin (see my comments in the preceding chapter), it was clear that they had not been used for hunting. I was left with the exciting feeling that I was looking at a simple and easily manufactured head for use as a fire arrow.

I forged a copy of the head with the 6-inch spike and glued and riveted this to an arrow shaft. I chose aspen to reduce weight. The shaft and the fletchings were made to the same dimensions as the armor-testing arrows. The weight of the completed, but unarmed arrow was 87 grams (1,340 grains).

A light linen bag, 6 inches long and 1 inch wide, was filled with gunpowder acquired from a licensed explosives manufacturer to medieval specification. It is important here to note that modern gunpowder, or black powder, is not the same as the medieval version, and under no circumstances should it be used as a substitute. I should also state that I have the relevant license to acquire and keep this type of explosive.

The filled bag was pushed over the bodkin spike and tied off with a leather thong. The whole head was then coated with genuine medieval rosin provided by armorer Roy King. We were ready to test our theory. The total weight of the armed arrow was 125 grams (1,925 grains)—exactly the same as the heavy quarrel-type head used in tests against armor. That arrow had made 200 yards of ground and had traveled well. It would be interesting to see whether this arrow, of the same weight, would travel the same distance or whether its aerodynamics would be affected adversely by a thermal change. I chose some safe ground on which to test, since I did not want to set the countryside alight. When all was prepared and water buckets were on hand, we began the tests.

The end of the bag was ignited (with a blowtorch) until it began to fizz. Then, as the flames started to roar from the front of the bag, I loosed the arrow into the air. It flew well, leaving a smoke trail behind as it traveled. When it hit the ground, a large puff of smoke and flame shot up, an indication that it was very much alight on landing. It had made 150 yards of ground, a result of drag coupled, perhaps, with a braking effect from the forward thrust of the flames.

The head and the ground were extinguished and we returned to rearm the head for further testing. Fig. 25 shows the head relit and burning vigorously. This I shot point-blank into a bale of wet hay some 15 yards away, which first began slowly to smolder, then to flame, and finally to burn properly.

The head was once more rearmed and shot at an old stable door. This proved a most interesting test. The exposed point of the bodkin slammed into the wood and split it. This allowed the head to move forward and so compress the bag of gunpowder, which then ruptured. This in turn exploded into a fireball and, coupled with the molten rosin (pine resin with the turpentine extracted), set fire to the stable door.

This proved a fitting end to our tests, showing to our satisfaction that this type of long spike head could work well, although mass saturation of incendiary arrows would be tactically necessary to ensure a satisfactory blaze.

I would like to thank those who have helped me with my tests which I hope have been of interest to the reader. I do not claim them to be definitive, but they do put forward arguments for the purpose of differently shaped medieval heads and, moreover, are based upon actual shooting tests rather than educated guess and repeated supposition.

Chapter Six

STRINGS AND OTHER EQUIPMENT

"As unto the bow the cord is, so unto the man is woman.
Though she bends him, she obeys him;
Though she draws him, yet she follows;
Useless each without the other"
(Hiawatha's wooing) —Longfellow (1855)

It would be quite improper for a book dealing with the war bow to omit that most essential of components, the bowstring. Strangely, for all its importance and age, the craft of stringing was not regulated until comparatively late in medieval times, and then only because the failings of its artisans were brought home emphatically to those who used their products.[1]

Henry V's campaign of 1415, ending in the utter defeat of the French forces by a small and desperate English army at Agincourt, was marred in no small way by the failure of bowstrings, often at inconvenient times. Although huge quantities were carried in reserve and archers were accustomed to having—as the saying goes—"two strings to their bows," the breaking of a string, with the necessity to restring quickly, possibly in the heat of battle, would have been an unwelcome task for the user, even if time and the situation allowed.

Some indication of the concern military authorities felt for the failings of bowstrings can be seen in the proportion of these to bows carried on Henry VIII's 1513 foray into France. The 5,200 bows were backed by 86,000 bowstrings: a ratio of 16 to 1.[2] In contrast, Henry's flagship *Mary Rose* was equipped with 250 longbows, supported by a mere 6 gross of bowstrings (864): a ratio of fewer than 4 to 1.[3] One wonders whether someone in 1513 was lining his or her pocket at the king's expense. As Ascham succinctly remarked over a century later:

> Although apparently a trifle, it is of much importance, as a bad string breaks many a good bow . . . and that because an inexperienced man may be more easily deceived in the choice of his string than in the choice of his bow that stringers should be the more diligently looked after by the proper officers . . . since they might deceive a simple man the more easily.[4]

He is prompted to conclude, "God send us good stringers for War and Peace"—a sentiment that his king would not dispute.

It would seem almost without question that even before they were organized into a guild, there had been a fraternity of stringers; indeed, when their guild was finally formed, it took the title "Ancient Company," suggesting a lengthy shared concern. However, unlike their more charismatic associates, the Worshipful Companies of Bowyers and of Fletchers, who formed their groups by choice, organization was thrust upon the stringers by an authority concerned about the quality (or lack of it) apparent in the work of some. Formed under something of a cloud, the bowstringmakers eschewed the title "Worshipful," emphasizing the age of their craft by the appellation "Ancient" and choosing for their corporate identity what is surely the most curious of mottos. Not for them the proud boast "Crecy, Agincourt, Poitiers" of the bowyers or "True and Sure" of the fletchers. Their choice was the enigmatic, not to say, cynical Nec Habeo: Nec Careo: Nec Curo, meaning "I have not. I lack not. I care not."

Some indication of earlier concern with quality follows from the fate of Alan Birchare, a London stringer who, on August 9, 1385, was found guilty of selling four dozen bowstrings considered to be "false and deceptive." The aggrieved purchaser reported him to authority, and for this misdemeanor, he was sentenced by the Aldermanic Court to be pilloried and have his bowstrings burned, one by one, beneath his nose—a punishment that probably shortened his life. This somewhat barbaric practice was substituted, in future years, by a fine of one pound of wax, a humane penalty but one that hit where it hurt most—the pocket since wax was a vital commodity in the manufacture of the bowstring.

Now, let us talk a little about the London company. Unlike many other companies and guilds, the stringmakers had no meeting hall. Their business was conducted in one of several city inns, the wheels oiled no doubt with good food and wine. At least two of these hostelries, The Mouth and The Vine, were friendly to archery and sponsored roving stakes in Finsbury Fields.[5] Unlike some other livery companies (the bowyers for example), the stringers, as they came to be known, had no roistering corporate song with which to accompany their meal. A dour lot, as their motto suggests, music seems to have played no great part in their affairs; the first mention of such entertainment comes in 1708, when at a celebration, £1.51 was paid for "music." The court took a dim view of the expense, however, and while paying the bill, it remarked frostily that "it was not to be made Presidente [sic] for ye future."

Having no livery, the company played little or no part in the city's political affairs. It did, though, perform both its national and its local duties immaculately. In 1562 it provided "two able men"—one with corslet and pike, the other with bow and a sheaf of arrows—for Queen Elizabeth's service at Newhaven (le Havre) in Normandy, although in the event, neither man was needed. Later in 1564, it supplied seven soldiers for a watch on the vigil of St. Peter.[6]

The stringers company also had a charitable side. In 1583 it contributed 7 shillings and 4 pence toward the relief of the poor in Nantwich, Cheshire "where were consumed with fire on the 13th December, 600 houses." Charity also extended to foreign individuals—stringers who lived elsewhere. Adam Adam, of Bewdley in Worcestershire, "a poor workman of the Longbowstring" and not the best advertisement for their motto, bid successfully for 33 shillings and 4 pence against his debts there. They looked after their own poor properly, in particular widows who received various payments "towards the relief of their necessities" from the poor box. Company members who had fallen on hard times were helped with supplies of basic material. Various payments of "hemp for thread" appear in the books, and a stock of the material appears to have been maintained with this purpose in mind.

As with the bowyers and fletchers, companies of bow-stringmakers existed elsewhere. One such was formed within the city of Chester, a place notable for archery (indeed, with its proximity to the Welsh border, a prime candidate for the development of the great English war bow itself).[7] The Chester company, while retaining the London company's motto, had, unlike them, both a shield and a crest. The shield consisted of "gules on a chevron argent, between three pairs of shin bones salterwayes [or, as we would say today, in saltire] argent three . . ." (subsequent text lacking). The significance of the three shin bones is not apparent today unless it was simply symbolic of mortality. The crest depicted a man clad in cloth alternately green and silver, carrying across his shoulder a staff on which were hung bungs, or knots of bow-strings. As an aside, one feels that the collective noun "knot" appropriated to bowstrings could not have been better chosen. "Bung" is a Continental word of middle Dutch origin and reflective perhaps of the source of the best strings. Another company, as yet unidentified, but perhaps of Coventry, used a shield on which three strung bows appeared above two coiled bowstrings, the whole surmounted by a hunting archer with bow at full draw. Whether any of these disparate heraldic designs were produced with the agreement of the College of Arms is in doubt, however, since those of the London company seem not to have been; these and others were likely to have been devised unofficially by the companies themselves.

A small group of bowstringmakers also lived and worked in Bristol.[8] Two families were involved: the Copys and the Sanckys, providing between them four stringmakers. Curiously here, in the case of at least one individual, there was evidently a close connection between string making and the surely disparate trade (or perhaps profession) of barber, since John Copy is shown in the apprentice records as a barber and stringer. One wonders whether, here at least, quality control was always paramount.

From Ascham we learn that there were two types of string, a "little" and a "great," chosen "according to the occasion of your shooting."[9] The distinction is interesting and may carry a possible explanation for breakages. The "great" string was "surer for the bow and more stable but slower in cast." In short, it was safer to use but did not make the same distance as the "little" string. This was "more fit to shoot far" but being lighter (for one presumes it to have been of fewer strands), it was more prone to breakage.

It may be that the military archer, wishing to make the greatest distance with his shaft would habitually use the lighter string, thus putting his bow at some risk. Perhaps the adage "two strings to one's bow" referred to a great and a little string?

Although latterly strings of green, or untreated, silk were used for certain purposes (primarily hunting, since strings made of it were deemed quieter), bowstrings were largely of hemp. "Well-chosen" English hemp from the female plant was specified in the bowstringmakers ordinances, and we must assume that as directed by authority, this was generally used. "Tubbed" and "Coleyn" hemp was considered inferior.[10]

Perhaps it was hemp from these sources that drew the blunt epithet "course" (sic) when 100 bowstrings were mustered at Higham in the County of Kent.[11]

Exactly what was meant by "tubbed" is not apparent, but it seems likely that soaking in water detracted from the quality of the fibers. "Coleyn" hemp was imported from abroad, perhaps from Cologne. It is noteworthy that despite the arbitrary dismissal of material from overseas, latterly at least, the finest bowstrings were made and supplied by stringers from what is now Belgium.[12]

For all that hemp was specified, fibers from the common nettle could be, and almost certainly were, used by country folk (after retting, or soaking, and then stripping) for bough, or drovers bows.

It is unclear at this stage whether the craft of stringing included spinning the thread from the prepared fibers. There is no reason to suppose that it did not, at least in part, to supplement bulk supplies from elsewhere, and one can envisage the master stringer's wife or daughter hard at the spinning wheel, keeping up with the demands of her husband and his apprentice.

The string itself was made of the longest threads of hemp, twisted tightly and held together with a form of water glue, a practice that continued into modern times, although some preferred a mixture of linseed oil and glue. Sadly, no examples of medieval strings survive; however, it is unlikely that much changed in the intervening period, and examination of an early nineteenth-century hemp string from my collection shows the loop to be thicker (4 millimeters) than the body of the string (2 millimeters) with the tail thicker still (5 millimeters).[13] Medieval loop holes would have been smaller (that of the example is 15 millimeters by 22 millimeters) to allow the string to lie centrally along the limbs, which was necessary with the string groove on the side of the horn nocks. Strings were protected from wear against the archer's bracer by whipping (today we would say by serving).

Advice given to those sixteenth-century officers responsible for archers included "seeing that their soldiers, according to their draught and strength [an exhortation suggesting a selection of bows varying in draw weight] have good bows, well nocked, well stringed, everie stringe whippe in the nocke, and in the myddes rubbed with wax."[14]

The advantage of silk, a costly alternative to hemp, lay in its resistance to breakage, and it is just possible that occasionally strings made from it may have found their way on to the battlefield. Undyed, raw, and green, strand for strand, it is considerably stronger than hemp and lasts longer than other materials without breaking, thus enabling thinner strings to be made. When properly prepared, a silken bowstring was deemed at that time by virtue of its elasticity to propel an arrow further and with greater force than the inert hemp string, offering a potential advantage for distance shooting.

It is time now to leave the string and turn attention to another important piece of archery equipment, the effectiveness of which far outweighed its simplicity. It was the archer's stake. Although the use of spears and such to form a hedge of spikes against advancing infantry or cavalry was not new, the specific introduction of a protective stake to guard an archer is as late as the mid-fifteenth century. It dates from the Agincourt campaign and foreknowledge of an intended French battle plan. Spies reported to Henry V that when the two field armies finally met in set-piece battle, it was planned that French cavalry should ride down the flank archers, get behind the English line, and charge the infantry from the rear. Henry then instructed his archers, and perhaps others (although the extent of his instruction is not entirely clear) to cut stakes, sharpen them, and be ready when necessary to angle them in the ground, their points at breast height. As history records, this was done, the French cavalry charge was halted, and the two armies met face to face.[15]

Although there were occasions when they were ineffective (notably at the battles of Verneuil, when hard ground made the driving in of stakes difficult, and at Patay, where through lack of discipline, the archers were ridden down before stakes could be inserted), from the time of Agincourt onward, stakes formed a fundamental part of archery armament. As late as 1547 330 stakes were in store at Berwick-on-Tweed and eight bundles at Pontefract Castle. Let us put the protective stake to one side to look at the archer's personal gear, and we will begin with his arm guard or bracer. But first, an introduction to this odd word.

The noun "bracer" (brace) derives from the Latin braccia (meaning "arm"), from which comes the French word bras, and by extension, gardebras, or alternatively, wardebras (the latter written occasionally as warbrasse). Anglicized, the term "bracer" has become "arm guard." Both the words "arm guard" and "bracer" are in use today (as is "wrist guard," a synonymous term peculiar to archaeologists and used by them when occasionally they find such things in Neolithic grave sites).

Mundane in function, desirable but not essential, the purpose of the bracer is two-fold. In neither, however, does it either brace or offer strengthening support. As an arm guard, it serves to cushion the impact of the string when released, when shooting technique is imperfect or when the bow is either low or inadequately braced (strung for use); i.e., the string is too close to the bow limbs. Its second important function is to keep a loose sleeve out of the path of the string to avoid a poor shot. Ascham, writing in 1544, adds another purpose, a strange idea that continued into the early nineteenth century:

> Little is to be said of the bracer. A bracer serveth for two causes, one to save his arm from the stripe of the string, and his doublet from wearing; and the other is, that the string gliding sharply and quickly off the bracer, may make a sharper shot.

For all that, however, he did not approve of its addition to the archer's gear.

> But it is best in my judgmente to give the bowe so much bent, that the string need never touch a mans arme, and so shoulde a man neede no bracer, as I know many good archeres which occupy none.

It would be natural for an archer at sea, leaning forward to counteract the movement of the ship, to shoot with a rounded stance, keeping the bow away from the body. In such a position, a bracer might well be thought superfluous.

That many good archers did not wear a bracer, or to give it its alternative description, an arm guard, we may perhaps infer from the comparatively few that have been recovered from the warship *Mary Rose*.[16] Just 24 serving an estimated force of over 300 archers. Of these, 22 are of leather, one is of horn, and one is of ivory. Of the leather bracers recovered, not all were being worn. Four were found in personal chests, while nine were associated with material stored at the stern end of the orlop deck. Five were directly connected with skeletal remains, and in this context, it might be assumed that they were in use.

Regarding their nature, shape, and general appearance, it is possible to categorize the bracers as either fine or coarse. This is perhaps a subjective judgment, and open at once to challenge, but significant if one considers the position in which certain of them were found.

The four recovered from what are believed to be personal chests are deemed to have been associated with men of quality and/or rank. Each might be designated fine. Three are neatly rectangular, one with cropped ends; two have a single and one has a bifurcated securing strap. Two are decorated, one is plain. The fourth is exceptionally fine, its border elegantly defined and its fleur-de-lis decoration suggestive of royal association. A number of accompanying stamped symbols might reflect the owner/wearer's personal seal. This bracer also has a single fastening strap.

The location of two bracers found in association with skeletal remains on the main gun deck is interesting; one particularly so, since it is of ivory. Considering the general quality of others recovered, it is difficult not to see this as belonging to someone of significance and potentially of rank.

It has been suggested that archers were stationed alongside each gun in order to provide covering support for the gunners as they reloaded. Although this suggestion should not be dismissed, I question whether the restricted space available would allow the truly effective use of a longbow and propose as an alternative primary reason the presence of a specialist archer, possibly even an artillier in support of one or more gun crews. It is an interesting question and some modest speculation is irresistible.

A second bracer, also fine and associated with skeletal remains, its decoration depicting the royal arms and thus highly suggestive of royal association, was recovered from a similar position; while two others, perhaps discarded but also fine and with significant decoration, were nearby.

It is known that archers were styled in two sorts: "archers principalls" and "archers mean."[17] It would be consistent with a status suggested by the quality of their bracers that those on the gun deck were "archers principalls," but there conjecture must end!

A bracer found in a chest within the carpenter's cabin is rectangular and simply decorated. Tools found in the cabin included doweling planes suggestive of arrow making, and one might fairly presume the carpenter to have knowledge of archery. The presence in the chest of an arrow and a silver ring embossed with arrows is further indication.

Ornamentation was a feature of sixteenth-century bracers, whether on the arm of a seaborne warrior bowman or that of a peaceable practitioner of recreational archery on Finsbury Fields. However, unlike his recreational compatriots whose decorated bracers are pleasing to the eye, the little that we know of the English "goddam" (as his Continental adversaries

Drawing and replica of an archer's armguard including an Ave Maria surrounding Tudor symbols and the royal arms. (*Author's photograph with acknowledgments to the Mary Rose Trust*)

styled him) suggests that he was no aesthete. If the comparatively few examples we have to study are in any way representative of his artistic taste, then the decoration with which he was presumably content was at best haphazard and at worst chaotic.

When examining his arm guard for available evidence, we may perhaps give him the benefit of doubt, since his equipment was designed for function and not for aesthetic appeal. One does not go to battle wearing one's best clothes. Perhaps these crudely patterned arm guards were workaday objects, replacing more artistic examples left ashore.

So, what were these patterns? They fall naturally into two styles—religious and secular. Of the 22 leather bracers recovered, 16 have stamped symbols of some form. These divide loosely into six with a religious theme and ten without. Those

with sacred motifs include two with Marian aves, each different and with distinctive lettering, surrounding the royal arms,
and a third with a gridiron, symbolic of the martyrdom of
Saint Lawrence. This latter is coupled with a wiredrawer's
gauge and, it is thought, may be connected to the Worshipful
Company of Girdlers, a City of London livery company with
whom the Wiredrawers Company had recently amalgamated.

Other religious symbols include St. Peter's keys (a reference
perhaps to the parish from which the wearer came), a group of
nimbuses, and among the more enigmatic of the embellish-
ments, a figure on a cross, assumed to be that of Christ, surrounded by what may be the tools of the Passion.

Of the secular motifs, carefully positioned fleurs-de-lis
appear twice on well-made bracers suggestive of authority. A
bearded man appears on another, similar in design to a book
cover recovered, and suggests a possible association with the
Stationers Company, perhaps of London. On the remainder
appear petals, either well-formed examples of Tudor roses
(again with possible royal connections) or crude indetermi-
nate representations of flowers, added perhaps by the archer
himself.

The presence of religious symbolism reflects the hold that
the Church then exerted over ordinary people. Today's secular
society looks on these images with avuncular condescension,
lacking a full understanding of their significance in sixteenth-
century thought. Although on most bracers, symbols are in
reasonable symmetry, on two this is not so. In the modern concept of order and discipline, the haphazard, almost frenetic
appearance of certain of these sacred symbols often overlaying
one another and in no apparent order is an enigma and suggestive of a disorderly mind concerned with quantity and not
quality. We have no way of understanding why they appear in
this fashion. We are not party to the purpose. Perhaps the
more talismanic symbols that could be crammed together, the
greater their efficacy. Who can know the working of a
medieval mind?

The two royal bracers are interesting in their own right, since, although superficially the same, they differ significantly in detail. While the "Ave" surrounding one is probably the more common *Ave Maria Gracia Plena Dominus Tecum Benedicte Tu* (or an abbreviation), the other is more obscure.[18] Certain of the symbols differ; one is lettered in uppercase, and the other in lower. One is bordered and one is not.

In addition to these sixteenth-century arm guards, one other seaborne bracer is known to survive. This was found in the vicinity of the keelson, or maststep, within the remains of a ship recovered from Newport harbor in South Wales during the late twentieth century and is a well-preserved example of some quality.[19] It is of interest in the context of the *Mary Rose* artifacts, since unlike those, it consists of two pieces of leather, a thicker outer layer and a thinner inner lining, which, being combined, have allowed two heart shapes to be cut and backed. Of rectangular shape with truncated corners—similar to a number of those recovered from the *Mary Rose*—it was seemingly fastened by a single strap, probably of leather. Although backing, or stiffening, a bracer was contemporary practice, to my knowledge, none of the *Mary Rose* bracers were so backed.

The origin of the Newport bracer is uncertain, while the meaning of the visible lettering is enigmatic and has not as yet been fully deciphered. It is possibly a dialect form of some seaboard European language. Some who have examined the lettering have seen a connection indicative of aggression. Others believe there may be some association between the word and the heart shapes.

The fastening of bracers was achieved by either strap and buckle (or strap and D ring) or by lacing. The former is more easily achieved. An example of the latter was recovered from the moat of Stogursey Castle in Somerset and can perhaps be dated to the fifteenth century when in 1455 it was attacked by Yorkists.[20] Crudely made, roughly eight inches long and ten inches wide, the Stogursey bracer is of thin, pliable hide and without any visible ornament. In short, it is a simple but functional object similar in certain respects to one recovered from the *Mary Rose*.

In contrast to the random and inartistic grouping of symbols on bracers from Henry VIII's flagship, a contemporary example in leather, recovered from London's Finsbury Fields shooting ground, is neatly decorated on each side of the upper surface with stylized trees and foliage and has, moreover, a thin leather stiffening piece running lengthwise behind the central portion.[21] A second, earlier example, also recovered from the general area and now in private hands, is of leather, elliptical in shape and remarkably similar to those shown on archer's wrists in a marginal decoration of the fourteenth-century Luttrell Psalter illustrating archery practice at the village butts.[22]

If the ivory arm guard recovered from the main deck of the *Mary Rose* is of English making, then it may have a parallel in one held by the Southend Museum.[23] This is 145 millimeters long and 125 millimeters in width, also undecorated, and may be compared with the dimensions of 114 millimeters by 67 millimeters of the *Mary Rose* example.

It is a matter for conjecture who made these leather bracers, and, for that matter, who fashioned those of ivory and horn. One presumes that the better leather examples came from members of the Cordwainers Company, dating from 1272, one of the oldest of the city livery companies, and that made of horn, from the Horners Company. Of the cruder versions, perhaps they were off cuts from leather sellers?

If the apparent lack of arm guards worn by bowmen aboard the *Mary Rose* is puzzling, then so too must be the seeming absence of finger protection. Roger Ascham, the contemporary commentator, remarks that "a shooting glove is chiefly for to save a mans fingers from hurting, that he maye be able to beare the sharpe string to the uttermost of his strengthe."[24] Those that used the shooting glove, and we must suppose that among them were soldier bowmen, were recom-

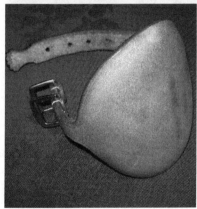

Recreation (above) of a leather armguard recovered from a fifteenth-century merchant ship in Newport (South Wales) dock. Note the fastening arrangement and presence of backing piece. (*Author, with acknowledgment to Newport Museum and Art Gallery*) Recreation (left) of an early elliptical leather amguard. (*Author, with acknowledgement to the London Museum*)

mended to have thicker leather for the pads of the forefinger and the ring finger, since, says Ascham, it is they and they alone that take the weight of the string. The middle finger "beareth no weight of the stringe at all." The comment may seem curious to some today, since many modern archers take most of the weight of the string on the middle and ring finger. In consideration of the pressure of a heavy bow string, it was recommended that a piece of cloth impregnated with "virgin wax, and dere sewet" be placed inside the fingers of the glove.

Ascham, an archer himself, was aware of the problem some archers face when pulling back the string of a heavy draw weight bow, for painful calluses can form on fingers. His remedy, and he advances two, is to take and split open (he uses the archaic term "spinet") a piece of goose quill and sew it within the finger of the glove as protection. Alternatively he recommends sewing a leather spacer between the fingers of the glove "which shall kepe his fingers so in sunder that they shall not holde the nocke so fast as they did."

In Ascham's day, the shooting glove embodied a purse in which were contained a linen cloth, wax for the string, and perhaps a small file. He was writing largely of recreational practice of course; although the men of quality and rank aboard the *Mary Rose* may

Detail from the fifteenth-century "Black tapestry of Zamora" showing a three-finger shooting glove. (*Wim Swaan.*)

well have possessed such things, there is no evidence that the ordinary archer was so equipped. It is unlikely that he would have been, for if he used anything at all (and evidence for any form of finger protection is lacking), then a simple piece of leather with three holes cut roughly would have sufficed. Today we know these latter as tabs, and they are an essential part of an archer's personal equipment. Bowstrings were whipped—or as we would say today, served—so, combined with hands and fingers toughened by manual work, this alone may have been sufficient safeguard.

The only broadly contemporary illustration of an archer using finger protection known to me comes from a fifteenth-century Flemish tapestry. This clearly shows a three-fingered open glove secured by a strap around the wrist. Curiously, this arrangement differs only in detail from three fingered gloves of the late nineteenth and early twentieth centuries, examples of which are within my collection.

A century later in Elizabethan times, it was recommended that each archer had a "shutting glove," and elaborate examples of these can occasionally be seen in contemporary drawings. Later still, however, when "ancient archer" William Neade persuaded Charles I to license the creation of the coupled bow and pike, a shooting glove, or indeed any other form of protection, is conspicuously absent from illustrations of the archer's drawing hand. Evidently he was assumed to have had no need of it!

L et us now consider the quiver. But first, a note of caution is appropriate here, for with this enigmatic object, things are not entirely as they may seem. We will divert a little. Today, archers sport a container for their arrows that they call a "quiver" when it should properly be called a "pouch." For until a little over a century ago, the term "quiver" was reserved for the large tin canister in which one's reserve supply of arrows was held. Only during roving would this tin canister have been carried. It was fitted with two rings through which a leather thong could be passed to enable it to be slung across a shoulder or suspended from a belt.

Those arrows needed for immediate use were carried by both ladies and gentlemen in a pouch; those of the ladies in a light metal and leather container holding no more than six arrows comfortably. A gentleman carried his either through his belt, the heads in a small bucketlike container suspended from the belt; in a leather pouch within the pocket of his shooting jacket; or if he were a member of certain senior societies, in a special long pocket let into the tail of his shooting coat.

It is from the ladies' pouch that the present description comes. That attractive olive-green metal quiver with its bulk contents and its often detachable top providing a compartment in which a spare string and other essentials might be held is no longer seen. It has been replaced by a wooden box (or in many cases, a cardboard one). Such is progress!

Let us return to the more remote past. The term "quiver" is believed to derive from a Near Eastern word kukur, used to describe an arrow case carried by horsed archers. It is thought, possibly, to be cognate with the vernacular middle English quequer and the gaelic corcaich. Whether the term was in use during the late medieval period is uncertain, and indeed, if it was in use, to what would it have referred? There are clues in various places. In 1508 the will of Thomas Tremayll contained a bequest of a bow with 24 arrows in a quiver, suggestive of a bulk container. Certainly Tudor arrow containers survive—a particularly fine example is held in the Museum at Hereford.[25]

Although the description "arrow case" occurs frequently— the inventory of Henry VIII's belongings contains "arrowe casses of red lether with girdells CC [200] held in the Arrow Loft at Calais"—so also does the term "quiver."[26] Again, from the inventory of Henry's belongings (but this time from what are perhaps his personal possessions, since they were kept in the "Littell studie next the King's Bedde Chamber") we find "Two quyvers one of greene vellat embredered with gould and the kinges armes, the other quever of grene and white vellet both unfurnisshed."[27] From these entries it might seem that the terms were interchangeable; however, other sixteenth-century references suggest that the quiver was a bulk container. At Calne in Wiltshire in 1577comes the description "To the Constable to feather a quiver of arrows, 2s 4d." In 1588 the Chamberlain at Bath in Somerset paid ten pence "for mendynge of five arrowe casses."

Before we leave the subject for something equally puzzling, can we learn anything from our fifteenth-century French source *L'Art d'Archerie*? Indeed we can. In translation of chapter nine (Of the way of shooting with the bow), we find reference to "drawing the arrow from his quiver in two motions." In the French version, under the title *De la maniere de tirer de l'arc*, we find "tirer sa flesce a deux fois hors de la

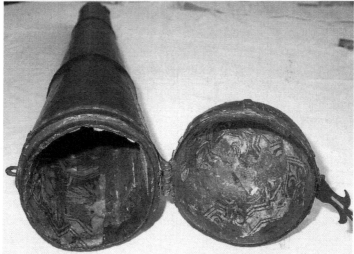

Top, replica "slashed" leather sixteenth century quiver. (*Author*) Lower, the decorated interior of a rare sixteenth-century metal arrow case (*Copyright Hereford Museum*)

trousse."[28] Since the word trousse means "case," clearly to the translator, "quiver" and "case" were synonymous terms. It is now time to leave the vexed question of description and turn to usage.

Remnants of arrows separated one from the other by holes in circular leather spacers have been recovered from the *Mary Rose*, each spacer designed for a sheaf of 24 shafts. Around the edge, closely spaced stitching holes can be just discerned, suggesting that—although no trace survives—originally the arrow shafts were contained within a protective material sleeve (possibly linen). Supporting the suggestion is the record of eighteenth-century antiquary Francis Grose who, while at Canterbury, saw "an ancient quiver about the size of a stocking" with just such a leather spacer roughly half way along. He surmised that it had originally contained arrows.[29]

We move now to the related matter of how the arrows were carried and used. Were these potentially unwieldy bundles carried on the archer's person? If that was the arrangement, were they removed and laid by his side to replenish from time to time, with a few held for immediate use under his belt? If the former, then an arrangement to keep the thing in place would be necessary. There are sixteenth-century references to arrow sheaves supplied with "girdles," and in one instance, money was paid to obtain "six girdles complete with hangings."[30] The suggestion is that the girdle was supplied complete with securing hangings to which the quiver was attached.

A contemporary (1560) Flemish painting of the martyrdom of Sainte Sebastien clearly shows an archer carrying a sheaf of arrows behind him, contained within what is probably a cloth bag, open at both ends.[31] The spacer cannot be seen but can legitimately be inferred. It appears from the painting that English spacers, and thus the arrow cases (if they are assumed), were smaller than the Flemish, and the sheaf would thus have lain closer to the archer's back, offering a more functional arrangement.

A particular source of information concerning archery dress and equipment comes from numerous drawings depicting English mercenary archers serving in Burgundian armies. Two such archers, shown shooting messages into a besieged town, are equipped with exceptionally large and stiff arrow bags, suggestive of more substantial construction than linen cloth (perhaps leather stretched over a wooden framework), or might this be just artistic license?[32] An interesting feature of this illustration is the appearance of two men, dressed as

Replica leather arrow spacer with light London Museum Type 16 headed arrows in position (*Author's photograph, with acknowledgement to the Mary Rose Trust*)

archers, one of whom extends his left arm with fingers outstretched and thumb uppermost in what seems to be a derogatory gesture, while his companion raises two fingers in that irreverent gesture that modern bow folk deem the "archer's salute." Whether it carried the present obscene message, who can tell?

Putting the matter of arrows in spacers perhaps beyond doubt has been poignant photographic evidence obtained during the recovery of *Mary Rose* material, when human remains were found on the seabed, directly associated with a bundle of arrows in a spacer. Other remains from within the ship and reported by the research director showed "a bundle of arrows contained within a leather spacer and attached to a 'waist thong' firmly attached to concretion around a man's spine."[33] For "waist thong" we can perhaps substitute "girdle."

It would be essential for arrows carried in this manner to be readily accessible, and a moment's thought will confirm that this can be achieved only if the arrows were carried point forward, since to do otherwise would snag the barbs on the spacer as they were removed. This being so, it begs the question: how were the spacers originally loaded, and following from that, with what type of head were the arrows fitted?

It is believed by many that for seaborne warfare, small, lightly barbed broadheads—Ascham refers to them—were favored at the time, since these would have been particularly effective against unprotected seamen. Experiment has shown that it is just possible to push a low-barbed arrowhead (London Museum Type 16, Jessop M4) through the spacer holes to load, suggesting that unless the shafts were headed after insertion, this was the type in use. Fletchings can be drawn through spacer holes without difficulty or damage, although a certain technique is necessary.

Let us consider the Tudor bowman in action. He would hold the bow in his left hand, his dominant eye notwithstanding, and he would withdraw his arrow from its container with his right hand; then turning his bow to the horizontal and holding his arrow below the shaftment, he would bring it over his bow to nock it on the string. This technique is described concisely in the twentieth-century translation of an instruction by the French author of *L'art d'archerie*, and it is likely that a similar sequence had evolved among English bowmen.[34]

An archer should poise his bow on the thumb of the hand in which he holds it when he shoots [to determine the point of balance which could, coincidentally but not necessarily be the geometric center] drawing an arrow from his quiver in two motions, the reason being that unless he had a very long arm, the arrows would remain jammed in the quiver from which the feathers would suffer.

In the matter of withdrawing through a spacer, many of the arrows recovered from the *Mary Rose* were bobtailed and of lesser diameter at the shaftment, thus facilitating withdrawal of the long triangular fletchings without damage. Additionally, our anonymous Frenchman tells us that the barbs of arrows were in the same plane as the arrow nock. If the withdrawal practice he describes was common in England then, because the cock or leading feather is invariably at right angles to the nock, an archer drawing head first could, by feeling the barbs do so in such a way as to present the cock feather uppermost,

English archers shooting messages into a besieged town. Note the large arrow cases and the primitive hand guns of the defenders. Note also two archers to the right of the picture offering gestures of defiance.

thus enabling a speedier shot. Furthermore, given a mix of arrowheads within a sheaf, he could readily identify the one that he wished to use without looking for it.

Having drawn and nocked his arrow, the archer had then to shoot—and he was not wanting for advice. Roger Ascham was withering in condemnation of some of his fellow bowmen. "Men have many faultes, which evill custome hath brought them to." His advice, followed by archers even today, was simple. Strength should be employed to the best advantage, and shooting performed to other's pleasure and delight.

He listed some of the antics he had observed while on the shooting line.[35] "Some will give two or three strides forward, dauncinge and hoppinge after his shaft, as long as it flyeth, as though he were a madde man" or "Some which feare to be too far gone, runne backwarde as it were to pull his shafte backe" or again "One lifteth up his heele and so holdeth his foot still, as long as his shaft flyeth." An honest man, he admits to many of these faults himself but adds that "I talke not of my shootinge, but of the general nature of shootinge."

Ascham was largely concerned with disciplining the recreational aspect of English archery, and with regularizing what he saw during practice at the butts. There is no evidence that he was aware of Continental practice, although if he was, then no doubt he would have been caustic in his appraisal, since matters were conducted rather differently in France.

Not for the French archer was the discipline of steady stance and controlled loose. There the act of drawing and loosing was a dynamic activity conducted in sequences of one, two, or three steps.[36] The one-step loose was done in two ways. "One is stepping forward with the foot of the bow-hand side, and the other by bringing back the arm, pushing out the bow and arrow and at the same time stepping back with the other foot; this step straightens the arm, but it must be a long and sharp step back." The other two ways involved taking either two steps or three steps back. "To shoot with two steps, a backward step must be taken with the hindermost foot so that on bringing the front foot down sufficient impetus is given to effect the loose." The three step method was even more demanding. "The front foot is moved forward, then the bow is thrust forward as explained above, and the hinder foot is brought back in such a way that when the arrow is loosed one can step forward with the front foot."

The French shooting line would have held no appeal for Roger Ascham, but it is with this line that we are now concerned. The French, who took to the war bow rather later than most (and replaced it with the handgun rather earlier than did the English), were systematic in their training.

Since in those far-off days, all archery was in preparation for warfare or for hunting—itself a form of warfare—it is

An unequal contest between a war bow and sling depicted in a fifteenth-century painting. Note the arrow bag in the left foreground.

appropriate that this book should include practice. Where the English were concerned with the development of distance shooting, in the execution of which they were encouraged by statute, the French had evolved a system by which personal technique was improved. This was known as shooting beneath the screen (*souz la toile*), and it was conducted in this manner. A screen was erected across the shooting range, the bottom edge being one foot above the ground for every ten paces between the targets as they faced each other across the field. Thus, if there were 100 paces between these, then the lower edge of the screen would be ten feet above the ground. This lower edge had bells attached. The archer then shot from one target to the other, endeavoring to keep his arrows beneath the screen. Arrows that brushed the screen would ring the bells.

A remarkably similar arrangement is mentioned in an early ballad of Robin Hood, when archers are said to have shot "under the line." In this game, arrows that went above the line were not only forfeited, but the archer concerned got a hefty box around the ears for his pains. The system is redolent of purpose, and the penalty suggests a training exercise of some sort—possibly in preparation for hunting, since it occurred within a woodland context, although accurate technique was equally necessary in warfare. No such salutary sanction is recorded in the Gallic equivalent.

Distance shooting, at which the English excelled, was also a feature of Continental practice, distances of 300 and even 400 paces being set and, one presumes, achieved. By statute, once they had reached maturity, English archers were forbidden to shoot at any mark closer than 220 yards with a livery, or standard, military arrow. This distance is regularly achieved by today's English longbowmen using heavy draw weight replica war bows and arrows of 52 grams and above.

Let us leave the modern shooter of the war bow to his pleasure, for in the following chapter we will examine the mustering and practice of his predecessor in more detail.

*Chapter
Seven*

STIFFEN THE SINEWS

*"Let every Village prove the Seat of Warr
Whose small Dimensions then need never fear,
When manly Archers once inhabit there."*
—Shotterel and D'Urfey (1676)

Mustering for military purpose in earlier, Anglo-Saxon, days was seemingly achieved by the appearance in a neighborhood of a horsed messenger waving a wooden sword, since such a sword has been discovered, bearing a runic message interpreted by some as a call to war.[1] The summons thus conveyed was no doubt recognized, at least in theory, by those concerned, as an order to prepare for service. A hit-or-miss system, perhaps, but presumably it was effective.

It would appear that the Anglo-Saxons mustered three distinct forces.[2] These included the "great fyrd," consisting of just about every able-bodied man who could find something usable as a weapon; the "select fyrd" of nobles and thegns with their trained house troops; and the "royal army" led by the king and having at its core his personal handpicked bodyguard or "hearthtroop," their loyalty ring-bound to him.

We have little knowledge of how this arrangement worked in practice. However, the outnumbered force that mustered under ealdorman Byrhtnod of Essex in 991, when he bravely (if with foolhardiness) confronted a numerically superior Danish army at Maldon, may have contained an element of each. Certain references within the text of a poem commemorating the event—one of few sources about the conduct of Anglo-Saxon warfare—are suggestive of this.[3]

Whenever there was opportunity to do so, an Anglo-Saxon leader personally supervised his men. There was ample opportunity for this at Maldon, since initially a channel of water separated the two sides. Byrhtnod evidently took advantage of this to put his men in proper order.

> Then there Byrhtnod began men to arrange
> He rode and instructed, soldiers he taught
> How they should stand and the position defend
> And required that their shields correctly they held
> Firmly by hand and not be frightened not at all.

Byrhtnod was the king's ealdorman for Essex and had his own house troop with him; however, the composition of his small army poses something of an enigma. Besides his house troops—men who had received his ring and who owed allegiance (not all of them loyal, as events subsequently proved)—also at Maldon, and named specifically, are three other combatants whose presence is a little puzzling if it was the select fyrd that the ealdorman commanded.

Dunmere, an unorne ceorl, or humble yeoman, such as one might find in a great fyrd, had his moment of glory recorded when after Byrhtnod fell, standing tall, he shook his throwing spear at the enemy and called upon each Saxon warrior present to avenge their Lord's death.[4]

Firm alongside his ealdorman and master was Wulfmere the Young, a boy not yet fully grown—unweaxen (a youth in warfare). It was he that drew the bloody spear from Byrhtnod's side and threw it back so effectively that he killed its owner. As the ethic of Saxon warfare demanded, he had slain the killer of his protector.[5]

Perhaps the most curious, however, is the presence of Æsferp, son of Ecglaf. He was a Northumbrian hostage placed (one assumes) in the care of Byrhtnod—although tantalizingly, we are not told why. King Ætheiræd had a fairly tenuous hold on the northern parts of his kingdom, so perhaps the hostage was there as an assurance of good behavior among his kinsmen. While perhaps not willingly present, he was obviously trusted, since he makes his appearance in the poem as an effective bowman, shooting at the enemy until either he ran out of shafts or the battle reached a stage where his accuracy was affected.[6] If he was of noble birth, then his skill with a bow would not be surprising, since in preparation for hunting, archery was particularly favored by the Anglo-Saxon great and good as a worthy activity. In fact, archery has had an appeal for the ruling classes of England for many generations. Although largely for sport, it developed hand and eye coordination and would be militarily advantageous in that respect.

Military training began early in a boy's life. In his *Life of St. Cuthbert*, Bede mentions that the seventh century saint "played at games" requiring physical stamina and quick thinking, including contact activities such as wrestling. Saint Guthlac, another in the extensive early English calendar of holy men, was not only a warrior at the age of 15, but a successful one, having joined a youthful war band, killed foes, and taken booty.

Stephen Pollington, in his work *The English Warrior*, draws attention to burials of young Saxon males between 12 and 20 years old accompanied by a partial set of weapons, a shield, and spear.[7] Such was the armament, perhaps, of young Wulfmaer who avenged his Lord at Maldon.

While there is no doubt that archers were present and served in warfare, it was many years before they achieved their long-deserved recognition. Through his 1181 Assize of Arms, King Henry II ordered that every adult freeman should provide himself with arms according to the value of his belongings, and bows would have been included for those of the lowest income.

The Assize was in effect a revival of the old system of fyrd duty, or obligation to defend home and county as necessary. While this obligation had not ceased, it had fallen into abeyance during the period immediately following the Norman occupation. Understandably, for their own safety, early Norman kings relied upon levees provided by their feudal tenants, backed up by foreign mercenaries, rather than the uncertain loyalty of a Saxon fyrd. When Henry II revived the practice in 1181, two generations had passed since the overthrow of Saxon king Harold II at Senlac, and the initial hostility was easing. The true, heavy draw weight war bow, however, was still a century away. It is likely that the weapon mustered by thirteenth-century Englishmen was the lighter hunting bow—although legend at least credits those Welsh archers who fought alongside the English with something more powerful.

Henry II had prescribed the bow as a war weapon for his possessions on the continent 60 years before; and there is a suggestion, probably well founded, that by regulating the bow in England, he was reflecting growing concern with its use, particularly in forested areas where the hunting of deer and other game for sport was held sacrosanct by the ruling class. Whatever the reason, from that time, archers formed a tactical addition to men-at-arms, first on foot as supernumeraries, then later mounted, as a vital tactical arm, more than proving their worth during the two succeeding centuries.

Writs of array, or muster, were issued regularly. One for July of 1264 serves to show procedure. In the county of Cambridgeshire, all knights and tenants were ordered to London. There foot soldiers were chosen to serve with the mounted troops. From each vill, or conurbation, a number of the fittest men were chosen, equipped with lances, bows and arrows, axes, swords, and crossbows (for this weapon had yet to be entirely superseded by the hand bow). Expenses for 40 days were provided. When all were gathered together, units of twenties and hundreds were formed.

Originally all able-bodied men between 15 and 60 were required to attend the general muster.[8] Barons, nobles with their personal retinues, and churchmen were excused— barons, since they were potential commanders with a special role; nobles, perhaps because their retinues were assumed to have regular warlike training; and churchmen, since in warfare their role was to shrive the participants.

Henry III's Assize of 1242 had been revolutionary in that it established the hand bow—the proto-longbow—as a national weapon. His writ reaffirmed military obligation, specifying the age of those liable for service as between 15 and 60 years; while the important Statute of Winchester (Edward I) in 1285 commanded that "every man have in his house harness [weapons] for to keep the peace according to ancient Assize." Edward also ordered that a "View of Arms" be held in each hundred every year.

After the Statute of Winchester, another important question was debated. Could the king require his armed subjects to follow him out of the country? The matter was important. No fyrd duty had ever gone that far. The subject was discussed, and it was agreed that by sanction of Parliament, the king might issue a Commission of Array authorizing those appointed to provide a given number of men from a particular district. They were required to provide their own arms.

> In special at the fyrst moustre, everie archere shall have hys bowe and arrowes hole, that is to wytte in arrowes xxx or xxiv at the least, headed and in a sheaf. And furthermore that everie archere do sweare that hys bowe and arrowes be hys owne, or hys mastyr's or captyne's. And also that no man ones moustered and admitted as an archere, alter or change himself to any other condition, without the king's special leave, uppon payne of emprisonment.

The burden of cost was a great consideration, however, and those responsible would have been relieved to learn that when men moved beyond their county borders, then their costs would be borne by the king.

Although the general principles to which these enactments conformed are well enough known, little survives of their operation in practice. Records are sparse, but details survive of

mustering arrangements within an English city during the mid-
to late fourteenth century.

It was decreed by order that there should be a "View of
Arms" in 1355 on "Monday, next after the feast of St. James
the Apostle" to "Preserve the peace of the Lord King" in the
County of Norfolk.[9] Thus it was that on July 27, the adult
manhood of the city of Norwich presented itself for review
before Justice of the Peace John Bardolf and his fellow justices.
Conesford was one of three wards, or leets, in Norwich, and
as was practice then, the responsibility for mustering its active
men folk lay on the shoulders of a constable, or rather on the
shoulders of two constables—Wiliam Skie and John de
Causton—since the leet was divided into two subleets, each
constable having a subconstable to assist him.

The total armed strength of the two parts was 180. Each
part had as its captain a centenar invariably fully armed and
carrying a banner with either four or five vintenars (titles used
during active service) below him and each vintenar with a
company of 20 men.[10] Of the first company, four were half-
armed men, including the vintenar, Thomas de Hornyngg,
who carried a lance and a pennon and had under his charge 16
men with no defensive armor at all.[11] Each of these carried a
staff (perhaps a quarterstaff[12]) and a knife, while several had
swords, and one an axe called a wyex.[13] The second company
was led by Walter Whitbred, also with lance and pennon,
together with two more half-armed men and 18 others, each
with staff and knife. John Latimer, again with lance and pennon, plus three fully armed and two half-armed men, had
charge of the third company with 16 rank-and-file soldiers,
each with the customary staff and knife. The fourth company
was under William de Biburgh, a fully armed man. His lance
and pennon sheltered one half-armed man, 14 staff and knife
men, six who carried swords and hatchets, and one who held
a sword and a double-edged axe. Finally there was John
Rokele, a fully armed vintenar with one other also fully
equipped. His contingent included 13 staff and knife men and
five with double-edged axe and sword.

Space limitations preclude more than just a summary of the remainder. The second subleet consisted of one centenar, four vintenars, plus a number of fully armed and half-armed men, while a rank and file of staffs and knives with a leavening of archers made up the number. Of 180 men, just eight in these two subleets mustered as archers, a situation markedly different from that of the three others leets that made up the city's wards. The leet of Mancroft included 56, Wymer had 61, and Over the Water had 43.

The weaponry mustered, or viewed, would seem to have been broadly divided between the close quarter, defensive staff, knife, and sword and the standoff bow and arrow. This was a balance presumably felt appropriate to prospective contemporary need.

Curiously, the subleet of Berstrete (the second half of the Conesford leet) included a woman: Petronella de Bokenham. As a widow, she had inherited the responsibilities of her late husband. Although she was permitted to provide a man in her stead, her position—if by circumstance she were unable to do so—is unclear. Fourteenth-century women were well able to look after themselves, and she might have been equally as effective with quarterstaff and knife as the man who should have represented her.[14]

To what extent formal training played a part in weapon viewing is vague, although reason, supported by that most tenuous of sources—the ballad—suggests that archers generally practiced in an informal way. Whether by now the lighter country weapon had been replaced by the true war bow is also open to question. Circumstantial evidence, although academically inadmissible, exists in early ballads and gestes (tales) to suggest that bows capable of great distances were in being, and these may have been forerunners of the fourteenth-century weapons carried by the Norwich archers.

Although an academic might frown, I make no excuse for delving into folklore for relevant reference. The "Ballad of Adam Bell," thought to be contemporary with the earliest of the Robin Hood gestes, refers in passing to the bow, the string, and the arrow.[15] "They bent theyr good yew bowes" (Yew was early recognized as the best of the bow woods) "and looked theyr stringes were round" (the compiler believes this to mean "in good shape," although a well-made string is rounded in the making). "For theyr stringes were of silk ful sure." This is an interesting early reference to this material as a source of bow strings. Silk would have been costly and not readily accessible to an ordinary man. The reference sets these men apart.

In the course of the ballad, Adam and his fellows move to a pair of butts. "Thyere twyse or thryse they shot about, for to assaye theyr hande. [try their hands] There was no shote these yemen shot thyat any prycke [mark] myght them withstand." This shooting impresses the king, who is watching, but William of Cloudesley, who is one of the archers, decries the width of the butts. "I hold him never no good archar that shoteth at buttes so wyde." That said, they move into a field "There set up two hasell roddes twenty score paces betwene." It is conjectural how far apart these actually were and indeed whether they bore any relation to reality. Twenty score is 400 yards; 20 score paces would be approximately 350 yards. This is within the proven limits of modern examples of the war bow using a light flight shaft, and we may give credence to the tale. "I shall assaye, syr," William says, "or [before] that I farther go." Then comes an example of accuracy, as he cleaves the wand in two—an indication, perhaps, that not only distance but accurate shooting were required of the early English archer. Cloudesley, with supreme confidence, then ties his son to a stake, an apple on his head and, moving back six score (120) paces—100 yards or thereabouts—"there he drew out a fayre brode arrowe, hys bowe was great and longe. He set that arrowe in hys bowe that was both styffe and stronge." Here we meet the nascent war bow and the arrow that stood stiff in it: the broadhead battle shaft. Predictably, father shoots an apple from his son's head, and all is well. (Readers will be reminded of a similar circumstance involving the Swiss William Tell, although he achieved success with a steadily held crossbow. With a potentially unsteady longbow William Cloudesley had demonstrably the more difficult task.)

An inspiring tale that doubtless went down well when it was told, it encapsulates something of the skill required of the common archer of the time. Men would have listened to gestes such as this, and they would have been driven to emulate them for distance and accuracy (although one fervently hopes that a stake subsequently substituted for a son). The date of the tale is uncertain, as are the dates of most early ballads. However, the verses conclude "All that with a hande bowe shoteth," a term suggesting that it predates the mid-fifteenth-century vernacular term "long bow."

The bow was of course also necessary for personal protection and for amusement in those far-off days. Men walking to market or between farms or to church would carry theirs and, when appropriate, would shoot hoyles (an early from of roving archery often shot at short distances to relieve the tedium of long country walks) en route. Some with less concern for others occasionally made nuisances of themselves. Thus from a coroner's report in 1249 we have: "two strangers passing through the town of Eston were shooting arrows in sport so that by misadventure, Alice, the daughter of John, was hit by an arrow so that she died eighteen days later. The strangers fled at once. It is not known who they are."

For many years men accepted archery as fundamental to their way of life, but things move on. With ever-increasing opportunities for passing his leisure time with other games and activities, coercion by worried authority became a necessity. There is the saying "one can take a horse to water, but one cannot make him drink"—a piece of homespun rhetoric as true for archers as for horses. Despite the majesty of a law that required his presence at the village butts whenever he had time on his hands, and on pain of dire consequence, the independent-minded Englishman often exercised his perceived right to do something else, usually more congenial and frequently much less morally uplifting.

It was left to the authorities, then, to devise a means by which he might be encouraged, and this took the form of periodic contests for both money and other valuable prizes. Here we will look into the complexities of archery practice that, although masquerading as recreation, was in reality preparation for warfare.

The town or village elders bore some responsibility for ensuring obedience to statute law, including the one that required regular attendance for archery practice; and among others, the local beadle often had the unenviable task of ensuring that all went well in this connection. It seems doubtful whether in earlier times any official undertook responsibility for actual instruction in the performance of the art, but latterly this task fell to an appointed corporal whose duty it was, among other matters, to pick out the "mishandy" and drill home some understanding about the principles as best he could.

Instruction was, however, in the main, a requirement devolved by authority to parents; and it is for certain that habits, whether good, bad, or indifferent, were for generations passed more or less enthusiastically from father to son as each lad became of statutory age to possess and use a longbow. It is unlikely that seven year olds, with their new bows, were present at the butts, or even required to be—archery for them was confined to the garden, and from the numerous coroner's reports recording accidental death during juvenile shooting, it would seem that supervision was not always as tight as it should have been.

Roger Ascham himself records that his mentor and master, Sir Humfrey Wingfelde, instructed him in archery from a young age, instilling in him a love of the activity that lasted throughout his life.[16]

Thys worshypfull man have ever loved and used, to have many children brought up in learnyinge in hys house amonges whome I my selfe was one. For whom at terme tymes he woulde bryng downe from London bothe bowe

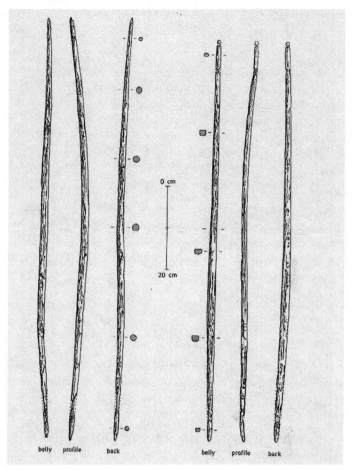

Sixteenth-century children's longbows recovered from Acton Court, South Gloucestershire. Note their distinctive cross sections. (*Drawing copyright the Bath Archaeological Trust. May not be reproduced without permission.*)

and shaftes. And when they should playe, he woulde go with them him selfe in to the fyelde, and se them shoote, and he that shot fayrest, shulde have the best bowe and shaftes, and he that shot ilfavouredlye shulde be mocked of his felowes, til he shot better.

Ascham does not say whether he was ever "mocked of his felowes"; in his seminal work *Toxophilus*, he describes himself as a mediocre archer, although his explicit writing suggests that there was perhaps an element of self-deprecation present. Certainly, if anyone knew what constituted good shooting, it was he.

There was evidently a regular element of competitiveness in earlier times, even for the very young, as the book of common council of the city of Chester records.[17]

For the avoiding of idleness, all children of six years and upward shall on week-days be sent to school, and on Sundays and Holy Days shall resort to their Parish churches where, in the afternoon, all the male children shall be exercised in shooting with bows and arrows for pins and points only; and that their parents shall furnish them with bows and arrows and pins and points for that purpose, according to the Statute lately made for maintenance of shooting long bowes and artillery, being the ancient defence of the kingdom.

By the greatest good fortune, two small child's yew bows dating from the mid-sixteenth century were found some 20 years ago during an archaeological excavation at Acton Court, a Tudor residence in South Gloucestershire. We thus have the opportunity to examine the weapons with which sixteenth-century six year olds were enjoying archery.

Reconstructions of these bows in yew (*Taxus baccata*) have been created by a professional bowyer, and thus, despite the degraded state of the originals, it has been possible to share informed comment about their construction and perhaps their purpose.

They are of particular interest because each has a distinctive section. One is plano-convex and the other is ogival, or elliptical. They therefore reflect the varied sections found in contemporary war bows and the suggestion that each was for a different function must be considered. In this we are guided by the author of the early sixteenth-century continental booklet, *l'Art d'Archerie*. He suggests that a bow of "square" section is best suited to butt shooting, while a "round" bow is more appropriate for distance. Here we have examples of each, and their presence begs the wider question of whether war bows recovered from the Tudor warship *Mary Rose* had separate purposes related to their sections.

Although the limb ends were damaged, there is some evidence for the coning of limb tips and thus the provision for horn nocks; however, no bow nocks were found and the replicas have thus been constructed with self-string grooves. Had they been horned, then the working length of each limb would have been extended; in consequence draw weights would have slightly lessened and the working arrow length increased a little.

The draw weights of the replicas are 25 pounds at 12 inches (the suggested arrow draw length for the plano-convex section) and 19 pounds at 13 inches for the elliptical section. Their draw-weights and overall lengths (964 millimeters and 1,021 millimeters respectively) together with the predicted arrow lengths are consistent with use by a young child. It is the opinion of the replicating bowyer that the originals were professionally made and tillered.[18]

The dates of the bows cannot be verified, beyond an assumption that neither is later than the 1550s when the moat in which they were found is known to have been filled in. It seems possible that their origin was the early 1540s, following the Statute of 1541, which required all boys over six years of age to practice archery.

Adults over 24 shot at 11 score yards or more, but teenagers of 16 and above were restricted in distance and equipment as we shall later see.

To make a useful distance even with a light shaft requires a bow in excess of 50 pounds in draw weight, but in those remote times, when England was largely an agrarian economy, farm and village lads were almost certainly capable of drawing a bow of suitable weight quite early in their teens. Since military service could, in theory at least, start at 15, if archery was their ambition, they would need to have been well on the way to mastering the heavier war bow by then. If it was not, then the lighter the bow, the better they were suited.

On those days when shooting was mandatory, the "butty-fields" must have presented quite a scene. Picture two groups: one composed of those anxious to gain experience and show prowess, with bets placed on favorites; the other reluctant and ever ready to slip away after mustering when the Beadle's back was turned. Somewhere among the throng of onlookers no doubt were ancient archers looking approvingly or critically at stance and technique, young girls eyeing their particular swain as he strove to impress, and the inevitable unruly gaggle of runny-nosed small boys, anxious for the day when they too would take their stand with the men to draw and loose their bearing shafts at the mark.

Standards of accuracy varied, but excellence did not always bring the expected reward, as the following account will show.

At Malling Town in Kent, one of Queen Marie's Justices, upon the complaint of many wise men and a few foolish boys, laid an Archer by the heels because he shot so near the white Mark at Butts. For he was informed and persuaded that the poor man played with a Fly, otherwise called a Devil or a Familiar; and because he was certified that the Archer aforesaid shot better than the common shooting which he had before heard or seen of, he conceived it could not be in God's name but by enchantment, whereby this Archer [as he supposed by abusing the Queen's liege people] gained one day some two or three shillings, to the detriment of the Commonwealth and to his own enrichment and therefore the Archer was severely punished, to the great encouragement of archers and to the example of justice, but especially to the overthrow of witchcraft.[19]

In a rather more friendly vein, on Easter Mondays during the sixteenth century at Chester (in the English county of Cheshire), reward for the best shot at the butts was provided by the city's newly married men—those who had been wed for less than one year. They were required to deliver to the city's

Guild of Drapers (with whom, one presumes, responsibility for organization of the day rested) in front of the mayor an arrow of silver to be awarded as the principal prize. Silver arrows were among the more common of awards for merit, exceeded in prestige, although not in value, by a crown of gold.

Communities varied occasionally in their interpretation or definition of statute law. However, in 1464 the court leet of the city of Coventry defined the duties of its citizen archers exactly and without compromise. "That no manner of persons of this city from henceforth shoot at a moveable [portable] target , but shoot at standing marks [marks permanently positioned] and butts, upon pain that he who does to the contrary shall lose at every default six shillings and eight pence."

Distances at which one shot evidently varied; beyond the age of 24 no man might shoot at less than 11 score yards. It is clear, as we shall later see, that distances for the younger ages were graded, although there is reason to believe that gradation was fluid and perhaps not rigorously enforced.

Preparation for warfare was mandatory for those archers who had enrolled in service. During the fifteenth-century civil war between the Yorkists and the Lancastrians, fighting on the side of Yorkist Edward IV was Charles, Duke of Burgundy, brother-in-law to the king. A thoroughly organized commander, his military ordinances are masterpieces of practical advice; and since many English archers served in his army, the following direction addressed to his captains is relevant.

Captains are to exercise their archers with their horses to get them used to dismounting and drawing their bows. They must learn how to attach their horses together by their bridles; to march briskly forward and to shoot without breaking ranks. The pikemen must be made to advance in close formation in front of the archers, to kneel at a sign from them, holding their pikes lowered to the level of a horses back so that the archers can shoot over the pikemen as if over a wall.

He continues:

Thus, if the pikemen see that the enemy are breaking
rank, they will be near enough to charge them in good
order as instructed. The archers must also learn to place
themselves back to back in double defence in a square or
circle, always with the pikemen outside them to withstand
the charge of the enemy horse, while their own horses are
entered in the midst.

Let us now look at the type of shooting legitimately open
to would-be bowmen, always bearing in mind that the result
of their practice might ultimately be tested in warfare.

In earlier times four forms were open. Flight, or distance
shooting: pricks, or clout, butts, or standing marks; and roving, or hoyles (a shorter form of roving). Prick and clout
shooting took place at distances between 160 and 240 yards
(8 and 12 score)—the shorter distance being reserved for the
younger lads (the "yonglyngs"). The mark, or clout, as it was
early known, was constructed of canvas stuffed with straw,
much as it is today, and was 18 inches in diameter. A white circle was painted upon the clout, in the center of which was
placed a wooden peg—the prick. The expression "to hit the
white" meant to hit the white circle, while "cleaving the pin"
meant to hit the peg.[20] However, for those under 24, there was
seemingly some regulation here relevant to arrow weight.
Arrows for flight and prick (clout) shooting were generally
lighter, but heavier for standing marks, or butts. The statute of
Henry VIII (1542) is explicit.

No-one under 24 shall shoot at any standing prick, except
it be at a rover, more than once, when he shall change his
mark, under penalty of four pence; that no-one under 24
shall shoot at any mark of eleven score or under with any
prickshaft or flight [arrow] under penalty of six shillings
and eight pence; that no-one under seventeen shall use a
yew bow under a penalty of six shillings and eight pence
unless his father or his mother shall be possessed of œ10

in land, or he himself 40 Marks; and that the inhabitants
of every city, town or place put and keep up butts and
shoot at them or elsewhere on holy days and at other
times convenient.

Although Henry was a committed archer, he was obliged to
move with the times. While smiling on the older weapon, he
encouraged the use of the handgun, unwieldy and uncertain
though it often was. His daughter Elizabeth was aware of the
value of archery, although she too was conscious of the march
of progress. In 1560 her muster arrangements included special
orders for improving the skills of arquebusiers, "the least efficient arm," whose abilities evidently left much to be desired.
However, despite its rapidly increasing obsolescence, Queen
Elizabeth urged that the use of the bow should be positively
encouraged in villages and that some acceptable means be
found to "draw youth there unto, that all and everyone being
viewed, arrayed and prepared, may be always ready to serve."
To the vintenar, or "twenty man," was handed the responsibility of achieving this very necessary improvement. For "acceptable means" we may perhaps infer "bribery"!

To assist him, and for the special benefit of the arquebusiers, a butt 20 feet wide and 16 feet high was to be erected
in some convenient place, away from the highway and the
public at large. In the midst of this monumental object—the
size of a small house—a roundel was to be put, 4 feet 6 inches
in diameter, on which were to be prominently marked black
circles and a white centerpiece. The arquebusier was to stand
150 paces (about 120 yards) away and, with the critical advice
of the vintenar at his elbow, endeavor to hit the thing. One
may imagine a degree of coarse humor on the part of watching
longbowmen.

Weapons were given to men "fit by their status and apt-
ness; the strong men to be bowmen," and those responsible for
training the warrior archer were concerned with a number of
important aspects. First, and most important, that he should
be suited to the task, since archery requires mental agility as

well as strength; second, that he should be capable of making long distances (for those over 24 years of age, statute laid down that 11 score was the minimum to be expected of him); third, that he should have accuracy at undetermined distances; and last (seemingly less emphasized, since despite its importance, it does not appear in statute), that he have accuracy at short distances.

The apparent embargo on lighter flight (clout) shafts imposed on those under 24 is particularly interesting, since the implication is that a heavier forehand shaft alone was to be used. One is reminded of the words Shakespeare put into the mouth of Justice Shallow (Henry IV, Part II) when informed of the demise of an archer called Old Double:

> Dead! He drew a good bow, and dead!—He shot a fine
> shoot—Dead!—He would have clapp'd in the clout at
> twelve score and carried you a forehand shaft a fourteen
> and a fourteen and a half that it would have done a man's
> heart good to see.

Although archery was in a real sense recreational and healthy, men were never allowed to forget that in handling their bows and arrows, they were preparing to be effective in defending their country in warfare.

By far the preferred system of shooting, and probably that most favored by the archer, was the still-popular activity of roving, since this offered freedom to roam, besides providing the opportunity to develop that vital accuracy at unknown distances.

Richard Mulcaster, first master of Merchant Taylor's School on Lawrence Pountney Hill in London City and an enthusiastic archer himself, set down the virtues of roving as he saw them in his work Positions.[21]

> He that shooteth in the free and open fields may choose
> whether between his marks he wil run or walk: daunce or
> leape: halloo or sing: or do somewhat els which belongeth
> to the other either vehement or violent exercises. And

whereas hunting on foot is much praised, what moving of the bodie hath the foot hunter in hills and dales which the roving archer hath not in variety of grounds? Is his natural heat more stirred than the archer's is? Is his appetite better than the archer's, though [despite] the proverb "help the hungry hunter"? Nay, in both these, the archer has the advantage, for both his houres be much better to eat, and all his moving is more at his choice. In fine what good is there in any particular exercise, either to help natural heat, to clear the body in the senses, to provoke appetite, to strengthen up the sinews, or to better all partes, which is not altogethyer in this?

Richard Mulcaster belonged to an elite archery society, Prince Arthur's Knights, and as a member, he would have had firsthand knowledge of the virtues of roving.[22] Although he extolled its values as an aid to health—a subject very close to his heart as a schoolmaster—he would have been aware that the society was primarily concerned with archery as a military exercise, for its original formation had been at the behest of King Henry VIII.[23] The king had witnessed citizens of London exercising in Mile-End Fields and had jovially suggested that they form a society, even naming them after his own dead elder brother Price Arthur, whose prowess with a bow had been well marked.

Richard Robinson, a minor Elizabethan man of letters, and self-styled historian of the society, reports that Henry actually granted a patent—sadly, now lost—in which he conferred title and purpose, In Robinson's words:

By patent of his princely prerogative (Henry) ordained, graunted and confirmed he unto this Honourable Citie of London, free election of a Chieftaine and of citizens representing the memory of the magnificent King Arthur and the Knights of the same Order, which should for the maintenance of shooting only, meet together once a year, with solemn and friendly celebration thereof.[24]

Interestingly, there is circumstantial evidence for a second society, possibly also archery based, which was commanded by a self-styled Duke of Shoreditch, whose entourage included other fanciful individuals such as the Marquess Barlow, the Marquess of Shacklewell, the Earl of Buckley, Baron Stirrup, and the like. The Duke appears to have been a senior member of the Goldsmiths Company, possibly its master; it was he and his company who appear to have sponsored the great archery procession and meeting of September 1583, described in such detail by Sir William Wood a century later.[25]

A third, even more shadowy organization, but one with evident militia connections, was the Black Train, led by one known as the Black Prince of Portugal.[26] They were reviewed by Alderman Thomas Offley while en route to Mile-End Fields for military and, from the context (since Offley was a senior member of Prince Arthur's Knights), what was probably also recreational archery practice.[27]

The ethos of the day was the medicine of archery training for warfare, sugared with the pleasure of a congenial pastime. As Thomas Churchyard, a contemporary Elizabethan poet succinctly put it in his poem in praise of the bow, "Thou art a fearfull foe in field, and yet a pastime brave."[28]

It is difficult not to see the September 1583 meeting closely connected with, if not directly arising from, a petition made earlier that year in June by the bowyers and fletchers companies who pleaded poverty because citizens were disregarding the various statutes requiring them to practice archery. The huge turnout of archers, over 3,000, each of whom had a bow and one arrow to shoot, is evidence for the success of the event; and one might expect that the dry and empty coffers of the bowyers and fletchers were suitably refreshed. The shooting took place toward a single butt (there is no reference to a pair) 148 yards distant.

The reason for this choice of length is not explained. However, it is a distance approximately 27 southern roods of 5 1/2 yards which may have been as familiar to southern archers as 20 roods of 7 1/2 yards (150 yards) would have been to those from the Midlands and the north of England. On the other hand, of course, it may just have been the maximum safe area available. How the master of the game managed to control an event that attracted many thousands of spectators, whose unruly behavior had already caused the cancellation of a banquet arranged by the Duke of Shoreditch, is a matter of some wonder. However, history does not record any casualties. Perhaps whifflers (a person of authority armed with a wooden sword or a stick employed for crowd control) were employed to keep the onlookers outside the statutory 40 feet from the butt.

Although in 1583 the great procession of archers, together with those who held them in esteem, along with the subsequent shooting, might loosely be called a muster, the term should correctly be applied to a rather more formal arrangement. Subsequent to 1573 the old general muster at which county forces were examined and put through their paces by some form of military exercise was accompanied by an occasional special, private, or particular muster at which a captain might inspect his own troops and, if necessary, order additional training.

L ike many an old soldier, the war bow did not die, it faded away. Obsolescent by the mid-1500s and obsolete a century later, meetings to improve archery skill were nevertheless still held in the first quarter of the seventeenth century, while the first occasion on which the bow was shot in contest as a recreational weapon took place in 1663, a year after its omission as a weapon from the national list of arms.

The occasion was the restoration of the monarchy and a natural wish on behalf of the City of London to dismiss any lingering doubts about their loyalty. Since much stiffening of sinew was involved, we will conclude this chapter with a brief account of the proceedings.

The meeting advertised "The truly ENGLISH and manly Exercises of Wrestling, Archery, and Sword and Dagger" to be held on St. Bartholomew's Day at Finsbury Fields, through the auspices of the lord mayor and his aldermen.

The Day began with the processing through the streets of the master of the game, pro hoc vice—Mr. William Smee, "richly clad in a sute of Cloth of Silver, the ground Grene Silke, accommodated according to Custome with one of His Majesties Horses and Royal Furniture, and two of his Grooms, with two Footmen of his Own and the City Trumpets." With due ceremony, Mr. Smee reached the mansion house where he knelt before the lord mayor (upon a cushion) and, in a speech resonant with patriotic fervor, drew attention to the bows and arrows that would be used: "All remaining Trophies of our French Conquests and the best evidences of our English Valour." Warming to the occasion, he drew attention to the lord mayor's exemplary accomplishment in publicizing the nation's honor through "reviving this Military Exercise" and concluded with a stirring exhortation to archers to take aim and—encouraged by the lord mayor's patriotic integrity, loyalty, and honor—to hit the mark.

At this event the pound arrow, the broad arrow, and the flight arrow were each shot using the war bow. Winners were Mr. Girlington (pound arrow and flight arrow) and Captain Taylour (broad arrow). Each appears to have been a member of the Honourable Artillery Company. The winning distance for the flight arrow was 22 score (yards is assumed) or 440 yards, personally checked (it is said) by Mr. Smee; a very respectable distance.

In keeping with ancient tradition, the archery was first, followed by the wrestling, and then the sword and dagger, won respectively by Mr. Henchman and Mr. Darby Bell. The Honourable Artillery Company, direct descendants of the Guild of St. George (formed in 1537 by Henry VIII), policed the proceedings, being led on this specific occasion by Sir George Smith, a steward of the company. And so ended what might be called a valediction for the old war bow, since from thenceforth we meet it only in peace.

Chapter Eight

SUMMON UP THE BLOOD

"You must not fight too often with one enemy,
or you will teach him all your art of war"
—Napoleon Bonaparte (1769–1821)

It was said of allied soldiers during the Great War that they were lions led by donkeys. This is altogether too broad a dismissal of frustrated commanders faced with impossible decisions, perhaps, but in much earlier times, when warfare was more fluid, it might be more truly said that the English bowmen and men-at-arms were lions led by tigers. For while there were those in medieval times whose tactical skills were occasionally found wanting and by whose ineptitude battles were lost and towns taken, there were many others whose exploits gained fierce loyalty from their troops and real respect from their opponents. These were men such as Sir Walter Manny of Hainault; Sir Thomas Dagworth; Sir William Bentley, the Earl of Derby; Lord Talbot, Earl of Shrewsbury; and Lord Scales.

We are fortunate to have a contemporary description of the men these tigers led. It is by a Spanish priest, Padre Fre: Antonio Agapida, traveling with an expeditionary force sent to Spain in the late 1400s. After careful assessment, he wrote of the English soldiers:

They were a comely race of men, but too fair and fresh for warriors: not having the sunburned hue of our old Castilian soldiery. They were huge feeders also and deep carousers and could not accommodate themselves to the sober diet of our troops but must fain eat and drink after the style of their own country. They were often noisy and unruly also in their wassail, and their quarter of the camp was prone to be a scene of loud revel and sudden brawl. . . . They were withal of great pride, yet it was not like our Spanish pride for they rarely drew a stilletto in their disputes, but their pride was silent and contumelius [contemptuous]. Though from a remote and barbarous Island they yet believed themselves the most perfect men upon earth and magnified their Chieftain the Lord Scales beyond the greatest of our Grandees.

We are not told who these men were, but from the context, it might seem that they formed the personal retinue of Lord Scales. The Padre continued with a summary of the fighting qualities of these "unruly" warriors:

With all this it must be said of them that they were marvellous good men in the field; dexterous archers and powerful with the battle axe. They did not rush forward fiercely but went into the fight deliberately and persisted obstinately and were slow to find out when they were beaten. Withal they were much esteemed, yet little liked by our soldiery, who considered them staunch companions in the field yet coveted but little friendship with them in the camp.

There are many examples of English longbowmen acting on their own initiative, some in the context of a set piece battle, others on less formal occasions. One surviving account shows this clearly. It comes from a history of the seaside town of Brighton on the Sussex coast. For many years there had been sporadic attacks by French raiders on coastal ports, some successful, others less so. When the sleepy fishing hamlet of Brighthelmstone—the forerunner of the present town—was attacked in 1514 or 1515 (the year is unclear), the local watch of six archers was ready and waiting. The history takes up the story:

> Prior John, great captain of the French navy, with his Gallies and Foists charged with great basilisks [guns] and other great artillery came on the border of Sussex and came aland in the night at a poor village called Bright Helmston, and before the Watch could he escrye [notice him], he set fire to the town and took such poor goods as he found: then the Watch fired the beacons, and people began to gather, which seeing, Prior John sounded his trumpet to call his men aboard, and by that time it was day. . . . Then six archers which kept the Watch followed Prior John to the sea and shot so fast that they beat the galleymen from the shore, and Prior John himself waded back to his Foist, and the English men went into the water after, but they were put back with pikes, or else they had entered the Foist, but they shot so fast that they wounded many in the Foist, and Prior John was shot in the face with an Arrow, and was likely to have died, and therefore he offered his image of wax before our Ladye at Boulogne with the English arrow for a miracle.

Local leaders were not wanting in initiative either. On July 26, 1545, following an abortive attempt by the French navy to destroy the English fleet at Portsmouth, the commander, Admiral Claude D'Annebault, sailed along the English coast en route for home. Thwarted in his endeavor to breach the English defenses (although he subsequently claimed to have sunk the English flagship *Mary Rose*), he sailed his fleet further along the coast to anchor in a bay between the recently changed outlet of the river Ouse at Newhaven and the old but now silted and largely disused port of Seaford. Here his frustrated men could look for easier pickings. Thus it was that when the tide was right, troops swarmed ashore, heading for the town, to cause mayhem in search of booty. The arrival had not gone unnoticed, however. The town's watch had seen smoke billowing from poor fishing hovels by the old mouth of the river Ouse at Bishopstone as D'Annebault's men made their way inland, and a rather special welcome had been prepared.[1]

Led by a local dignitary, Nicholas Pelham, who by useful coincidence had a country house at Bishopstone and thus a vested interest in the outcome, the town's Portmen (with others from the locality), armed with bills and bows, were waiting, concealed in a low-built fort. Hidden from view by a lightly constructed wooden structure bridging a fast-flowing tidal river, they waited until the French had crossed the bridge. Once on the farther bank, the wooden structure was quickly destroyed by the billmen. The archers then pinned the troops against the river bank with accurate shooting from their bows and were close to destroying them before their plight was noticed by those on board ship. To rescue them, D'Annebault was obliged to have ship cannon laboriously unloaded and ferried ashore. Maneuvering them across a shingle beach proved difficult, however, and it was not until they were finally in position that he was eventually able to rescue the remainder of his beleaguered troops.[2]

It was a weary, dispirited, and depleted rabble that struggled back across the river to finally make their way back aboard, leaving Pelham and his portmen victorious. The would-be marauders then raised anchor and made sail for France, Admiral Claude D'Annebault having decided that enough was enough; he would risk no more confrontations.

Although as a boy, I roamed the nearby hills, coastal erosion has taken toll of the place and sadly, neither river, fort, nor bridge survive, having long since succumbed to wind and tide. But the bravery of those local men lives on. Nicholas Pelham became a hero, and although he died at the early age of 43, his exploits were commemorated by the following epitaph, inscribed upon his tomb within St. Michael's Church at Lewes.

His valours proof, his manlie vertue's praise
Cannot be marshall'd in this narrow room,

His brave exploits in great king Henry's days,
Among the worthye hath a worthier tombe.
What time the French sought to have sacked Sea-Ford,
This Pelham did RE-PEL-EM back aboard.

A picture of these bowmen of old is slowly emerging: one
of men strong in mind and body, able to act on their own initiative when required by circumstance; men loyal beyond
reproach to both comrade and country, subject occasionally to
misplaced exuberance, but responsive to firm and decisive
leadership. In the course of this chapter, each characteristic
will appear.

They were fortunate in their commanders, these bowmen,
skilled in the art of war as they were, trained almost from birth
to lead. These were men such as Sir Walter Maunay (his name
was anglicized to Manny), commander on land and sea, and a
legend in his own lifetime; Sir Thomas Dagworth, victor at St.
Pol de Leon, and responsible for the capture of French commander Charles de Blois at Roche-Derrien; the Earl of Derby,
whose relief of the Auberoche castle set a new standard in
audacity; and finally John Talbot, whose exploits spanned a
generation and whose death in battle spelled doom for the
English cause. Their faith in the quality of their soldiers was
absolute; here we will briefly assess their skills.

Walter Manny was present at so many successful engage-
ments that it is difficult to single out one of more note
than others. Although he had served with distinction during
Edward III's campaign against the Scots, it is as a commander
during the French wars that he became best known.

By 1337 matters between Philip VI of France and the
English king had reached breaking point. The French king had
confiscated all English territory in France, invaded Gascony,
attacked Jersey, and raided Portsmouth. In response Edward
did what any red-blooded English king would do, he repudiat-
ed his homage to Philip and prepared to regain what he con-

sidered his rightful possessions. Since the pressure of domestic issues militated against the immediate dispatch of a major force to France, operations began with a small expedition led by Sir Walter Manny, Admiral of the North,[3] against the island of Cadzand.[4] The engagement was in every sense successful and a baptism of fire for the English and Welsh archers whose barrage of arrows covered the landing of the men-at-arms.

Once ashore the English drew up in a formation that was to become all too familiar to their enemies: men-at-arms in line, with archers on each flank. The French garrison was no match for Sir Walter and his men, and what little resistance was offered was quickly crushed. Although it was a powerful indication of things to come and Philip's introduction to the war bow, Edward was in no financial position to follow up the advantage, and victory at Cadzand was of little strategic value.

One of the most successful of contemporary military combinations was the coupling of the Earl of Derby with Sir Walter Manny. Each was vastly experienced in all forms of warfare and (the key to victory in so many battles) well able to use their bowmen to maximum advantage.

Now that King Edward was provided with money, in June 1345 Derby was sent with a small army of 500 men-at-arms and 2,000 archers across from England to France, landing at Bayonne. From there he marched his men to Bordeaux, where he was greeted rapturously by the pro-English inhabitants.

News of his arrival reached the French commander, the Count de l'Isle, who promptly began to marshal an array at Bergerac, a town some 12 miles to the east of Bordeaux. Once comfortably in position, and surrounded by an impressive panoply of barons and knights, he awaited Derby's next move with resolution and perhaps just a touch of apprehension. The move was not long in coming. The Earl and Walter Manny set out for Bergerac, camping at the friendly castle of Montcuq while Manny's scouts reconnoitered the area toward the town. Their subsequent report suggested that the French positions were not particularly formidable. Derby and his commanders were lunching early when the scouts returned, and upon hearing the news, Manny is recorded as saying to the Earl of Derby, "My lord, if we were good knights, and well armed, we might this evening partake of the wines of these French lords who are in garrison at Bergerac." The idea obviously appealed to Derby, for with the ready agreement of other commanders, preparations were swiftly made. Quickly arming themselves, men-at-arms and archers mounted and, with banners prominently displayed, set off in good time to meet de l'Isle and his forces.[5]

Bergerac is a town partially surrounded by the river Dordogne and accessed by bridges. The approaches to these were defended by many soldiers, supported by a large group of poorly armed country folk. Taking them would not be easy. As the English drew near, the archers dismounted, braced their bows, and prepared to shoot. The longbow was a weapon new to the foot soldiers defending the road into the town, and the arrows that rained down upon them forced them back against the waiting men-at-arms, severely impeding their movement.

Into this melee the mounted English knights rode pell-mell; with lances in their rests, they dashed into the midst of the French infantry, spearing and riding them down at will. Positioned on either side of the road, the English bowmen kept it clear while the first of the bridges leading into the town's suburbs was stormed and taken, thus allowing the English to enter and consolidate their position.

Predictably, Sir Walter Manny is said to have been the first to penetrate, advancing so far that for a time he was cut off and in great danger. However, Lord de l'Isle, with the remaining French nobles and knights, now retreated into the castle and, once all were in, let down the portcullis.

Derby regrouped his forces and, the following day, drew them up in battle array for a direct assault upon the town and its castle. This proved unsuccessful, and a council of war was held to decide the next move. It was agreed that a better chance of gaining access was from the side fronting the river,

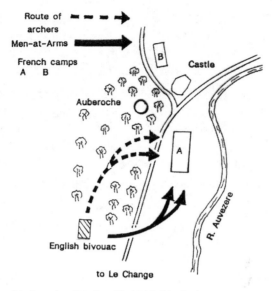

The Battle of Auberoche, October 31, 1345. (*Author*)

and to achieve this, with his commanders' agreement, Derby sent to Bordeaux for a fleet of small boats. Some 60 of these arrived promptly by the following evening. At sunrise the next day, with full complements of men-at-arms and archers, the boats moved forward and the assault began. The river side of the town was protected by a wooden palisade, and it was from behind this that a large company of Genoese crossbowmen, shielded in addition by their pavises, now engaged the English bowmen. These old adversaries kept each other occupied all day, with many casualties on each side, until finally the palisade was broken down. With further resistance now futile, Lord de l'Isle and his commanders left the doomed town and castle precipitately and in disarray and headed to La Réole a few miles distant.

All is not always well, even in the best regulated armies, and Derby was occasionally guilty of a lack of foresight. Following a mature judgment not to attack a particularly strongly defended town, he had retired some distance and had set up camp for the night. About midnight, 200 mounted men-at-arms from the town burst into the camp and, killing many men as they slept, captured the Earl of Oxford, one of Derby's principal commanders, and bore him off in triumph. To their credit, the English, now fully roused, armed and horsed themselves and hotly pursued the departing Gascons, catching up with them outside the town gates. A short battle ensued in which the Gascon knights more than held their own and Derby's men were obliged to retreat to camp licking their wounds and without the missing earl.

In the morning, Derby, with brows well furrowed, we may surmise, held counsel with his remaining commanders. Oxford was too significant a man to leave behind, and, moreover, Derby himself had a reputation to maintain. It was agreed to seek an exchange, and negotiations were begun. A bargain was eventually struck. Two French earls and two viscounts were considered fair trade, and a relieved Oxford was returned to English hands, pride dented and a little worse for wear, but otherwise in excellent fettle.

Once more back to full strength, Derby pressed on, his new goal being the strategically important walled town and castle of Auberoche. A terse message to the inhabitants threatening them with the sword was enough to transfer allegiance from King Philip to King Edward, and, leaving Sir Frank Halle and two knightly comrades in charge with a "sufficient garrison," Derby turned for home. Some may think that castle garrisons were of substantial numbers; after all, castles are large, imposing things. Matters are brought into perspective, however, when we read, for instance, that during this campaign, a group of just 30 archers with an esquire was thought adequate for defense and detached from Derby's force to "sufficiently garrison" and defend the strategically important castle of Langon.

Having sent the Earl of Pembroke to Bergerac and garrisoned other gains, Derby and Manny settled down in Bordeaux. Their stay was to be short, however, for, reenter the Lord de l'Isle. Reasonably certain from the disposition of his troops that Derby had finished campaigning, he sent word to

An incident during the siege of the town of Auberoche, previously taken by the Earl of Derby and Sir Walter Manny. A captured messenger has been catapulted back into the town.

those counts and barons who were on King Philip's side to meet him at Auberoche, where they would besiege and retake the castle.

Governor Halle could know nothing of this, of course; his first intimation of approaching trouble was the sight of thousands upon thousands of French troops mustering in the meadows below the town, followed shortly afterward by the arrival of four huge stone-throwing devices. Once laboriously wheeled into position, these commenced to batter the towers and walls constantly through day and night, doing immense damage and forcing the inhabitants to live permanently at ground level.

Sir Frank was a worried man. His "sufficient garrison" was clearly insufficient to cope with the force facing him. With a bloody and inevitable end in prospect, in desperation, he dispatched a messenger to Derby seeking immediate succor. Sadly, the unfortunate fellow was discovered and catapulted back inside with his letter strung around his neck to arrive dead at Sir Frank's feet. Although the governor could not know this, Derby had a spy within the French camp and knew of the messenger's fate. Anxious to safeguard the castle, he sent to Pembroke at Bergerac for him to join in a relieving expedition and waited impatiently for a day. However, when Pembroke did not arrive, Derby decided to set off alone, with Manny and his own small force of some 400 lances and 600 archers.[6]

They bivouacked that night at Libourne, some six miles from Auberoche, and the next day moved to the outskirts of a wood that reached to the border of the French encampment. Derby ordered horses to be tethered and the men to observe silence. While waiting (in vain as it happened) for Pembroke to appear, he and Walter Manny moved quietly through the trees to the forest edge. There before them they could scarcely believe what they saw. Smoke from cooking fires coiled lazily heavenward, and a hint of garlic lay on the early evening air. The French were preparing a leisurely meal. Men lounged by their tents, crickets chirped in the meadow grass, and all was peace and tranquility. Drinking in the scene, the two commanders returned, and after a brief council of war, it was decided that the opportunity to take advantage of this unreadiness must not be neglected. From his slender force, Derby positioned his 400 lances at a point on the forest's southern edge some 300 yards from the French camp and spaced his 600 archers along the tree line. On command the latter were to volley arrows into the groups of French as they ate, while, in the ensuing confusion, the cavalry would charge full tilt through the tents, slashing and lancing all in their way.

Consider the scene. One moment all is sweetness and light. Dinner is concluded. François has permitted himself a second bouteil de vin, groups of men are chatting together, and the dice are out. Lord de l'Isle is relaxing on his couch, his valets busying themselves clearing away the remnants of his recent meal while, with hands clasped over full bellies, sentries are drowsing at their posts.

Suddenly, from the forest edge comes the sound of trumpets and a mighty roar from six hundred English throats: "Derby and Guyenne." Then wave upon wave of bodkin-pointed battle shafts flash in the early evening sun, hang momentarily in the sky, and descend like a storm on the unprepared French. Before the situation can be fully grasped, thundering down upon them from the south, lances couched, come 400 fully armored, determined men-at-arms.

Knights struggle to put on armor, but surprise is complete. In a matter of minutes, 1,000 English troops have overrun and scattered a force seven times as numerous, capturing or killing the principal French commanders and taking Lord de l'Isle prisoner. From the castle walls, Sir Frank Halle watches in astonishment as a French army of over 7,000 men disintegrates before his eyes. Without further ado, he opens the castle gates and with his small garrison sweeps down and into the fray.

After his men had systematically cleared the last few pockets of resistance, Lord Derby entertained his captives, as protocol required, joining them in their interrupted meal. Meanwhile, apologizing profusely for the delay, a tardy Earl of Pembroke arrived, to be greeted by a jovial Derby who, dismissing a belated offer of assistance, invited his laggard brother-in-arms to help him finish a venison pasty.

Sir Thomas Dagworth was a professional soldier; a captain drawn from the gentry rather than the aristocracy and thus not of noble birth, as were many of his contemporaries, he was among the most able and trusted of Edward III's commanders. Like others of his type, he was charismatic by nature, with achievements that were invariably spectacular, and accomplished, moreover, with the smallest of forces. He was a product of Edward's military revolution, as were Manny, Chandos, and Bentley. This revolution had substituted the nonaristocratic professional soldier, drawn to war for profit and gain, for the gentler-born aristocrat whose allegiance to the king required military service but whose domestic activities demanded his presence at home on his estate.

Dagworth was trusted and idolized by his men for, although he understood and was almost certainly fluent in the Norman French still spoken by the nobility he served, his native language was the English he had learned at his mother's knee. When he addressed his troops, it was in the vernacular tongue. In common with other contemporary commanders, the core of his small armies was always mounted bowmen, and he used them to effect. Thomas Dagworth came to prominence in 1345 under the general command of the Earl of Northampton, another soldier who stamped his authority firmly on the battlefield. In company with Northampton, Dagworth had already met and soundly defeated a French army led by French field commander Charles, Count de Blois, at the village of Cadoret and, after an intensive three-day siege, had helped in the capture of the town and castle of Roche-Derrien.

He was then placed in charge of a flying column of lances and mounted bowmen with orders to impose Edward's rule upon the countryside. This he did successfully, mopping up a number of places until he was finally cornered by Charles de Blois at the town of St. Pol De Leon. Dagworth's small force of little more than 300 lances and 400 archers was vastly outnumbered by the opposition, but it nevertheless repulsed an attack by the first French line. The second line, however, fresh to the conflict, overlapped the flanks of Dagworth's force and closed in for the kill, to be met by the 400 English archers. Coming into their own and taking skilful and deadly aim, they poured in such a stream of arrows at point-blank range that the second line dissolved into chaos. De Blois was defeated for a second time and, with the remnants of his army put to flight, was lucky to escape with his life.

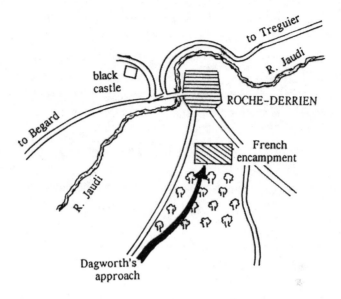

The Battle of Roche-Derrien, June 20, 1347. (*Author*)

This victory at St. Pol de Leon made a big impression among French military circles at the time and added very significantly to the respect accorded Edward's archers at Crécy a year later. If just 400 archers could produce this result, what would 5,000 do? The matter merited serious consideration by the French.[7]

Charles de Blois spent several months recovering from his ordeal, but with the battle of Crécy and its consequences intervening, it was not until the late spring of 1347 that he was once more able to gather sufficient troops to meet the English in open combat. With a cosmopolitan army of Bretons, French, Normans, and other nationalities, it was his determined objective to retake the town and castle of Roche-Derrien, and he set about the task systematically.[8] He first prepared an extensive camp to the south of the town. This was laid out in rather curious fashion—a curious construction like a large village with streets, houses, shops, and even a market. In addition he placed a large force to the west of the town on an old earthwork known locally as the Black Castle.

Important to subsequent events, as we shall see, were his peremptory instructions. This force was under no circumstances to move, except on the express orders of de Blois himself.

Charles de Blois had brought with him nine large siege engines, one of them so huge that it could throw stones of over 300 pounds in weight. With everything in place, bombardment commenced. By lucky (or unlucky) chance, one massive boulder landed directly on the governor's house, effectively demolishing half of it. His lady wife, inside at the time, was so shaken by this that she pleaded for the town to be surrendered. The governor, though, was made of sterner stuff, and although three weeks had elapsed before help was at hand, he resolutely held out. It was Dagworth who was charged with the responsibility for regularizing the situation, and he eventually appeared on the scene with what may have seemed to some a pitifully small relieving force. But these were the cream of Edward's fighting troops; here once more were the 300 lances and the 400 mounted longbowmen who had dealt so effectively with de Blois and his army at St. Pol de Leon. A minimalist by inclination, Dagworth knew well the quality of the men he commanded.

He was well aware through spies and reconnoitering outriders of the disposition of de Blois' camp, and he may also have known of the explicit instructions given by de Blois to those at the Black Castle. He had decided on a typically distinctive course of action. Leading his men personally in the darkness of a June night through the forest to the south of the camp, he arrived at its outskirts just before dawn. No sentries had been posted, since de Blois had believed Dagworth would approach from the west. Having tethered their horses and now on foot, the English emerged from the trees, charged across the intervening space, and entered the camp. Surprise was complete. There was mayhem. Knights were in their tents asleep and, slashing guy ropes and demolishing tents as they went, the attackers carried all before them.

A period etching showing English archers against the French. (*Author*)

Although the center of the camp fell without any real opposition, the outlying areas remained untouched, and it was from there that a counterattack was prepared. This was successfully repelled, as was a second; but it was still dark, and in the poor light a third, better-organized than the previous two, proved more difficult to withstand. The English, still outnumbered, were, despite the ferocity of their initial impact, forced to give ground. In one melee, Dagworth himself, fighting for his life, was wounded and briefly captured. A prompt counterattack rescued him, however and he fought on.

Despite their initial advantage, things were not looking at all well for the small English force. With some degree of discipline now imposed, the French were fighting back strongly and Dagworth's back was to the wall. However, with the arrival of dawn, peering through a steadily improving light, the governor was able to size up the situation. Realizing the predicament that the relieving force was in, he opened the town gates and dispatched the few hundred men that he could spare from his garrison. These proved enough for Dagworth to regain the initiative, and with the tide now against them, the French gave way and fled the field.[9]

Charles de Blois, meanwhile, unable to don his armor in the confusion, had been fighting furiously. Wounded in several places and bleeding profusely, he was captured and sent to England where he convalesced to a full recovery in the Tower of London. History records, for no apparent reason, that en route he was serenaded by eight guitar players. One trusts their skills were such that his mind was relieved of other matters.

Dagworth's subsequent dispatch to his king is a masterpiece of terse understatement.

> Very dear and much honoured lord, you will wish to know the news from Brittany, that Sir Charles de Blois had besieged the town and castle of La Roche-Derrien and had in his company 1,200 men at arms, properly speaking, knights and esquires, and 600 other men at arms and 600 archers of the country, and 2,000 crossbowmen, and men of the commons whose number I do not know. This Sir Charles had caused great entranchments to be made around his position, and outside his fortifications he had caused all manner of ditches and hedges to be filled or razed for half a league's breadth around him, so my archers could not find an advantage over him and his men, but had in the end perforce to fight in open fields. And he and his people knew of my coming against them through their spies, and they were collected and in arms all the night. And we came against them, my companions and I on the twentieth day of June, in the hours before dawn and by the Grace of God the affair went in such a way that he lost the field and was entirely defeated. God be praised therefore. And I had in my company around 300 men at arms and 400 archers.

Dagworth's dispatch might seem contrary to another account, but it would have been to his credit perhaps to embellish a little. Despite his popularity with his men, and his undoubted loyalty to his king, Dagworth may have been a volatile fellow. He was murdered in an ambush following a heated quarrel with an erstwhile ally of the king, Raoul de Caours, in 1350. Thus Edward and England lost one of their finest fighting captains.

The victory at Roche-Derrien had the saddest possible outcome. After the victorious Dagworth had returned to England and the celebrations had died away, the French retook the town, slaughtering all the inhabitants. The brave garrison, allowed to leave without harm, was subsequently massacred to a man within a neighboring town.

We have seen how success could be achieved against odds by skilful, if unusual, tactics. It is now time to look at two battles in which faulty decisions led to disaster.

With weak King Henry VI enthroned, England's hold upon its French and Norman possessions was tenuous in the extreme. Charles VII of France, a strong and capable ruler, had reorganized his forces and now had an army that if not the equal of that of England, was at least disciplined. Estimates of its strength varied around 12,000 mounted lances, supported by crossbowmen and archers whose weapons differed little from those of the English goddams.

With English-held territory in Normandy diminishing almost by the day as Charles advanced, something had to be done by Henry, and fast, before the prizes so hardly won by his father slipped away. The principal city of Rouen had fallen, by treaty not by force, but a consequence had been the loss of Lord John Talbot as hostage. The terms of his subsequent release required that he would never again bear arms against Charles—terms that Talbot, ever the honorable man, observed until the last.

Awake at last to the real possibility of losing even a foothold in Normandy, a vacillating English government came to its senses, and an army was raised. With its natural leader, Talbot, now unavailable, Sir Thomas Kyriell was put in charge. Kyriell was a militarily competent, although independently minded, tactician with, as it proved, a penchant for disregarding orders when they did not suit his personal ambition. His force was small, just over 2,500 men in all, and when it eventually set sail after an enforced stay of several months in Portsmouth, Kyriell had instructions to march directly to Bayeux.

Sir Thomas was very much his own man, however. Disregarding his directive, after he had cajoled a reluctant Duke of Somerset, governor of Normandy, to provide him with additional troops and by scraping around various garrisons, with his force now grown to some 4,000 strong, he evidently felt able to indulge in some extramural activity. Thus it was that en route to Bayeux, he besieged and took the town of Valognes, and with this success to his credit, he resumed his leisurely march toward Bayeux.

Meanwhile, dogging his footsteps and never far behind was a substantial French force of some 3,000 men led by the young and impetuous Comte de Clermont, while approaching him from a different direction was a second and more potent threat, a column of 2,000 men led by the formidable Constable de Rochemont, a man with much experience of English tactical warfare. Each independently posed a threat to Kyriell, although if met separately, they were a threat with which he could probably have dealt. However, if the two columns joined, then matters would be very different. Although he was well aware of Clermont's position and was confident of success against him, events suggest that while he would have had men out scouting, Kyriell may not have known of de Rochemont's column until too late.

He left Valognes unhurriedly on April 12 and crossed the wide but shallow tidal river Vire without incident. He was particularly vulnerable at this point, but Clermont was well aware of the fighting qualities of the English when in defensive mode and made no move against him. Once safely across, Kyriell acted strangely. Instead of pressing on to Bayeux as he had been instructed, he once more acted on his own initiative. He rested his men amid the pleasant orchards and gardens of the

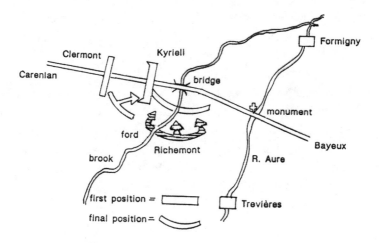

The Battle of Formigny, April 15, 1450. (*Author*)

little village of Formigny while sending an officer and a party of men to Bayeux some ten miles distant. The purpose is unknown, but perhaps it was to seek approval for a further military adventure before reaching his goal.

Meanwhile, Clermont had not been idle. Knowing of de Rochemont's force, he had made contact and had suggested a joint attack on Kyriell. With this agreement secured, he then pressed forward until eventually the English force came into view. It is difficult at this stage to determine the French battle plan, but if events had unfolded as they had been designed to do, then it was both effective and masterly.

Engagement with Clermont was now imminent, and Kyriell arranged his battle lines. Although his army was unbalanced, with a preponderance of lightly armed archers and just 800 dismounted men-at-arms as a nucleus, he felt confident of victory. His flank archers occupied themselves as usual with positioning stakes and digging potholes to embarrass the cavalry, and once this was done, the English waited for an attack.[10]

It came in the form of a cavalry charge and was dealt with comprehensively by the archers, who then turned their attention to the advancing infantry, as a French account says, "impetuously," and this would accord with our knowledge of Clermont himself. Faced with volleys of arrows at point-blank range, this attack also disintegrated.

Other attacks were indecisive, and for a while there was stalemate. However, matters then took a rather ominous turn. Clermont had brought with him two large culverins, and these now came into play. For a time these successfully blasted their shots into the flank archers. Galled by this, in desperation, the archers broke ranks and charged; they killed the gunners and began to haul the guns back to the English lines. However, while so occupied, the French attacked again; with his archers in disarray, Kyriell was in some difficulty. He either could not, or would not, support them, and they were severely mauled by the better-armed French men-at-arms.

Despite this setback, Kyriell was having the better of the fighting, and Clermont was within an ace of fleeing the field when Richemont arrived on the scene. Following a quick consultation, Richemont agreed to attack Kyriell's left flank while Clermont, with what forces he could muster, would resume his attack on the right.

Matters were now grim. In short order Kyriell had to rearrange his troops to meet threats from either flank, and it is a credit to his command skill and the innate discipline of his men that he swung his battle line almost to a right angle and, pivoting around a bridge over a brook, did his best to beat off a combined attack.

It is unlikely that Kyriell's left flank archers had sufficient time to consolidate and protect their positions with stakes and potholes against a cavalry charge while his remaining men-at-arms fought doggedly against hugely greater odds and increasingly successful attacks. Finally his small army lost all cohesion and disintegrated into pockets of fiercely contested resistance. One small group of men-at-arms made a fighting retreat and gained Bayeux, as did another group of archers. Kyriell himself was captured and made prisoner.

To their undying glory, one party of 500 English bowmen fought stubbornly on amid the trees and bushes of an apple orchard by the brook side, selling their lives dearly and dying to the last man. We do not know the names of these yeomen archers, but in the true spirit of an English soldier, they fought doggedly and died with bravery. It is to our discredit that beyond the occasional mention in stuffy books of history, their gallantry has gone unremarked across the years. How well it would be if half a millennium later a lasting memorial could be raised to their heroism.

With Formigny, the writing was on the wall. Normandy was as good as lost. At Castillon, two years later, a war that in desultory fashion had spanned five reigns was brought ignominiously to an end.

Fought in October 1453, the battle of Castillon was marked by the death of Sir John Talbot, Earl of Shrewsbury. Believed to be almost 80 years old at the time of his death, Talbot was not just the senior military commander but the most celebrated tactician of his day. Although the conditions of his release from French capture required that he did not again take up arms against them, Henry VI had few qualms about his choice as a leader of a relieving army into France.

The circumstances were a little unusual. With the English defeat at Formigny, Normandy had reverted to French control, a circumstance not at all to the liking of wine traders in the strongly pro-English port of Bordeaux. In 1452 a delegation of leading Burgesses crossed the Channel in secret to plead with Henry for help to restore the status quo, and with a substantial element of his economy under threat, Henry agreed. Accordingly a small army of 3,000 archers and men-at-arms was put together under Talbot's command and, arriving at Bordeaux, had the desired effect. The French garrison beat a hasty retreat, and Talbot settled in to decide his future tactics.

All was well for a while, the lucrative wine trade began again, and Talbot was joined by his son, Lord de Lisle, with a further contingent of 3,000 men. However, Charles of France was not disposed to let things lie. Bordeaux was his—he would regain it come what may, and he began to assemble a huge army. Well aware of what havoc even a small English force could cause to one vastly superior in size, Charles prepared not one army, but three, and arranged for them to approach Bordeaux from three separate directions. Once together they would be joined by a reserve force, commanded personally by the king, and all would be set, either for a battle between field armies or a siege.

Talbot was a shrewd tactician, however and, knowing through spies of Charles' plans, had decided his own strategy. He would wait at Bordeaux until the first army arrived, then engage and defeat it before regrouping in readiness to deal with the second, and finally the third. Had this plan been operable, it is probable that it would have succeeded, Talbot and de Lisle's combined forces of 6,000 men being adequate to deal with a French army of even double that size. However, lying in the path of Charles advancing army was the small walled town of Castillon. The burgesses were aware of Talbot's plan but were unhappy to be thrown to the wolves for the greater good of Bordeaux and demanded his support. Talbot deliberated, but the vociferous complaints of town elders reluctantly persuaded Talbot to abandon his original intention and depart to defend their town. The French force threatening Castillon was considerable; it included, in addition to between 7,000 and 10,000 archers and lances, a large number of gunners and guns. In overall command was Jean Bureau. Not only was Bureau a clever tactical commander, he had made artillery his particular concern, and it was these that formed his formidable first line of defense. It seems unlikely that Talbot was aware of the strength of the French position.

Bureau had constructed an encampment to the east of the town, its rear protected by the river Lidoire, its front facing the river Dordogne. Around the perimeter of a high embankment he had positioned his cannon, while to protect his western flank and guard a bridge across the Lidoire he had placed a strong force of archers in the priory of St. Laurent. In the

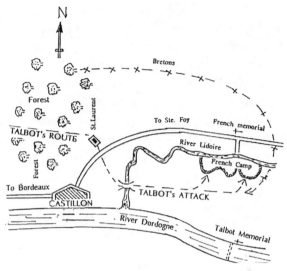

The Battle of Castillon, October 1453. (*Author*)

woods to the north of his camp he had located a substantial force of Bretons. Only the barest detail of these arrangements appear to have been known to Talbot, although Bureau was a fearsome opponent and his knowledge and use of artillery was well known. Had he been aware of the strength of Bureau's position, Talbot may have acted differently. However, without delay he assembled a mounted force of 500 lances and 800 archers as an advance guard, leading them himself, and leaving his foot soldiers to join him when they could, while Bureau, learning from scouts of Talbot's intention to support Castillon, sat back to await events, secure behind his guns.

They were not long in coming. Talbot moved swiftly through the forest, his journey uninterrupted by the Breton force. He arrived at the priory before dawn, and the unhappy archers within, many still in their beds, stood little chance. A number escaped across the bridge however and made their way to Bureau's encampment. All was going well for Talbot so far. He had just settled down to an early breakfast when a panting messenger arrived to report that men on horseback had been seen galloping away from the encampment. Therein lay a problem. If Bureau was moving away, then tactically Talbot had lost the initiative. He was isolated from his power base at Bordeaux, and liable to attack from not just one, but three armies. Hurriedly he marshaled his men to try to intercept Bureau and bring him to battle. Moving across the bridge and en route to the encampment, however, the true position was revealed. The horsemen seen had been valets moving the horses away from the encampment to make way for the incoming priory archers and possibly the Bretons. Bureau was not only in position but was leveling his guns.

Talbot was in a dilemma. His back was now to the fast-flowing River Dordogne, and barely half of his small force was with him. However, he was not prepared to retreat. Although outnumbered six to one, he knew the quality of his men; if they could only surmount the embankment, he was convinced of their superiority once inside. Dismounting his troops, Talbot, riding a white palfrey, his white hair covered by a purple velvet cap, deployed them around the perimeter of the encampment and, when they were in position, gave the order to strike. To shouts of "Saint George and Talbot" the attack began.[11]

Against a devastating barrage from the French guns, men tried vainly to mount the sheer sides of the 10-foot-high parapet. The task proved virtually impossible, although by now small numbers of Talbot's foot soldiers were arriving, and they hurled themselves into the fight. Inching his way against intense opposition, Sir Thomas Evringham, a commander under Talbot, succeeded in reaching the top and planting a banner but was instantly killed by point-blank cannon fire.

Despite this almost insuperable obstacle, the outcome was finely balanced for a time. However, the Breton force then arrived from the woods. Conspicuously absent from the initial action but sensing the English in difficulties and wishing to be there at the kill, they joined in. With his right flank now under threat, Talbot withdrew part of his attacking force to deal with the new situation, leaving the area by the encampment gate weak. Seeing this, Bureau mounted a counterattack from within and drove the English back toward the Dordogne.

Talbot made a fighting retreat, enabling many of his men to ford the river, but pressure from the French proved too much, and the defensive line broke. It was now that Talbot suffered his own nemesis. A stray cannon ball glanced off the side of his palfrey, which fell, trapping him by the leg beneath it. As he struggled to get clear, his son and his personal guard stood over him in protection, but they were overwhelmed and killed. Although Talbot was now upright and defending himself ably with a sword, he was struck on his unprotected skull by a French battleaxe and fell dead. Thus ended the life of one of the most charismatic and respected English commanders, and with him went the last hopes of English rule in France. Castillon fell, and Gascony and Bordeaux were lost. The Hundred Years' War had reached its ignominious end.

John Talbot's military feats are the stuff of which legend is made. His ingenuity and tactical military skills made him one of the most feared of English commanders at set-piece battle and ambush alike. His body rests in sacred peace within the parish church at Whitchurch, Shropshire.

Had Kyriell obeyed his instructions and not chosen to fight at Formigny and had Talbot held to his original plan, it is arguable that things may have evolved differently. But history is full of "if onlys" and "might have beens"; what is gone is gone, and we are left with the here and now!

Notes and References for Further Reading

Chapter 1

1. A. Curry, *The Battle of Agincourt, Sources and Interpretations* (Woodbridge: 2000). Specifically, "The Brut," Cambridge University Library: Ms Kk 1.12.

2. Ibid. Specifically, "Vita et Gesta Henrici Quinti," ch. 27.

3. Ibid.

4. Ibid. *Translated from the Chronicles of (Jean) Waurin (vol. 1) and (Jean) Le Fàvre (vol. 3) and the Chronicle of Enguerran de Monstrelet, vol. 2.*

5. Ibid. *Chronique normande de Pierre Cochon,* ch. 30.

6. See n. 4, ch. 148.

7. See n. 2.

8. See n. 6.

9. H. D. H. Soar [Greybeard, pseud.], "Some Thoughts on Nestroque, An Agincourt Battle Command," *Journal of the Society of Archer Antiquaries* 44, no. 10 (2001). See n. 4.

10. The penetrative power of an arrow alters exponentially with the apogee of its ballistic curve; that is, the point at which velocity has decayed sufficiently for gravity to take charge. The variable is the angle at which the arrow is shot, the optimum angle for distance being between 42° and 45°. The circumstance is important in connection with the effectiveness of the arrow storm. Experiment by specialist war bow archer Mark Stretton has been conducted to assess the potential penetration of a war arrow at various distances. The results appear to show that having regard to the angle at which the arrow is discharged, penetration is as great at 220 yards as at 60 yards and 120 yards, while it is relatively less between 160 yards and 180 yards. Variation of penetrations within a tightly packed multi-foam nine inch thick target ranged between 9 inches at point blank range, through 7 1/4 inches at 60 yards, 8 1/2 inches at 80 yards, 8 1/4 inches at 100 yards, 7 3/4 inches at 120 yard, 6 5/8 inches at 140 yards, 6 1/8 inches at 160 yards, 6 inches at 180 yards, then 7 6/8 inches at

200 yards, and 7 3/8 inches at 220 yards. The arrow used weighed 72 grams and was armed with a London Museum Type 10 short bodkin. It was shot from a self-yew war bow replica made to Mary Rose Trust specifications of 144 pounds draw weight.

The revealing conclusion would appear to be that the arrow has least penetrative effect between 140 and 180 yards. Beyond that distance the apogee of the ballistic curve following the acute angle of shot is sufficient to allow for a significant gravitational effect upon velocity as the arrow approaches earth. It has of course to be said that penetration is a matter of degree. I am indebted to Mark Stretton for permission to mention the above.

11. See www.paintedchurch.org. I am indebted to Anne Marshall, Associate Lecturer, The Open University (UK) for permission to utilize her research.

12. H. Stein, *Archers d'Autrefois: Archers d'Aujourd'hui* (Paris: Longuet, 1925), app. vii, ch. 1eme.

13. C. J. Longman, H. Walrond, et al., *The Badminton Library Archery* (London: Longman's Green & Co., 1894), ch. VIII.

14. Ibid.

15. Ibid.

16. Anno 6 H. VIII cap. 2.

17. Eliz Anno 8. See also Megson, *Such Goodly Company* (Privately published: 1993), ch. 1, note 11.

18. C. S. Knighton and D. Loades, *Letters from the Mary Rose* (Sutton: Stroud, Glos. 2002).

19. Dr. M. Rule, *The Mary Rose* (London: Book Club Associates 1982).

20. Bristol Record Society, *The Great Red Book of Bristowe*. Ordinances (1479) of the bowyers and fletchers of Bristowe.

21. *Rules of the British Long-Bow Society, Organisation—Tackle*, 4th ed. (2001).

22. C. N. Hickman, F. Nagler, and P. E. Klopsteg, *Archery, the Technical Side* (National Field Archery Association, Redlands, California 1947).

23. *Mary Rose Archaeological Report, Part Three* (The Mary Rose Trust, in print).

24. R. Ascham, *Toxophilus, the Schole or Partitions of Shotinge* (London: 1544).

25. See n. 12. Appendix vii, ch. 3ieme.

26. *Exeter Riddle Book* (Anglo-Saxon Books: Norfolk, 2002).

27. J. Porter, *Beowulf, Text and Translation* (Anglo-Saxon Books: Norfolk, 2000), lines 3114–3119.

28. S. Pollington, *The English Warrior from Earliest Times until 1066* (Anglo-Saxon Books: Norfolk, 2002).

29. G. Rausing, *The Bow, Some Notes on its Origin and Development* (Manchester: Manchester Museum, 1997).

30. A. A. MacGregor, *Over the Seas to Skye* (Edinburgh: W & R Chambers 1926). The story of Donald the Black.

31. By Statute of James I of Scotland, 1424, "All men busk them to be archers fra they be twelve zeir [year] of age, and that in ilk ten poundis worthe of lande, their be made bow markes, and specialle near paroche kirkes, quhairin upon halie days men may cum and at the least shute thrise about and have usage of archerie."

32. C. E. Whitelaw, *Scottish Arms Makers* (London: Arms & Armour Press, n.d.).

33. G. Davies, *Early Stuarts 1603–1660* (Oxford: Oxford History of England, 1959).

34. *To prove the Necessitie and Excellence of the use of Archerie* (London: Richard John 1596). A treatise produced in support of "decaied" bowyers whose trade had diminished through the nonobservance of archery practice.

35. J. B. Black, *The Reign of Elizabeth 1558–1603* (Oxford: Oxford History of England, 1959).

Chapter 2

1. The length of the Japanese *yumi* has been stabilized at 2.3 meters. See Jackson S. Morisawa, *The Secret of the Target* (New York: Routledge & Kegan Paul, 1984.) Bows of the tribes in the Brazilian province of Xingu average 2.47 meters. See E. G. Heath and Vilma Chiara, *Brazilian Indian Archery* (Manchester: Simon Archery Foundation, 1977).

2. R. Ascham, *Toxophilus.*

3. W. Middilton, *The Boke for a Justice of Peace, Never so well and Dylygently Set Forthe* (London: 1544; reprinted Oxford University Press 1921). See also B. H. Putnam, *Early Treatises on the Practice of the Justices of the Peace in the Fifteenth and Sixteenth Centuries* (Oxford Studies in Social and Legal History VII)

4. Sir J. Smythe, *Certain Discourses Military Concerning the Forms and Effects of Divers Forms of Weapons, and Chiefly of the Mosquet, the Caliver, and the Long Bow. As Also of the Great Sufficiencie,*

Excellent and Wonderful Effects of Archers (London: 1593; facsimile Cornell University Press 1964).

5. R. S., *A Briefe Treatise to Proove the Necessitie and Excellence of the use of Archerie* (London: 1596).

6. J. Bartlet, *A New Invention of Shooting Fire Shafts in Long-Bowes, Wherein Besides the Manner of Making Them, There Is Contained a Briefe Discourse of the Usefulnesse of Them in Our Modern Warres, by Sea and Land. Published by a true Patriot for the Common Good of His Native Countrey of England* (London: 1628).

7. R. Shotterel and T. D'Urfey, "Archerie Reviv'd, or the Bow-Man's Excellence, an Heroic Poem, Being a Description of the Use and Noble Vertues of the Long-Bow, etc. . . ." (London: 1676).

8. S. Rose (ed.), "The Navy of the Lancastrian Kings," *Accounts and Inventories of William Soper, Keeper of the King's Ships 1422–1427* (London: Navy Records Society, 1980).

9. J. Ritson, *Robin Hood, Poems, Songs, and Ballads* (London: Ballantyne & Hanson 1785, 1885). "The Noble Fisherman," (Robin Hood's Preferment).

10. Anon. Elizabethan ballad, retouched by Thomas Percy, "Sir Andrew Barton, Knight." May be found conveniently in K. Hare, *The Archer's Chronicle* (London: 1929).

11. An arrangement that applied as recently as 1982 during Britain's Falklands conflict when S.T.U.F.T (ships taken up from trade) provided much of the support for the British battle fleet.

12. In conversation with me, Cmdr. Peter Whitlock Royal Navy, lately Executive Officer on board H.M.S. *Victory*, expressed his personal, if unkind, opinion that after her final refit, the warship *Mary Rose* would have had all the handling characteristic of a wet haystack!

13. R. Galloway, *Archery International Magazine* 2, no. 9, (Feb./Mar. 1982), p. 40.

14. C. Cruikshank, *Henry VIII and the Invasion of France* (Stroud, Glos.: Sutton 1990).

15. S. Pope, *Bows and Arrows* (Berkeley, California: University of California Press 1923).

16. R. Ascham, *Toxophilus.*

17. Ibid.

18. H. Hartzell, *The Yew Tree—a Thousand Whispers* (Cottage Grove, Oregon: Hulogosi Communications 1990). "Whether the first churches were built near yew trees because the early Christians recognised them as holy from their experiences on the Continent, or whether the trees were actual places of pagan worship, the church-

yard, 'God's Acre' was built around them and they became participants in the lives and deaths of parishioners."

19. See ch. 1, n. 13. See also H. Riesch, "Yew Exploitation and Long
Bow Trade in the 16th Century," *Journal of the Society of Archer
Antiquaries* (1996).

20. R. Williamson, *The Great Yew Forest*, (London: Macmillan
1978), quote. See also n. 17.

21. J. Stowe, *A Survey of London Written in the Year 1598*, facsimile
(Stroud, Glos.: Sutton 1994).

22. Ibid.

23. T. Roberts, *The English Bowman* (London: C. V., 1802). It may
also be noted that a yew bow backed with ash and dated 1650 is held
by the Royal Company of Archers in Archer's Hall, Edinburgh. It is
said originally to have belonged to a Mr. Bisset of Lessendrum,
Aberdeenshire. A contemporary Aberdeen bowmaker (bowyer) was
Thomas Mayen.

24. Commissions of array involving the mustering of bowmen included one for Leicestershire in June 1642, which required the array and
training (sic) of bowmen armed "but with bows and arrows," together with "armed men," and "men-at-arms." Each was to be provided
with his own weapons. Carlyle, Cromwells's Letters & Speeches, vol.
1 (London: Carlyle 1846), p. 153. Likewise, in November 1643, the
Earl of Essex issued a precept for raising a company of archers in
London for the "service of the king and parliament."

25. A. Barfoot, *Everyday Costumes in Britain* (London: Batsford
1961).

26. J. Duff, *Bows and Arrows* (New York: Macmillan 1927).

27. Dr. A. Hildred, Research Director and General Editor, *Mary Rose
Archaeological Report, Part Three* (The Mary Rose Trust, in print).

28. I am indebted to the National Museum of Ireland, Dublin, for
permission to reproduce a photograph and summarize dimensions of
this most interesting weapon.

29. H. D. H. Soar, "Bowyers and Fletchers of Bristow," *Journal of the
Society of Archer Antiquaries* (1989). Preceding the ordinances by
which the guild was to be governed was the following:

Trustinge the saide Bowyers and flechers hereafter to Kepe and con-
tynue in good and honnest rule with the saide hoopers And to be
Contrybutoryes in alle ordenary charges with the saide hoopers
accordinge their forsaide Peticioun Haue graunted them this Article
folouyng yerely to be duely observed and executid for the better Rule
of the saide Craffte and common wele of alle this towne. Yevin

[given] in the Guildehall of Bristwe forsaide the xixth. Day of May the yere of the Reign of Kyng Edward the 111jth [Fourth].

30. J. Duff, *Bows and Arrows* provided the basis of this fictional account.

31. See n. 28.

32. Mr. Bert Oram was a farmer and a countryman steeped in country lore. An expert longbow archer and National British longbow champion, he regularly shot with a yew bow. He made it a condition of his will that he should not be laid to rest near the yew tree in his native churchyard. His request was honored, and his grave lies a suitable distance from the church yew.

Chapter 3

1. W. Shakespeare, *King Lear*, Act IV, Scene III.

2. J. Ritson, *Robin Hood, Poems, Songs, and Ballads*, "Robyn Hode and the Potter" Second Fitte, v. 20.

3. Sir. J. Smythe, *Certain Discourses Military*.

4. T. Roberts, *The English Bowman, or Tracts on Archery* (London: Privately Published 1801).

5. W. Shakespeare, *King Richard III*, Act V, Scene III.

6. R. Ascham, *Toxophilus*.

7. See n. 4.

8. J. Gendall, "The Arundel Archive of Arrows and Arrowheds," *Journal of the Society of Archer Antiquaries* (2001).

9. A. G. Credland, "The Longbow in the 16th and 17th Centuries," *Journal of the Society of Archer Antiquaries* (1989). See extract from R. Holmes, *Academy of Armory* part 1 (Chester 1688) included therein.

10. J. Davies, "Military Archery and the Inventory of King Henry VIII," *Journal of the Society of Archer Antiquaries* (2001).

11. H. Stein, Archers d'Autrefois et Archers d'Aujourd'hui, appendix V.

12. Aspen wood to be used for arrows only and not for pattens (clogs). 4 HV. 1416. Also "Aspen that is not fit for arrows may be used for pattens." 12 Edw. IV. 1473.

13. I am indebted to colleague Janet Gendall for drawing this to my attention.

14. See n. 11

15. J. Gerard, *The Herball or Generall Historie of Plants* (London: 1597).

16. Today, "fistmele" is regarded as the distance between closed fist and outstretched thumb; this is however correctly the definition of shaftment. Source: *Oxford English Dictionary*.

17. Personal correspondence with Adrian Morgan, archery historian and experimenting fletcher.

18. Discussion with Charles Warmingham, now deceased. Head Marker and Bowyer/Fletcher to the archery society The Woodmen of Arden 1785.

19. Private correspondence during 1935 in my possession. Each was a member of the Royal Naval College, Greenwich. B. P. Haigh was concerned with aerodynamics.

20. J. D. Latham, and Lt. Cmdr. W. F. Paterson, RN, *Saracen Archery* (London: Holland Press 1970).

21. R. Ascham, *Toxophilus*.

12. By kind permission of Bristol City Records Dept.

23. See n. 9.

Chapter 4

1. The term knight derives for the Anglo-Saxon "cniht," a youth, a servant, or the junior and subservient member of a guild, or a junior warrior. By the fourteenth century however it had gained in status and although ordinary men could be knighted on the battlefield for prowess (carrying the financial penalties associated with advancing prestige!) the title was largely associated with respected men of class and breeding. From its humble early beginnings it has advanced through chivalric military association to become today's honored status.

2. There is an enigma concerning Malemort. In 1228 he was assisted by William the Smith, who was to be paid 6 pence a day, and William the Fletcher, who received 4 pence. John Malemort received 4 pence a day. In 1229 there was a pay raise of 2 1/2 pence a day and 1 1/2 pence a day for the fletcher. By 1232, however, while Malemort received his recorded 10 1/2 pence, there is no mention of the others. The suggestion is that either Malemort did it all himself, which seems unlikely, or that from the 10 1/2 pence, he employed and paid a journeyman fletcher and perhaps an apprentice, neither of whom are named.

3. See Dr. A. Webb, "John Malemort—King Quarreler," *Journal of the Society of Archer Antiquaries* (Part one, 1988; part two, 1989).

Chapter 6

1. J. E. Oxley, *The Fletchers and Longbowstringmakers of London* (London: Unwins 1968). See part two, "A History of the Ancient Company of Longbowstringmakers," chapter I.

2. C. Cruikshank, *Henry VIII and the Invasion of France.*

3. Dr. M. Rule, *The Mary Rose—the Excavation and Raising of Henry VIII's Flagship* (London: Book Club Associates 1982).

4. R. Ascham, *Toxophilus.*

5. E. B. and J. J., *Ayme for Finsburie Archers—or an Alphabetical Table of the Names of Everie Mark Within the Same Fields* (London: 1601), modern facsimile by University Microfilms. Note: Neither mark appears in the 1628 version.

6. See n. 1.

7. See ch. 3, n. 9.

8. H. D. H. Soar, "The Bowyers and Fletchers of Bristow."

9. See n. 4.

10. See n. 1.

11. Inventory of Armories of Henry VIII. P. 106. Item 4020. Public Record Office, Kew.

12. In past times, the ancient family of Giselencke of Belgium enjoyed an unrivaled reputation for the manufacture of bowstrings and horn nocks.

13. From my collection.

14. Sir. J. Smythe, *Certain Discourses Military.*

15. R. Holinshed, Holinshed's Chronicles of England, Scotland and Ireland 1586–1587. Mention is made of "certain persons also were appointed to remove the stakes, as by the movement of archers occasion and time should require." To my knowledge, this is the only reference to this service.

16. "Ordnance, Artillery, and Munitions for War," vol. III, *Mary Rose Archaeological Report, Part Three* (The Mary Rose Trust, in print).

17. Mention of these categories is made within a contemporary document "The Army Against France." I am indebted to Dr. Ann Stirland for this information. Capt. Richard Oliver-Bellasis, Royal Navy, was a keen archer who was elected to membership of the Woodmen of Arden in 1922.

18. A possible interpretation is "Virgo Ante Partum Et Post Partum Permanet Amen." I am indebted to Abbot Watkin and Dom: Philip Jebb, MA, of Downside Abbey School for their helpful suggestion.

19. The assistance of Dr. Mark Knapman, Dept. of Archaeology & Numismatics, Cathays Park, Cardiff, and Dr. Kate Hunter of the Newport Museum and Art Gallery is gratefully acknowledged, enabling a replica bracer to be made by cordwainer Wolfgang Bartl.

20. May be viewed at Somerset County Museum, Taunton. Accession No. 314. Dig No. 74.

21. Museum of London. Accession No. A.26607.

22. G. Egan and E. Pritchard, *Medieval finds from Excavations in London: 3. Dress Accessories c. 1150–1450. Strap Loops.* (London: Museum of London Dress Accessories Publication 1991) P. 229 Fig. 43.

23. *Southend upon Sea Borough Council.* Southend Museum, Human History Division.

24. See n. 4.

25. Hereford City Museum.

26. *Inventory.*

27. *Inventory.*

28. H. Stein, *Archers d'Autrefois et Archers d'Aujourd'hui,* appendix V.

29. Bodelian Library, Oxford. MS.TOP.Gen. e.70 fo. 24p.

30. Bristol Central Reference Library. Papers relevant to the Port of Bristowe. Ship Trinitye Smith. Manifest.

31. A. G. Credland, "The Medieval War Arrow," *Journal of the Society of Archer Antiquaries* (1982). Plate 1 "Martyrdom of St. Sebastien," anon. ca. 1560.

32. C. Bartlett, and G. Embleton, "The English Archer c. 1300–1500" (2) *Military Illustrated—Past and Present* 2 (Aug./Sept. 1986), p. 19.

33. Dr. M. Rule, *Excavation and Raising of Henry VIII's Flagship.*

34. See n. 28.

35. See n. 4.

36. See n. 28.

Chapter 7

1. S. Pollington, *The English Warrior from Earliest Times till 1066* (Norfolk: Anglo-Saxon Books, 2002). See reference in "Call to Arms" to a discovery in Arum, West Frisia.

2. C. W. Hollister, *Anglo Saxon Military Institutions* (Oxford: Clarendon Press 1962).

3. See n. 1, appendix iii.

4. Ibid. Line 255.

5. Ibid. Line 155.

6. Ibid. Lines 265–272, inclusive.

7. See n. 1.

8. By writ of Henry III, 1252. See also Stubbs Select Charters, p. 153. Excused from mustering they may have been, but some of the great and good were required to observe conditions of sergeanty, a personal service to the king and thus a form of muster, which were little short of ludicrous. For example, Brienston in the county of Dorset was held in "grand sergeanty" on condition that the tenant should supply a man to go before the king's army when he made war in either Scotland or Wales, for 40 days, barefoot and bareheaded, in his shirt and linen drawers, holding a bow in one hand and an arrow without feathers in the other. The purpose of this (and one presumes there to have been one) is not explained.

9. Rev. W. Hudson, *Norwich Militia in the Fourteenth Century Norfolk Archaeology* Vol. 14. (Norfolk: Norfolk and Norwich Archaeology Society 1901).

10. A fully armed (armored) man would wear a bacinet with aventail on his head and a pisan to cover his neck. His body armor might vary but in general was of two parts. A doublet of leather, or a quilted and stitched purpoint , or an acheton . Over this went a plat, or breast-plate, front and back. Instead of plates, alternatively one could have a hauberk, or haubergeon of mail (also possibly a paunce de maille, or shirt of mail between doublet and plate). His arms were protected by brassards or avantbras from wrist to elbow and a rerebras from elbow to shoulder, either of mail or steel. Elbow pieces, cotes de fer, or gauntlets were of mail or plate. A surcoat was worn over the armor, not for defense, although it prevented the armor from shining in the sun, but as a means for distinctive ornament. The Norwich color was red.

11. There appears to have been little significant difference between a fully armed, and a half-armed man. The latter may have lacked a pisan, however, and perhaps some other of the finer touches were omitted.

12. J. Strutt, *Sports and Pastimes of the People of England* (London: R. Griffiths & Co. 1838).

13. A bipennis, or double-headed axe, having one face vertical and the other horizontal.

14. Without overstressing matters, the few old English poems devoted

to women emphasize their strength of character and refer to them in terms similar to those used to describe warriors: elle riste—courageous—and collenferh e—bold in spirit. If called upon by circumstance to do so, Petronella may well have been as capable in battle as many of the men.

15. It is impossible to be exact about the dates of the Robin Hood and the Adam Bell gestes. It would seem obvious that they existed in oral form before being printed in the mid-fifteenth century, and some think—myself among them—that the archery references suggest a period when the heavier bow was coming into use; that is, approximately the mid-thirteenth or early fourteenth century. For views on the subject of age of the gestes see R. Dobson, and J. Taylor, *Rymes of Robyn Hood* (Stroud, Glos.: Sutton 1997) and J. C. Holt, *Robin Hood* (London: Thames & Hudson, 1989).

16. R. Ascham, *Toxophilus*.

17. The 1511 Henrican Statute [Henry VIII] required all male children to have and use a bow from the age of six years.

18. During the relevant period, five Master bowyers are known to have worked in nearby Bristol. See H. D. Soar, "Bowyers and Fletchers of Bristowe:" *Journal of the Society of Archer Antiquaries*, 1989.

19. *The Discoverie of Witchcraft* (London: 1600). The date of this travesty of justice is not given, but Queen Mary I reigned between 1553 and 1558.

20. As this verse from an old poem concerned with the art of shooting with a crossbow shows, longbowmen were innovative in their selection of "whites."

> *Thies longbowmen, they use a pretty feat,*
> *In myddes of the butte thei set an oyster shell,*
> *They care not if the white be litle or grete,*
> *The cause whereof forsooth I shal you telle,*
> *Like as the fissher will tak on hym to sell,*
> *An Ele in Themys by prodding with his spear,*
> *So sure be they the prick for to come near.*

21. R. Mulcaster, *Positions* (London: 1581).

22. H. D. H. Soar "Prince Arthur's Knights—a London Society of Archers," *Journal of the Society of Archer Antiquaries* (1988).

23. Circumstantial evidence vide a poem by R. Robinson (1583) suggests 1542 or 1543 as the possible year of its original formation.

24. R. Robinson, *The Auncient Order, Society and Unitie Laudable*

of Prince Arthure and his Knightly Armory of the Round Table (London: 1583).

25. Sir W. Wood, *The Bowman's Glory, Archery Revived* (London: 1682).

26. Ibid.

27. See n. 22.

28. R. L., *The Ancient Honour of the Famous City of London Restored and Recovered* (London: 1663).

Chapter 8

1. A. McKie, *King Henry VIII's Mary Rose* (Stroud, Glos.: Sutton 1973).

2. H. D. H. Soar, *Of Bowmen and Battles*—Battle of Blatchington Hill (Tolworth, Surrey: The Glade Ltd. 2003).

3. The reader may understandably be puzzled by the title Admiral of the North, enjoyed by Sir Walter Manny, and more particularly because his perceived role was largely on land. However, in those far-off days, warfare was an all-embracing activity. Whether one commanded on land or at sea bore relation only to the task at hand. Walter Manny was equally effective on sea and land. In his role as admiral, he was present as the seaborne captain of one of those ships led personally and successfully by Edward III against a combined French and Castilian fleet off the Sussex coast at Winchelsea in 1350.

4. J. Froissart, *Oevres 2* (Bruxelles: Cadzand, 1870), p. 429–437. See also Col. A. H. Burne, *The Crecy War from 1337 to 1360* (London: Eyre and Spottiswoode 1955). A popular account.

5. J. Froissart, *Chronicles* (London: Chapter Hill, 1852), p. 127–135. See also Col. A. H. Burne, *The Crecy War.*

6. Ibid. "The Count de l'Isle, Lieutenant to the King of France in Gascony, lays siege to the Castle of Auberoche."

7. Col. A. H. Burne, *The Crecy War.* This is the first field battle in Brittany where in contemporary documents the work of the English longbowmen is specifically mentioned.

8. Ibid.

9. Had the strong force placed by Charles de Blois disobeyed his specific order to remain in position and entered the fray, then matters could have ended very differently. Dagworth was taking a considerable risk.

10. Col. A. H. Burne, *The Agincourt War* (London: Eyre and Spottiswoode 1956), ch. XVIII "The End in Normandy." A popular account.

11. H. Talbot, *The English Achilles, the Life and Campaigns of John Talbot, 1st Earl of Shrewsbury* (London: Chatto and Windus 1981). See also Col. A. H. Burne, *The Agincourt War*, ch. XIX "Castillon." See also Jacob, *The Oxford History of England 1399–1485* (Oxford: OUP 1961), p. 505–507.

Recommended Additional Reading

J. Bradbury, *The Medieval Archer* (Woodbridge: Boydell, 1985).

A. Curry, *The Battle of Agincourt—Sources and Interpretations* (Woodbridge: Boydell, 2000).

A. Curry and M. Hughes, *Arms, Arm our and Fortifications in the Hundred Years War* (Woodbrige: Boydell, 1994).

D. Featherstone, *The Bowmen of England* (London: Jarrolds, 1967).

C. Hibbert, *Agincourt* (London: Batsford, 1964).

M. Jones, "Edward III's Captains in Brittany" in *England in the Fourteenth Century*, W. M. Ormond ed. (Woodbridge: Boydell 1986).

C. W. C. Oman, *The Art of War in the Middle Ages* (Ithaca, NY: Cornell University Press, 1963).

M. Powicke, *Military Obligations in Medieval England* (Oxford: OUP, 1992).

C. J. Rogers, *The Wars of Edward III—Sources and Interpretations* (Woodbridge: Boydell 1999).

————, *War, Cruel and Sharp* (Woodbridge: Boydell 2000).

Index

Acknowledgements

The preparation of this book, a companion volume to *The Crooked Stick*, has been a demanding but rewarding task in which I have been greatly encouraged through the support of numerous friends and colleagues both practical and academic. I have been helped immensely by the tolerance of Bruce H. Franklin, my publisher; the perseverance of Veronica-Mae, who has patiently corrected my punctuation; and the discipline of Christine Liddie, my editor, who has translated my scribblings into an acceptable form.

It is with pleasure that I acknowledge the help of my friend and master arrowsmith Mark Stretton, whose two detailed chapters on arrowheads, their making, and their awesome power when shot, are explicit of his skills and who, along with war-bow maker Joe Gibbs and traditional master fletcher Chris Jury, has provided many of the photographs with which this book is illustrated.

I acknowledge with gratitude the cooperation of the Mary Rose Trust, in particular Dr. Alexzandra Hildred, Research Director, and Finds Moderator Andrew Elkerton. In so doing I strongly commend the excellence of the Trust's Portsmouth Museum to those who wish to see the bows and arrows I have described in their evocative context.

I am most grateful for the invaluable assistance of Dr. Keith Watson of the University of Portsmouth and for the help given me by Dr. Kate Hunter, Newport Museum and Art Gallery. Thanks are also due to Dr Mark Redknap, National Museums and Galleries of Wales. I thank Dr. Andrew Halpin and Finbarr Connolly of the Irish Antiquities Division, National Museum of Ireland, for their assistance with my inquiry concerning the Ballinderry crannog longbow, and I gratefully acknowledge permission to reproduce an image. I am also appreciative of the kindness of Hereford City Museum Heritage Services in allowing me to illustrate a Tudor archery quiver, and in particular I thank David Stevens for his help in this regard. I also thank Anne Marshall, Associate Lecturer, the Open University, for allowing me to reproduce two of her photographs of church wall paintings.

Finally, if in the course of browsing these pages the astute reader should find inaccuracy, then the fault is clearly mine.